The
WRITER'S
MIND

The WRITER'S MIND

INTERVIEWS WITH AMERICAN AUTHORS
VOLUME II

Edited by Irv Broughton

The University of Arkansas Press
Fayetteville London 1990

810.9
W 9561
V. 2

DESIGNER: Chiquita Babb
TYPEFACE: Linotron 202 Plantin, with Peignot Bold
TYPESETTER: G&S Typesetters, Inc.
PRINTER: Braun-Brumfield Inc.
BINDER: Braun-Brumfield Inc.

The paper used in this publication meets the minimum
requirements of the American National Standard for Permanence of
Paper for Printed Library Materials Z39.48-1984. ⊗

LIBRARY OF CONGRESS CATALOGING-IN-PUBLICATION DATA

The Writer's mind.
    1. Authors, American—20th century—Interviews.
2. American literature—20th century—History and
criticism.   3. Authorship.   I. Broughton, Irv.
PS129.W75 1989   810'.9'005   88-29203
ISBN 1-55728-058-4 (v. 1)
ISBN 1-55728-059-2 (v. 1 : pbk. : alk. paper)
ISBN 1-55728-096-7 (v. 2)
ISBN 1-55728-097-5 (v. 2 : pbk. : alk. paper)

ACE-8284
91-7694

For Bob Fishburn,
Travis McKenzie,
and Gerry Cook,
loyal friends

CONTENTS

ACKNOWLEDGMENTS

Special thanks to Yvette N. Willard of The University of Arkansas Press and Connie Broughton for their editing assistance. Also, my appreciation to Dave Ling and Bob Zeller for help along the way.

Some of these interviews have appeared in the following magazines to whom grateful acknowledgment is given: *Mill Mountain Review* and *The Western Humanities Review*. Also, I would like to acknowledge the following authors and publishers for their courtesy in granting permission to reprint the selections in this book: Fred Chappell for excerpt from *Dagon: A Novel*. Harcourt, Brace, World, Inc., copyright © 1968 by Fred Chappell.

Ann Darr for "Send a Biographical Note . . ." from *The Myth of a Woman's Fist: Poems by Ann Darr*. William Morrow and Co., copyright © 1973 by Ann Darr.

James Dickey for "On the Coosawattee" ("Below Ellijay" section) from *Helmets* by James Dickey. Wesleyan University Press, copyright 1964 by James Dickey.

Julia Randall for "A Valediction" from *Moving in Memory* by Julia Randall. Louisiana State University Press, copyright ©1988 by Julia Randall.

William Jay Smith for "Galileo Galilei," "The Ten," "Saga," and "Death of a Jazz Musician" from *The Traveler's Tree: New and Selected Poems* by William Jay Smith. Persea Books, copyright © 1980 by William Jay Smith.

Photo of Issac Asimov by Kurt Muller; photo of Ann Darr copyright © 1987 by Irv Broughton; photo of Elizabeth Spencer by Piroshka Mihalka; photo of Richard Wilbur by Constance Stuart Larabee; photo of Richard Hugo copyright © 1974 by Irv Broughton; photo of Philip Levine copyright © 1989 by Irv Broughton; photo of George Garrett copyright © 1980 by Irv Broughton; photo of Ursula K. Le Guin by Richard Conrad; photo of Miller Williams by Constantine Christofides; photo of James Dickey by Teri DeBruhl, South Carolina Educational Television.

INTRODUCTION

I originally intended *The Writer's Mind* to be a one-volume collection of interviews with all of the contemporary writers I really loved, but the size and extent of the project led The University of Arkansas Press to this, a second volume, and after this, a third.

The thing that rings loudly for me in Volume II is seeing how writers work, and, in a sense, how they relate to their public. This is in many ways a most ungarretted (excuse me, George) group.

These are writers who are clearly social beings. Not socialites or climbers, but members of contemporary society. And from this group I think I learned that the consequences of writing should not be isolation or withdrawal. A simple lesson, but an important one for any person living in the world who writes or aspires to write. The stories and stereotypes of the writer in some dimly lit Paris or Greenwich Village hideaway are a romantic image, but little else. It is the work that counts no matter where it is done.

These writers have a quality of spirit and good humor. There is James Dickey, a people's poet with his rich oratorical style and wide subject matter; Philip Levine, who knows that tripe is more than stomach tissue; and George Garrett, a versatile, giving writer and teacher, who I'd bet knows a joke or two about tripe—or at least a limerick about Edna St. Vincent Millay. Then there is Elizabeth Spencer, a writer of genius whose chatty honesty made me feel I was talking to a neighbor; William Jay Smith, a most gracious, erudite man, whose humanity is always abundantly clear; and Richard Wilbur, a Poet Laureate of America, elegant, intellectual, clear, a gentleman. The human quotient of all these writers could be equally detailed.

These writers are grouped in this volume by date of birth, which doesn't make them a homogenous bunch. I offer here a variety of interviews with writers who work in fields as diverse as science fiction, poetry, translation, the novel, the short story, the essay and editorials, criticism, and screenwriting or playwriting.

This collection will give the reader a picture of the writer at work as well as a picture of the writer's earthbound place or places in the world.

"Could I remount the river of my years,
To the first fountain of our smiles and tears,
I would not trace again the stream of hours
Between their outworn banks of withered flowers,
But bid it flow as now—until it glides
Into the number of the nameless tides."

LORD BYRON

". . . there were metaphors for everything:
sometimes all his past life appeared to
him in the image of a gleaming snail track
over a damp garden walk; or a black iron
cube two inches square; or a shred of
discolored cuticle, or a frayed shoelace."

FRED CHAPPELL

HORTON FOOTE

Horton Foote started out to be an actor, studying at the Pasadena Playhouse and then in New York City. He also taught playwriting and worked in production management before the writing took hold.

Few have written for stage, television, and motion pictures with the

3

success and acumen of Horton Foote. He has written more than fifteen major television dramas for NBC and many others for CBS, ABC, and PBS. His plays include *Texas Town, Only the Heart, The Trip to Bountiful, Gone with the Wind, The Dancers,* and *Celebration.* His screenplays include *Baby, the Rain Must Fall; Storm Fear; Hurry Sundown; Valentine's Day;* and *Tender Mercies,* for which he won an Oscar. He was nominated for an Oscar for the movie version of *The Trip to Bountiful.*

The screenplay for which he is most recognized, *To Kill a Mockingbird,* won him an Academy Award as well as a Writers' Guild of America Award. The film is a modern classic and captures the spirit of the South—and of the novel—in a remarkable way. Foote lunched with the novel's author, Harper Lee, the week before our interview, and she told him the book was now in its forty-fifth printing. "She thinks the film is the reason it continues to do so well," he said. He seemed both pleased and modest.

Into his seventies he continues to work, producing films and writing, evoking the spirit and life of his father on whom his cycle, *The Orphans' Home,* is based.

INTERVIEW

IRV BROUGHTON: You have a great love for the common people. Where do you think you got that?

HORTON FOOTE: I don't think people are common really.

IB: How do you define them?

HF: I don't know how you would define them. I do know what you mean. I was raised in a small southern Texas town. I've come in contact with all kinds of people. You learn to value them. If you're sensitive at all to people I think you understand that there's dignity in everyone. Certainly everybody is striving to do the best in terms of what they understand best to be. And if they're defeated, as many people are, that's moving, too.

IB: How about *Harrison, Texas?* Where did that idea come from?

HF: Of course, I live in Wharton, the town I write about. I kind of wanted to be more impersonal about it, to find a kind of metaphor that wouldn't be so restrictive. So I just chose a different name. Actually the name Harrison is part of my family name.

IB: When you write about people close to you, does that ever get you in trouble? Sometimes writers tell tales.

HF: Actually, not so much with the kind of writing I do—I'm not a literal reporter, you know. I think Katherine Anne Porter said that a certain kind of writing goes through three stages. There is the experience, then there's the memory of the experience, and then what your active imagination does with that memory. So actually when it finally becomes—I don't mean to sound pretentious, but for the lack of a better word—a work of art, it's not recognizable at all.

5

IB: Does it take you a long time to incorporate an experience? I know a writer who says when something happens in his life, it takes him ten years or so to be able to put it into his work.

HF: I don't think there is any real rule about the law of time or anything. It is true that there is time involved. Sometimes it's a long process, sometimes not so long.

IB: Your mother, I understand, wrote to you every day. Do you think she had a secret wish to be a writer, too?

HF: Well, I don't think she did really. I don't think that ever occurred to her. We came from a large letter-writing family. She not only wrote me often but she would also include the letters from four or five other members of the family. They were all writers in that sense.

IB: What was your mother like?

HF: I thought she was an extraordinary woman. But she was a very small woman, really, and had a lot of strength. Devoted to my father. A musician, she played the piano wonderfully. She had been sent off to a conservatory to study music as a girl.

IB: How did your acting experience impact on your writing later?

HF: I'm very grateful for it. I would recommend to all playwrights to get some experience either in acting or directing or at least study acting. Because I think it's like a composer. If you're writing music, you have to know the instrument and know what it can do and what it can't do.

IB: What do you think the main thing you've learned from that acting experience is?

HF: Well, certainly I learned fairly early what one could act and what one couldn't act. You just know that there are certain qualities of writing that are not dramatic and you can't act them. They may be beautiful within themselves but they're passive, they're not active. You learn what makes a scene active, you learn what's the spine of a play or the spine of a work—what makes it cohere. An actor has a second instinct about that because they have to deal so much with the structure of it. That is, actors that I like.

IB: How does it feel as a writer to have actresses like Geraldine Page or Lillian Gish take your work and perform it?

HF: You know on the one hand it's humbling, on the other hand it's exhilarating. It's humbling because you realize how dependent you are, what a collaborative art film or theater is. You know you are dependent on the talent around you, really. It's exhilarating in the sense that you realize that there is something, perhaps more elastic, in the work than you thought because if two performers as different as Lillian and Geraldine can be moving and insightful in the same part, there's something strong about the part. It's almost like two great piano virtuosos taking the same piece of music, yet it sounds very different.

IB: Do you have a playwriting hat and a screenwriter's hat? In other words, is your mind set or your approach different when you're writing one as opposed to the other?

HF: No, not really. You're conscious of the strengths and limitations of the media you're working with. Both have their strengths and both have their weaknesses. You just simply have a kind of unconscious measuring rod that you just finally are able to say to yourself, "Well, this won't work in the theater or this won't work in film, this will work in theater, this will work in film."

IB: Are there some criteria?

HF: Actually it's kind of personal taste. What I might choose to think works in cinema or film, another person would say, "Oh

7

no, it would be boring, and don't do that." There are three films as different as possible that I'm devoted to that I've seen this year. One is John Huston's *The Dead*. I doubt if many people reading that story of James Joyce's would have said spontaneously, "Yes, this can be a film." But, in one sense, it breaks all the canons of what the film schools teach you about screenwriting. And I think, therefore, it's a very valuable lesson to show writers they shouldn't limit themselves. The others are films like *Jean de Florette* and *Manon of the Spring*—which is an entirely different structure and scope and yet to me a very daring one and it works wonderfully. So I'm anti-rules in that sense. I think, if you have your own sense of aesthetic, you just have to follow your own instinct.

IB: There must be some things you have to concern yourself with when you translate a play to the big screen. Could you enumerate some of those?

HF: There is one thing which you naturally look for, which is that very ambiguous term, "opening up." I say this is ambiguous because I think you have to be very careful with it. Most tendencies are to take a play which works well within its confines and turn it into a travelogue. You say, "Oh yes, let's get it out, let's do all the scenes we can in different places." And you dissipate the play. What you're left with too often are a lot of scenes that you use just to get them out in different locations and they don't mean anything. But on the other hand, it's very difficult—and *The Dead* is one of the few that, I think, is successfully done—to stay for a long, long time in a room or two rooms. So your instinct says, where can I legitimately use the gift of cinema which is to take in the world and not be confined to physical limitations of the theater. But you must be careful.

IB: What sort of mistakes do people in film schools tend to make?

HF: Well, I think, first of all, there is a great lot of film school clichés. One is that one should use as little dialogue as possible—everything should be in terms of the visual. I don't deny that's very potent and very powerful, but I think it finally gets to be mindless. I think this is my one quarrel with some of our young film directors. If it's their point of view, they are not really truly educated, in that their point of view mostly is referenced to other films or to television shows that they've seen. They leave out literature and they leave out music. They leave out a lot, really.

IB: You're a very fast first-draft writer, aren't you?

HF: In a sense that I usually write, . . . well, my drafts usually come after a lot of meditation. That's a kind of vast word, I know, and I don't mean it in a religious sense so much. But I think a great deal about what I'm going to write and walk around and kind of rehearse it inside myself a lot. So by the time I get to actually writing, a lot of it has been worked out inside me. So that's why I think the first draft comes usually quickly and I revise a great deal after that.

IB: What's the shortest time it's taken you to write a screenplay or play?

HF: Each one has its own demands and I don't think of it as slow or fast. I simply think of trying to find the proper form for the idea. That's very relative, you know, because there are certain things that could change it for you. You take a step and then you can see it performed, then you think, "No, I want to do a little bit here." Or I have a couple of things I put aside that I thought, "Oh well, not quite right" and, lo and behold, six or seven months later I pick them up and I think, "Well, they are exactly what I wanted and I don't want to do anything to them. So it's all very subjective. Katherine Anne Porter had this thing about the bureau drawer. The last story she published she felt dissatisfied with it and put it away. I think she forgot about it and thirty years later she found it. She was going to revise it, and she read it over and said, "No, certain things happen when you put them away in drawers. Certain magic properties take over."

IB: Can you talk about one script or play where you were influenced to change it by the performance?

HF: My play *Courtship*, which later became a film. I think when I saw that performed I felt I wanted to eliminate a great deal of what I thought was unnecessary about it and get it down to purer form. The same was true with *On Valentine's Day*.

IB: What sort of things did you change?

HF: To me, the ideal is always through elimination. In other words, to get rid of what is excessive or what is unnecessary—which is kind of a constant pruning—or getting down to the essence of the work, and that's really all I did. I just found certain things now that were unessential.

IB: So basically you tend to write long?

HF: Sometimes. Sometimes not at all. Sometimes I didn't change a bit. Again you have to think in terms of the work.

IB: How intense do you get when you get into a writing period?

HF: Oh, I get very obsessive, to the despair of my friends and family. I wake up in the middle of the night sometimes and get up and go to work.

IB: Can you talk a little more about that?

HF: I guess I'm a compulsive writer in that sense. It's hard to shake it off. It just kind of takes me over.

IB: Do you start thinking like characters or being like characters?

HF: I start thinking like the characters but I don't know about being like the characters. I don't think that's possible, probably. I hope not. I wouldn't want to be like some of them. But sure, you do all these experiments. You try to get inside, you try to find points of view—even with the people that you don't like that you write about.

IB: Any particular example of people that you write about you found difficult?

HF: Well, actually no, but you do end up finding something to identify with in all of them. So you end up not wanting to be like them, but if I do, I usually wind up with some kind of sympathetic response. I'm not particularly fond of the first wife in *Tender Mercies*, Dixie, or her boyfriend, the agent. But I certainly felt finally a sense, I hope some sense of understanding, to make people understand a little bit about them.

IB: What did it take to make you understand or appreciate them?

HF: Well, that's a very difficult process to explain. I don't know that I could. You just try to see them whole, and I think if you really understood, completely understood anybody, you couldn't help but have sympathy for them no matter what they did.

IB: You adapted Faulkner's "Barn Burning." Could you talk about that?

HF: I did three things of Faulkner's you know. *The Old Man* was the first one I did with Geraldine Page on "Playhouse 90" and then *Tomorrow*, which I did first on "Playhouse 90" with Kim Stanley and Richard Boone, and then later in the theater I did it with Robert Duvall and then we made that into a film.

IB: What was it like to adapt the great William Faulkner?

HF: Well, that's the last thing you can think of is "the great William Faulkner." It would intimidate the hell out of me. I just had to jump in and do it. Robert Duvall thinks *Tomorrow* is some of his best work. The story was taken from a short story. In that short story there are only five lines, or maybe a paragraph, describing a certain woman, who certainly permeates the story but you never see her, he doesn't give her a name. He calls her black complected, and that's about all. Well, that really was what began to fascinate me and how I kind of got into the story was thinking about this woman. I gave her a name and over the first half of the screenplay is about this woman. I was very nervous. I thought, well, what's Faulkner going to say about this. I never met him, but evidently he was pleased because he allowed me to share the dramatic copyright of his work. This was very generous and almost unheard of at the time. In *Barn Burning* I had great trouble with the end because it's a perfectly beautiful ending but it takes place in an area that's very hard to dramatize. It takes place inside the little boy's mind. That's very, very difficult to do. I think it's effective and I think we came as close as possible in solving the end. But I don't know that the end can ever be solved.

IB: How did you do that?

HF: Well, I simply had to take what was subjective and put it in a different form. Take it out of the subjective and try to find certain actions that would indicate to you or help you understand what Faulkner handled so sensitively in the subjective.

IB: *To Kill a Mockingbird* is a classic; it's just wonderful. Could you talk about writing the screenplay?

HF: Oh, that was a long time ago. I had a way to get into it because I grew up in a town not unlike Harper Lee's town. I was given a technical problem to solve by the producer who felt that it shouldn't cover a number of years—as the novel does—but to try to get more sense of unity, a unity of one year. So that was a technical thing I accomplished by pulling the action all into one year.

IB: What was the toughest thing about doing that?

HF: There wasn't anything tough about it because I felt so at home in the material. I had to be patient about certain things and I had to think about certain things, but it wasn't tough. It actually was a very happy time. It's tough when it doesn't work. As long as you feel it's working, I don't ever think it's tough. It may be long, it may be laborious, and it may be exasperating at times but it's never tough. It's only tough if you feel it's nothing, just flat, and you don't know how to make it easy.

IB: That was a first person book, wasn't it? What's the key of writing from the first person?

HF: I don't think there is any key to it. It's just that together with the director you figure that there will be a point of view involved in this as much as possible. We didn't follow that strictly. Everything wasn't from the point of view of the little girl but a lot of it was from the point of view of the children.

IB: Do you remember any conflicts or any little minor arguments you had over the approach, any scene or anything?

HF: None. The only conflict we had, which was quickly resolved, was we tried to do it in Harper Lee's hometown. It had changed so and in those days they didn't like to go out, they wanted to keep it in the studios. So we went back to Universal and the designer called me in and said, "Look, I just want you to check out this house I'm going to build." I took one look at it and hollered because it looked like Tara in *Gone With the Wind*. I said, "Oh, no, they didn't live in that kind of house." They lived in the kind of house I'm living in right now, that I've lived in my whole life. Well anyway, I told them what kind of house it was. So they found a house in Pasadena that was being condemned for a thoroughway and they moved it on the lot and that was the house they had.

IB: There's that scene with the children listening in *Mockingbird*. Did that come from your youth?

HF: John Hart did an interview for the "Today" program and he asked me about that. I said, "Here's my porch and my mother and father sat out here every night and this was my bedroom. And I went to bed every night listening to them talk about everything that happened in the town." And I said, "That's what those kids did." And that's the way I got that whole scene of listening and I rearranged the scene where Atticus hears about Tom Robinson and all of that, and the sheriff coming and asking him to take the case. I put it there on the porch so the kids could hear it.

IB: Let's talk about that experience. That's a pretty profound experience for a young child to be privy to all that information.

HF: Well, I think most of the children are. It's kind of commonplace.

IB: Do you think having the traditions of the South is beneficial to the writer?

HF: It just depends on what you want to do with it. My brother was raised the same way and it all bored him to death. He'd get up and leave the room if they started talking about something like that.

IB: Do you remember anything that shocked you as a young child?

HF: Children aren't shockable in that sense, and I was raised around the facts and nothing was ever hidden, whether intentionally or unintentionally. So at an early age I had quite a realistic view of life. I knew everything didn't turn out well and that everybody didn't live happily ever after.

IB: Who was more of a pessimist, your mom or your dad?

HF: Well, I don't think that either was a pessimist. I think that my father, since a lot of my growing-up-time was during the Depression, was worried more because he had a living to make for his family. Being in a community that depended on cotton and therefore the weather, I think he often felt very vulnerable to the elements.

IB: How desperately do you feel those Southern roots? You're obviously a man rooted in the land and the South. Do you really feel that?

HF: Oh, absolutely.

IB: What's the feeling?

HF: Well, this is where you belong. I don't mean to be sentimental about it because I don't feel about it sentimentally, but it's just a sense of home. Now I've lived many places and may live many more places before I leave the earth, but it's always inside me someplace. I love New York City, but it's not my home. I lived in New Hampshire and my children spent a great deal of time there and some of them have a close sense of identity with it. I admired it and like the people, but it wasn't my home.

IB: Is writing a kind of mystical process to you?

HF: Well, I don't like the word "mystical" because I think that has the wrong kind of connotation, but I certainly think there are many elements about writing that you have to depend on the unknown and the unseen. Otherwise it isn't something you can make a blueprint of. There is the unforeseeable in it and that you just have to trust.

IB: You have to trust—meaning?

HF: Well, you have to trust your talent, you have to trust your instincts, you have to trust wherever these ideas come from, wherever these solutions come from. I don't understand technology very well. For instance, I don't understand how a CD plays because I don't see a needle. But my daughter, with complete confidence, explains to me that there is something definite I can't see that's playing it. That it's like a needle. So now I have faith that there's something there playing it, that it's not doing it by itself. A little bit like the process of writing. You can't see it, and you can't worry about it or nothing happens. To me, it's like how a garden works. If you plant a seed to grow and if you go back every five minutes and dig around to see how it's growing, you won't see anything. But, if you plant the seed and you understand that the rain and the sun and certain properties in the seed that you can't see now—but are there— affect things, and you give it three months and something will happen. It's a little bit like writing. You have to water it, and you have to keep the weeds away but there's a part of it you can't force.

IB: So what you're saying is that at times if this would happen it may be better to let your work alone?

HF: There are times that I would simply walk away from something and say, "Look, I've done all I can do now and I just better put it on the back burner because I'm going to worry it to death. I'm going to dig it up too much."

IB: Does that happen rarely?

HF: You can't say when. It doesn't happen all the time, but it happens.

IB: What was the strangest kind of baptism or experience you had in writing a teleplay? Obviously you probably didn't know much about the technology then.

HF: Nobody did. I guess the great fear was that you couldn't prompt the actors and you couldn't stop it. So the great fear, as far as the actors were concerned, was—what if they forget their lines? That was terrifying to the writer. It only happened once and I don't want to tell you who she is because she is a great actress and I don't want to embarrass her. But in a play of mine she did forget her lines and there was a moment of almost thirty seconds of silence—while the other actors were trying to get her back on track. It was just terrifying. What can you do? I was sitting in the control room. She couldn't see me and I couldn't communicate to her. Everything was done, all the shots were called from the control room and the actors were out in the studio. You couldn't talk to them, they couldn't talk to each other, nothing. Finally the actor with her had sense enough to improvise a line that led her into what she was supposed to say. But there was thirty seconds of total silence.

IB: What's your main debt to playwriting as regards to screenwriting?

HF: I think it gives me a respect for form and technique, the willingness to try many different approaches; a realization of the importance of character to the action, to the story, and language.

IB: What did you learn from your teleplay experience in terms of your movie writing?

HF: Well, actually not too much, to tell you the truth. Because when I wrote them it was mostly when there was live TV, which meant that you couldn't stop the action. And you couldn't cut and you couldn't edit, do any of those things—it was just a continual performance. We also had so little money in our budget and space was so small that we couldn't do more than two or three or four sets. Four was considered a great extravagance.

IB: Do you remember a favorite teleplay? Was there one that really stands out in your mind?

HF: Well, no, I worked for two years with a producer named Fred

Coe and in those two years, I would be hard put to pick a favorite. Actually, they are all now published as one-act plays and almost constantly being performed. The one that is probably best known today is *The Trip to Bountiful* or *Young Lady of Property.*

IB: How much did *The Trip to Bountiful* change?

HF: It went from that into a Broadway play with Lillian Gish both on television and on Broadway. But actually the thing is that it didn't change radically but we never would take the trip, so to speak. Even in television because in those days we were confined in the studio and of course then we couldn't do it. So that's really basically it. The basic change was that we were able to follow her as she went home.

IB: What was the hardest thing about adapting *The Trip to Bountiful* into a motion picture?

HF: It's simply like shifting gears. It's not a question of hard or not hard, it's just a question of perception. You just suddenly have a whole different thing to perceive when you think in terms of film.

IB: You've touched on this to some extent, but do you think film is devoid of language these days?

HF: I think it's boring, when it is. I think often the language is elemental and so kind of rudimentary that it's just deeply boring. But I think that the balance is coming back.

IB: Real words, real people talk, and real sentiments?

HF: I think that could be boring, too. A sense of language which is more than reality. Because to me, effective language is selected language. It isn't just reporting. One has a good ear and one doesn't have a good ear. You can be a great writer and not have a good ear. Eugene O'Neill is a great writer from my point of view but he has a tin ear.

IB: So you don't think it is possible for someone with a tin ear to get better?

HF: Well, no, I think it's something that's a gift. I don't know what it is. It's inherent in the style of writing. The great stylists have a great ear for language. Someone can be an effective writer and not be a great stylist. There is no more effective play to me in the English language than *Long Day's Journey Into Night*— there he comes nearest to hopefully achieving a style. But you take *Strange Interlude*, or even *Ice Man Cometh*. *Ice Man Cometh* certainly works theatrically but to me it works in spite of the style of writing. Now you take Shaw and then Chekhov who combined them both, you have the real ball game.

IB: How much of a bonus is it to be able to hear a distinct regional dialect—like in the South. Do you think it helps the writer?

HF: I think it gives you a language, I think it gives you something to work with. Then again, in being born in the South, there is no guarantee of anything. There are plenty of bad Southern writers. Plenty of sentimental Southern writers. The South is just like any place else. I think the main strength of the South is the oral tradition, and because Southerners do have a vivid sense of language which, unfortunately, is being homogenized very rapidly.

IB: Talk about *Tender Mercies*. What was the toughest thing you wrestled with in getting Sledge's character?

HF: Actually it was very hard because I didn't really know any country and western singers of any repute. What you often do is substitute. I've known many a famous actor or actress. So actually it was kind of a composite of famous actors or actresses I've known who've lost their careers through drinking. Some

19

of them have been able to pull up and come back and some haven't. So I had all of these things in front of me.

IB: So you drew on that?

HF: I drew on that and I drew on my knowledge of country music and the ones I knew that were not famous. It all really comes down to being a composite.

IB: You've been quoted as saying you don't censor your first draft. Can you explain why that's important?

HF: I just say OK, I'm going to make the biggest fool of myself as possible and just go right ahead and don't stop. I just let it get out. Sometimes I just run out of steam and I don't get the first draft whole-done, and I go back and start again. Often my first draft is a very complete draft. It may not be the one I use or anywhere near what finally takes place. But it's in my own handwriting and very few people can read it but me.

IB: You say you're willing to make a big fool of yourself. Where did you get that idea? Did you ever worry that the first draft had to be just right?

HF: No, I never did feel that. I don't know. I learned on-the-job, so to speak. Nobody ever taught me how to write. Along the way you pick up things. Along the way, people that you love, admire, and respect, you listen to, and you learn. I mean no one ever sat down with me. I was an actor and then I wanted to write a part for myself to act in. That's how I got started. Then I became very passionate about writing and forgot about acting. I just jumped into it.

IB: Is there a favorite scene in *Mockingbird* that moves you the most when you see the movie?

HF: I'm very fond of the scene, which many people wouldn't even pay attention to, when she's asking Atticus about her mother and why Jem is getting a watch and she's not getting a watch. That's not in the book, but I think it's kind of a lovely scene where Atticus is handling her so delicately. It has a delicacy that is very touching to me the way Atticus explains it to her and Jem.

IB: How about another scene that you're particularly proud of from the movie?

HF: I think the scene that moves everybody so much is Harper's scene, which I trust we do justice to; it's "Stand up, Miss Jane Louise, your father is passing"—in the courthouse. She's sitting next to a black man and it's when he's leaving and everyone stands up and she doesn't do it and the black man tells her to stand up.

IB: Let's talk about any scenes that you're most proud of from *Trip to Bountiful*.

HF: Well, it's like talking about who are your favorite children. I think the scene in *Bountiful* is when Geraldine says, "I half expect my mother and father to come out that door since I've been here." I think she is magnificent.

IB: Is there any quintessential thing that you find yourself saying? Is there some thread like the love of family, the closeness or something?

HF: No, I don't think so. I have enormous compassion for the human condition. A great admiration for what people have to put up with and endure—the way they survive or don't survive.

IB: It isn't easy.

HF: No, neither one is easy. To survive isn't easy. To be defeated certainly is terrible.

IB: Have you ever found yourself making rules and then breaking them?

HF: Yes, certainly.

IB: Is it futile to make the rules?

HF: I mean you just do. At the time you think, well, you know. Everybody says, "Well, the perfect play is such and such." "*Oedipus* is the perfect play—a unity in time, place, and action." You go crazy. Then you read *King Lear* and Shakespeare breaks every canon—there is no unity of anything. It's just all over the place. So you soon learn that there is no way to get to heaven. Everyone has to make his own journey. I can't tell you how to get to heaven.

IB: Some people say, though, that you need to know the rules before you break them.

HF: They say all that stuff. Just get in and do it. Get in and write, that's the main thing.

IB: Do you keep notebooks?

HF: Yes, I keep notebooks and I write things down as they occur to me or things I should do so as to not forget them. You don't like to get too analytical on this because that will kill it. I don't want to get too analytical after it's done either because I think, "Oh well, that will be a formula, that's what I've got to try not to do," and that kills everything.

IB: Do you think it was inevitable that you became a writer?

HF: I don't know that. I don't know what else in the world I would have considered to do in any great sense. I say this very humbly. I know that if I had to stop writing, it would be very difficult for me. Because it's more than a profession, it really is a deep thing for me. If there was nothing I'd ever do ever again, I would still write every day.

IB: Do you have a regimen by which you write—say, three hours a day?

HF: I write some every day, but I don't ever say three hours because I would break it. I often write much more than three hours. I admire a writer that can do that. Certain writers write in the morning and read in the afternoon and visit with their families in the evening. Lovely, but I can't do it.

IB: So do you normally write in the morning?

HF: All the time. Sometimes in the middle of the night.

IB: One poet has this poem about how he got up at night and wrote this poem. He didn't really remember it, but when he got up in the morning there was this wonderful poem in his own hand-writing. Does it ever strike you that way?

HF: Absolutely. You just say "Where in the world did this come from? Who does this belong to?" Particularly when you've seen things written and you go and see a play done after you haven't seen or read it for fifteen or twenty years. You just get chilled at your heart because if someone said, "Now leave the room and write this again"—you couldn't do it.

WILLIAM JAY SMITH

William Jay Smith is a large, shy man, but not by any means distant. There is a certain urbanity and dextrous wit to him. Just before the interview I remembered something I heard him say to an ambling student who was consulting with him on a poem. The student had used "forever" in the poem, and Smith responded with firmness and a smile, "It might make eternity longer if you leave out the forever." The student smiled and dropped the word.

Smith was educated at Washington University, Columbia University, University of Florence, and Oxford University as a Rhodes Scholar. He served for two years in the Vermont House of Representatives where he wrote his now notorious "Minor Ode to the Morgan Horse," in which he spoke of all the other possible state animals and concluded with the line, "I will vote, of course, for the Morgan horse." The poem was reprinted in newspapers across the country, and he was made the official poet of the House of Representatives. Later he taught at Williams College and Hollins College, from which he retired as Professor Emeritus of English. Smith's numerous honors include prizes from *Poetry* in 1945 and 1964, a Ford Foundation grant, the Loines Award from the American Academy of Arts and Letters in 1972 and the Henry Bellamann Award for poetic achievement in 1970. He received a D.Litt. from New England College in 1973 and is a member of the American Academy of Arts and Letters, where he now serves as vice president for literature.

From 1968–1970 he served as consultant in poetry to the Library of Congress and from 1970–1976 as an honorary consultant in American Letters. He also has taught at Columbia University School, where he is on the Executive Board of the Translation Center and one of the editors of the journal *Translation*, published by the center. He has translated Spanish, French, Italian, Russian, Swedish, and Hungarian poetry.

William Jay Smith edited *Light Verse and Satires* by Witter Bynner and was one of the principal translators of *Nostalgia for the Present* by the Russian poet Andrei Voznesensky. With F. D. Reeve, he edited *An Arrow in the Wall: Selected Poetry and Prose* by Andrei Voznesensky, which the *New York Times* chose as one of the sixteen best books of the year.

He has published more than fifteen books of poetry, the latest being *The Traveler's Tree: New and Selected*, and more than a dozen books of poetry for children, including *Laughing Time*, published in 1980. His critical essays and reviews were collected in *The Streaks of the Tulip: Selected Criticism*. And he has published an autobiography of his early years, *Army Brat,* of which Ralph Ellison wrote, "It reminded me of the memoir of another Missourian, Mark Twain's *Life on the Mississippi.*"

Smith is part Cherokee Indian, and in recent years, he has explored his native American roots.

IRV BROUGHTON: You've been a sort of roving ambassador of American letters, haven't you?

WILLIAM JAY SMITH: I suppose I have. I hadn't planned to be— it happened over the course of time. I think it really began in earnest when I was consultant in poetry to the Library of Congress. Because I was interested in foreign literature, I organized an international poetry festival in the spring of 1970. I invited eight poets from different countries along with their translators.

IB: To where did you travel?

WJS: As consultant to the Library, I went on a cultural exchange visit to Japan and East Asia in 1969 and then to the Soviet Union in 1970. There had been no cultural exchange with the Soviet Union for some years, and I was the first American writer to go there after a very long period. I spent a month and traveled for two months afterwards in Eastern Europe—to Poland, Romania, Hungary, and then to Greece, Cyprus, Israel, and Turkey. I've been going back to Eastern Europe ever since and also to the Soviet Union and Hungary because I've been translating poets from those countries.

IB: Were there any instances of communication failures during your travels?

WJS: I was a delegate at the Budapest Cultural Forum in 1985, and we were talking about the reception poets had in various countries. The members of the Soviet delegation had been attacking us Americans rather severely all along because they resented our attacks on their obvious failure to observe certain basic human rights. I said that I had found that poets in the Soviet Union—unlike many other people there—were very much appreciated and valued. If I got into a taxicab in Moscow and told the driver that I was a poet, he would take me all over town without charging me a cent. Later on in the day, a member of the Bulgarian delegation spoke up and said that Mr. Smith had said horrible, slanderous things about Soviet cab drivers, which was a complete misunderstanding of what I had said. So I came back and said that I had not attacked taxi drivers. I got on very well with them as a matter of fact—even at the moment in New York where most of them were Soviet émigrés.

IB: You've met some great writers during your travels. Didn't you meet Yukio Mishima?

WJS: Yes. A lecture agent in New York had been in touch with his publisher, and she (at that time she was my agent also) asked me if I would see him and ask if he would be willing to come lecture in the United States. When we were in Tokyo, he arranged to meet my wife and me at the Imperial Hotel. He had a very strict schedule and was free only in the late afternoon. He met us around four o'clock and we had a very pleasant time. We were leaving the next day for Kyoto and then the northernmost island Hokkaido before returning to Tokyo. He said that one of his plays, *Madame de Sade*, was being produced and that he would like for us to come to see it. He sent us tickets and a translation of the play by Donald Keene to our hotel, and when we returned his wife came by in her car to pick us up. We went to a marvelous production of the play in a little theater on the high floor of a building in the business district and to a reception there afterwards. Around eleven o'clock he took us to dinner at a magnificent French restaurant where we sat up the rest of the night talking.

IB: What was he like?

WJS: He was very charming and witty—Western in so many ways that it was hard afterwards to understand that he was so keen on Old Japan and old Japanese values. He said he couldn't come lecture. He couldn't take the time away from his work and, besides, there would be a lot of silly women who would come up with very silly questions at the lectures. He gave a very amusing impersonation of such a woman asking about André Gide. And then, when he traveled abroad, he was always mistaken for a cabin boy off some ship because he looked so young.

IB: What did you think when you learned that he had committed suicide?

WJS: I was really quite astonished because it didn't seem to fit in with the picture of him that I had as the poised gentleman so aware of Western culture. Of course, when you read the accounts of his early life and his fascination with St. Sebastian and all that, I think you understand his attraction to violence and death.

IB: What are the advantages and disadvantages of being a general man of letters as you are?

WJS: If a writer has done work in a number of fields, that diversity can be helpful in his career, but at times it can also have certain disadvantages. When I give readings of my poems around the country, some people who come know me only as a writer of poetry for children while others come who know me only as a writer for adults. It's sometimes very strange. Other people don't know that I've written any prose at all, that I've written any criticism, or done any translations. But I feel that the center of my work has always been poetry and everything else I've done has gone back and strengthened that.

Some people thought of *Army Brat* as just another poet's memoir that would not have any interest except for readers of poetry, which turned out not to be true. Some of the readers who responded most strongly to the book were not readers of poetry at all.

IB: What were your first translations?

WJS: I began French early on and tried in high school to translate certain passages of Victor Hugo. Then, in college, I majored in French and tried to translate some of the poets I was reading, poets like Jules Laforgue, whom I read even before I read T. S. Eliot. I wanted to learn more about these poets and there is no better way to learn about a poet or a country than through translation. It was one of the great misfortunes that we knew nothing about Vietnam when the Vietnam war was taking place. If we'd done more translations of Vietnamese literature and had known more about the culture of that country, we'd have appreciated the situation there a little better.

IB: You do a lot of translation and it seems to me that your translations don't sound like your own poetry, as those of many translators do. Is it hard not to impose your own style on the poet you are translating?

WJS: I think it is very difficult because what you do as a translator is try to step into someone else's shoes and then write a poem as he or she would have done it. And that's not easy. But I think that one should translate only those poets for whom one feels a certain affinity. If you try to translate someone you feel no affinity for, then you're not going to be able to bring it off. And furthermore, one has to have a sense of humility. What happened with Robert Lowell was that his arrogance took over when he dealt with the poems of Baudelaire. He thought that he could improve on them, which was nonsense, of course.

I've spent so much time on translation because I have benefited so much from it. I've learned a great deal from the writers I have translated. I think I became aware of this when I saw how much Eliot and Pound had learned from their translations and rewriting of foreign poets.

IB: Did you know Lowell, by the way?

WJS: Yes, but not well. I saw him many times over the years. I admired him but we were not exactly on the same wavelength. I was much more in sympathy with Richard Wilbur, Elizabeth Bishop, and Theodore Roethke.

IB: Ever meet Roethke?

WJS: Yes, I knew him quite well over a period of years. I was with him for one whole year in Florence. He was there on a Fulbright Fellowship and I used to see him two or three times a week when I was attending the University of Florence. I saw the very first versions of many of the poems he was working on then, poems that have since become quite famous.

IB: What did you get from your relationship with Roethke?

WJS: I learned from him about W. H. Auden, Louise Bogan, and Stanley Kunitz—those poets he thought so highly of. And I learned to appreciate how much work he put into his own poems.

   Because there were so few students then at the University who were capable of following his classes in English, the Americans who were living in Florence at the time went regularly to make the attendance look decent. He was a strange teacher. He was always terribly nervous before class and would behave as if he were facing a physical ordeal of some sort—almost as if he were stepping into a ring for a wrestling match. His reaction was very physical—he would perspire heavily and pound up and down reciting the poems he was planning to discuss. He was an excellent reader of poetry. I found those sessions quite fascinating, and I learned a good deal from them.

IB: Any stories about Roethke that show anything about his character?

WJS: Ted could be very gloomy on occasion and look absolutely terrifying. I suppose this was his Prussian side showing itself. I remember once I went to see him with my son David, who was then just five years old. It was about ten o'clock in the morning and Ted was just getting up. He had a terrible scowl on his face and was making acid remarks about everything. He went on and on with this very depressing commentary for more than an hour. Then just as we were leaving—as we were about to go through the door—little David looked up at Roethke and said, lifting his bright, adoring face, "Uncle Ted, tell us some more jokes." (Laughs.) Of course, at that moment Ted absolutely collapsed like a bowl of jelly. He loved children and here was this wonderful little boy who had seen right through his gloomy facade.

IB: Ever found anyone you couldn't translate?

WJS: I was asked once to translate some poems of Jorge Guillén, the Spanish poet. I tried and found that I really couldn't do it— even though I admire his work very much. I found that he has a way of writing that is simply alien to me. I think this goes back to what I said about the feeling of affinity you have for the poet you're translating. Lorca is another matter. I feel great affinity for him and have translated a number of his poems.

IB: Let's talk about your most difficult translation.

WJS: I've translated a number of poems by Sándor Weöres, the Hungarian poet. There is a book of his called *Eternal Moment: Selected Poems* that is just now appearing in England and America. Edwin Morgan and I have done most of the translations in it. One long poem in this book is an elegy on the death of his mother, a magnificent poem but an extremely difficult one. I worked very hard to translate it. It's done partly in metaphysical language with many allusions, religious and otherwise, and it's very packed, very dense. It contains a great variety of metrical patterns. The tone also shifts frequently. In English at times he sounds like Richard Crashaw with the same extreme, very vivid, religious metaphors, and then again in the same poem he can be quite simple and musical with folk rhythms. This translation took me several months, although I didn't work on it the whole time.

IB: What about having to really change some elements of a translation?

WJS: In the poems of the Russian poet Andrei Voznesensky, you have many references to religion, to the Orthodox Church, and then also references to earlier Russian writers and historical figures—or even buildings. I translated a poem of his called "Saga." It's a love poem and takes place in Leningrad, but he never mentions the name of the city. In it he refers to two buildings, the Admiralty and the Stock Exchange. To anyone who knows Leningrad, those are immediately recognizable as two of the most famous buildings there. With Voznesensky's permission, I brought into the poem the name of the city, making it clear where the poem takes place, which is important because he is talking about the dampness of the city and the water all around. That's the kind of thing you often encounter and you have to find some solution. "Saga" is a song in the original Russian and I'm pleased that I was able in the translation to keep the rhyme scheme and the metrical pattern.

Saga

You will awaken me at dawn
And barefoot lead me to the door;
You'll not forget me when I'm gone,
You will not see me any more.

Lord, I think, in shielding you
From the cold wind of the open door:
I'll not forget you when I'm gone,
I shall not see you any more.

The Admiralty, the Stock Exchange
I'll not forget when I am gone.
I'll not see Leningrad again,
Its water shivering at dawn.

From withered cherries as they turn,
Brown in the wind, let cold tears pour:
It's bad luck always to return,
I shall not see you any more.

And if what Hafiz says is true
And we return to earth once more,
We'll miss each other if it's true;
I shall not see you any more.

Our quarrels then will fade away
To nothing when we both are gone,
And when one day our two lives clash
Against that void to which they're drawn.

Two silly phrases rise to sway
On heights of madness from earth's floor:
I'll not forget you when I'm gone,
I shall not see you any more.

IB: What's the main mistake that beginning translators make?

WJS: It is perhaps not to concentrate on the language into which the poem is being translated. The translator must concentrate on his own language. For instance, many beginning translators, when translating from French or from other Romance languages, will translate the definite article when in English it should be omitted. The beginner often feels that he is not being true to the original if he omits the article in English. But, of course, it must be omitted—it's just a difference of language. I think you have to be extremely careful and know the rules of your own language.

IB: What have you gained from your work in translation—in terms of your own poetry?

WJS: One very good thing about translation is that when a poet is stuck in his own work and not writing his own poems, it is always a good idea for him to keep in touch with his own language and to be constantly working with it. So I like to think that if I'm not writing my own poems, I'm trying to get someone else's into English. I've learned about my own language and my own craft through translation.

IB: The epigraph of your poem "The Tin Can" refers to a Japanese expression, doesn't it?

WJS: Yes, the epigraph gave me the idea for the poem. It seems that in Japan when a writer wants to get away from everything and get some writing done, he says that he is going "into the tin can." My poem begins with a description of Japan, where in fact I had never been, but when I did go there I found that the Japanese felt that in writing this poem I had shown great familiarity with Japan. I suppose this was just intuition.

IB: You explored the use of the long line in writing "The Tin Can," didn't you?

WJS: I've always felt that it is important in poetry—even in lyric poetry—to have a dramatic structure, so I turned to a longer line when I felt that I had material that needed a larger frame. "The Tin Can" was one of the first poems in which I used this long line. One of the dangers of using the long line is that everything begins to sound like prose, and I think that you have to avoid that. There has to be a rhythmic pattern to the whole thing. You can't just assume that because you're writing a longer line you're going to give up the basic musical qualities of poetry. Someone pointed out to me that "The Tin Can" is full of spondees and I think that's very true. I wasn't aware that I was making such use of them as I wrote it. But I think that using them was a way of building up tension in the poem—coming down very squarely with two beats, one after the other.

IB: Your poem "Galileo Galilei" is a haunting one. Could you talk about its origins?

WJS: It's a kind of dream poem, but actually I got the first four lines from a friend when I was a student at Oxford. He told me that these lines came to him in a dream and when he awoke he wrote them down. He couldn't continue with the lines, and he gave them to me—as a sort of challenge, it seemed. I thought about them off and on during the day. I had just been to Florence and had stayed with friends in the village of Pian dei Guillari up above the city, where Galileo lived when Milton went to see him. The whole city had become a kind of dreamscape for me and when I couldn't sleep the following night, I wrote down the poem, which for me still has the quality of a dream—and apparently it has had for many of my readers as well.

Galileo Galilei

Comes to knock and knock again
At a small secluded doorway
In the ordinary brain.

Into light the world is turning,
And the clocks are set for six;
And the chimney pots are smoking,
And the golden candlesticks.

Apple trees are bent and breaking,
And the heat is not the sun's;
And the Minotaur is waking,
And the streets are cattle runs.

Galileo Galilei,
In a flowing, scarlet robe,
While the stars go down the river
With the turning, turning globe,

Kneels before a black Madonna
And the angels cluster round

With grave, uplifted faces
Which reflect the shaken ground

And the orchard which is burning,
And the hills which take the light;
And the candles which have melted
On the altars of the night.

Galileo Galilei
Comes to knock and knock again
At a small secluded doorway
In the ordinary brain.

I tried to focus in this poem and in some others on an inner landscape—on that area between sleep and waking, which is an exploration of the psyche that can often be quite terrifying. Exploring the psyche in such instances is like bringing things up from a deep well. You have to send something down in a sense and then you find that you bring back something quite unexpected. That's what one does in exhuming one's dreams. One drinks from a deep well and feels refreshed in subtle ways that can go into one's work.

IB: What's the best poetical advice you ever received?

WJS: I remember that phrase of Whitman's, "Make the work," and I think that's terribly important. It's important not to give up and to keep working. You need a very tough skin because when you send poems out into the world, they can be misunderstood, and it can be very difficult to accept such misunderstanding. My son Gregory is a sculptor, and I think being a sculptor is perhaps even more difficult than being a poet. Greg has had to face rather stupid criticism at different times from people who don't understand anything about his medium and who make very silly remarks. I've grown accustomed to the same sort of thing with my poetry, and I've told Greg that he must develop a tough skin. Some poems of mine such as "American Primitive" were turned down by some of the best editors in the country. Now these poems are in anthologies and are translated into other languages all over the world. But I must say that before they appeared I had some very strange comments from people who should have known better.

IB: Example?

WJS: One critic said that the trouble with "American Primitive" was that it looked as if I was speaking of Uncle Sam because of the stovepipe hat, which is just absurd. Others didn't understand the poem at all—didn't understand that I was talking about a man who had hanged himself. They simply had not read the poem.

IB: What is your Muse like?

WJS: I used to have a beautiful old Italian postcard that showed a poet at his desk—a bearded figure leaning back in his armchair—and there before him was a lovely, ethereal feminine form rising through the air. The caption was "The Poet and his Muse." I used to keep that card on my desk as a joke because it's absolutely the opposite of what I consider the Muse really to be. For me the Muse is indeed the "White Goddess"— really quite terrifying, beautiful, but with the terror that comes with great beauty. I present a figure somewhat like that in my poem, "Slave Bracelets," and also in a light way in a poem called "The Ten," which is about women in general and, in the end, I think, about the Muse:

The Ten

"... one of the best-dressed ten women."
—A newspaper reference to Mme. Henri Bonnet

Mme. Bonnet is one of the best-dressed ten;
But what of the slovenly six, the hungry five,
The solemn three who plague all men alive,
The twittering two who appear every now and again?

What of the sexual seven who want only to please,
Advancing in unison down the hospital hall,
Conversing obscenely, wearing no clothing at all,
While under your sterile sheet you flame and freeze?

What will you say of the weird, monotonous one
Who stands beside the table when you write,
Her long hair coiling in the angry light,
Her wild eyes dancing brighter than the sun?

What will you say of her who grasps your pen
And lets the ink run slowly down your page,
Throws back her head and laughs as from a cage:
"Mme. Bonnet is one, you say? . . . And then?"

IB: What do you owe Wallace Stevens?

WJS: Stevens was a master of language and I greatly admire him. I spent ten months during World War II on Palmyra Island, a coral atoll a thousand miles southwest of Honolulu, six degrees above the equator. One of the few books I had with me at that time was Wallace Stevens' *Parts of a World*. I was fascinated by the great variety in that book and by the way Stevens dealt with language. That book was one of the most important influences on my poetic development.

IB: You never tired at all of that one book—in ten months?

WJS: No, never. And, of course, I had read the earlier Stevens as well—*Harmonium* and many of those poems had stayed with me.

IB: Do you memorize poems?

WJS: Yes, of course I do.

IB: Someone has theorized that memorizing poems can be destructive—that memorizing a poem kills it.

WJS: That's ridiculous. I think that's absolutely absurd. I can't think why it would ever kill anything to know it well. I'm just sorry that I didn't learn more poems early on. I remember when I conducted a poetry workshop at the Suffield Writer's Conference years ago, I had on one side of me Padraic Colum, the Irish poet, and on the other, the anthologist and poet Louis Untermeyer. If I referred to any well-known poem in the English language, Padraic Colum knew it by heart and could recite it right off. He said that there were few books when he went to school in Ireland, and he had to memorize all the poems. So he became a walking anthology, and wonderful to behold. I was sorry that I had been made by some bad teachers to memorize some very bad poems, which I can still quote—instead of having been made to memorize wonderful ones which I would also have remembered.

IB: What sort of bad ones?

WJS: There was one called "Somebody's Mother." I even had to write it all out. It was in the fifth grade, I think. It begins:

Somebody's mother was old and gray
And bent with the chill of a winter's day.

And it goes on and on. Somebody's mother comes out and it is snowing heavily. A little boy helps her across the street and when she gets home at night she says, "He's somebody's boy." It is one of the worst poems in English, and I can still recite great parts of it, especially if I've had a drink or two.

IB: Ever want to expunge it from your memory?

WJS: In a way, but it's like the parodies of Lewis Carroll. He was so aware that children like to make fun of very pompous poems. And we did the same sort of thing when I was in school. For example:

Under the spreading chestnut tree
The village smithy stands.

The smith a mighty man is he;
The muscles in his brawny arms
Are as strong as rubber bands.

(Laughs.) We were then simply having great fun with poems that seemed a bit too pompous for our young ears.

IB: Can you say something about the feeling you had when you first ran across a poem that wasn't one of the terrible ones?

WJS: I think it must have been a passage from Shakespeare. I remember hearing for the first time the opening of *Twelfth Night:*

If music be the food of love, play on;
Give me excess of it, that, surfeiting,
The appetite may sicken, and so die,
That strain again! It had a dying fall:
O, it came o'er my ear like the sweet sound,
That breathes upon a bank of violets,
Stealing and giving odor!

That seemed to me miraculous—and it still does. So much of the Shakespeare that I read or heard in school was really important to me. I also had a very fine teacher in high school who was passionate about poetry. She wasn't even one of my regular teachers, but rather a homeroom teacher, and she would open the school day with a poem by Robert Herrick. That was a revelation to me because the language of Herrick's poems was so simple and yet so magnificent. I suppose having poems like those presented to me daily was the greatest introduction to poetry that I could possibly have had.

IB: You're part American Indian?

WJS: Yes, Choctaw.

IB: You're interested in tracing your roots?

WJS: Yes, I talk about that in *Army Brat.* I've been in touch with the

Mississippi Choctaws, the branch from which my mother came. And I've been to the reservation in Mississippi. Some of the Choctaws stayed behind when they were supposed to move on to Oklahoma. Some of my mother's family came a little later to Arkansas and Oklahoma. I have a cousin who was a member of the first legislature in Oklahoma.

IB: What were the watershed periods in your literary life?

WJS: I was on shipboard for almost two years and I did a good deal of thinking about poetry and also writing poems in that time, and that was a very important period. And then right after the war, I spent three years in Europe, two of which were in Italy. I think that was important for me because I was able to concentrate on writing and slowly to develop a style of my own. I'd say that those two early periods were very important for my later work.

IB: What did Florence mean to you?

WJS: When I was there in '49–'50 and then again in '55–'57, it was a quiet, but wonderfully civilized place to live. I met a great many people in a very easy way. Italy at that time—just after World War II—was like Paris after World War I. Many writers came there, and I met people I would never have been able to meet in any other way. I met them casually and was able to see them over a period of days or weeks or years.

IB: Whom did you meet?

WJS: Harold Acton, who became a good friend, I used to see regularly, also Bernard Berenson and W. H. Auden.

IB: What was Berenson like?

WJS: He was always very reserved and formal in his gatherings at *I*

Tatti. I remember once when I was there working in his library (he used to let people come in to use it), and he didn't know that I was there. He came into the library dancing along like a little boy, calling to his secretary to come to lunch, and when he saw that I was there, he was quite embarrassed—or seemed so—because he was revealing a very natural side of himself that he seldom revealed. He drew himself up and asked me to stay for lunch, which that day I was unable to do. Through Berenson I met many people. And he took a great interest in everyone's work, including mine. Knowing him was very valuable to me.

IB: What was your fondest moment in Florence?

WJS: I was very shy in those days, and I regretted afterwards that I did not make any literary pilgrimages. I could have gone, for example, to see the Sitwells in their villa nearby, and I could also have gone to call on Sir Max Beerbohm. I now wish that I had. But I was shy then, and I would never have thought of doing anything like that, or I would have been petrified if I had.

IB: You were that shy? How else did your shyness manifest itself?

WJS: I remember standing in a pub in Oxford between Dylan Thomas and John Betjeman, unable to say a word while Thomas and Betjeman conducted a rapid-fire conversation about writers one after another. I felt as if I were in the middle of a tennis court while balls were whizzing back and forth. I later came to realize that the British in general abhor a vacuum in a conversation and rush on saying whatever happens to come into their heads when often in reality they have nothing to say.

IB: What's the key to writing children's verse?

WJS: I remember how I started. I had been listening to my four-year-old son David, and I began to put down some of what he was saying. I would continue with his statements and turn them into little poems, which he then thought that he had actually written. And, of course, in a sense, he had.

I think that anyone who writes for children has to remember what it was like to be young, and many writers can't remember. I recall that once after I had finished my first children's book, *Laughing Time*, I read it to an art critic friend. He thought that I'd gone out of my mind because he couldn't remember at all what it had been like to be four years old. But I thought that I was right, and indeed I was—the poems have had great appeal for children.

IB: What were your first memories?

WJS: I suppose I remember playing in the heat in Louisiana and Arkansas and the smell of tarpaper—that kind of thing— sensations of heat, smell, taste connected with smell. I remember the way the floors looked and the smell of bacon and biscuits.

IB: Didn't you know Marianne Moore early in your career as a poet?

WJS: Yes, I did. She was in a way the one who really launched my career. I was about to publish a first book of twenty-one poems. It was being printed by hand by the Banyan Press. The Press had just completed the printing when the editors of the little magazine *Furioso*, in which two of the poems had appeared, sent a copy to Marianne Moore. She wrote back about one of my poems, "Cupidon," calling it a "permanence, a rare felicity," and the editors sent me this comment. Of course, I was beside myself with delight. I wrote to her and asked if I could quote it. The Banyan Press put a special little band around the book with her comment on it. And she said that she had confidence also in my other work. I had not met her then, but Barbara Howes and I were married shortly afterwards, and we asked her to come to our wedding party and she came.

After that we had some correspondence, and I used to see her from time to time.

IB: Ever been in awe of a poet?

WJS: I was greatly in awe of Auden. I found it very difficult to converse with him. I don't think that I was alone in that respect because you couldn't carry on any kind of small talk with Auden—you just couldn't. I used to love to listen to him, but I felt very awkward putting questions to him. When I got to know him better, it became less difficult, but it was never easy.

IB: What was he really like?

WJS: He was a workhorse, very insistent on keeping to a certain schedule, which he would not break for any reason. Auden came once to visit us in Vermont. After he had moved to Austria, he wanted to get an international driver's license but he'd been turned down on the driver's test in New York City. He wanted to take the test again, but this time in Albany, which was just an hour away from our Vermont residence. He practiced driving in preparation for the test. His way of practicing was to take the car out of the garage and then put a stick down in the road and try to back up to the stick. He'd get out and go back to see how close he had come and then throw the stick down again. He was really one of the worst drivers I have ever seen. Every maneuver was impossibly awkward. He was absolutely confident that he was getting along well. He went over to Albany, took the test, and failed miserably. He blamed those who had tested him, saying that they just wanted to force him to go to driving school. It was a racket, he said. The truth was that he never should have been allowed behind a wheel—he was just a terrible driver.

IB: What is your view of poetry and politics?

WJS: I think that it is very important for a poet to be actively involved in what is going on in his country and in the world, but it is difficult to write poems with a political bias. I was totally opposed to the Vietnam war, but I found it difficult to put that particular sentiment into poetry. Actually in my poem, "What Train Will Come?" there are a number of references to the war and to that whole period. But when I wrote the poem, I was writing about violence in general and not just about the war. And perhaps that is why the topical references have not bothered readers many years later.

IB: Your poem, "Death of a Jazz Musician," is a kind of dream.

WJS: Not really. The poem started with a local bar and a jukebox:

Death of a Jazz Musician

I dreamed that when I died a jukebox played,
And in the metal slots bright coins were laid;
Coins on both my eyes lay cold and bright
As the boatman ferried my thin shade into the night.

I dreamed a jukebox played. I saw the flame
Leap from a whirling disk which bore my name,
Felt fire like music sweep the icy ground—
And forward still the boatman moved, and made no sound.

Hungarian television recently did a film on my poetry and translations. They did a dramatization of that poem in Hungary with my voice below reading the poem in English. There were actors on a barge on Lake Balaton, with the figure of the jazz musician stretched out and jazz music being played. And the jazz musician was wearing *my* clothes.

IB: Actually wearing your clothes?

WJS: Yes, because they wanted to make me the musician, you see, and they had my face—the actor's face—covered with a ski mask and studded with coins. It is a very startling dramatization.

IB: Your book *The Traveler's Tree* contains a number of epitaphs. Have you ever written one for yourself?

WJS: I thought that the very last lines of the title poem, "The Traveler's Tree," might serve as my epitaph. It sums up the whole journey that has come to an end and addresses the reader in these words:

Then cross the threshold and enter the dark house.
You will be welcome. I will be waiting. I will be there.

ISAAC ASIMOV

Isaac Asimov has been described as "the nearest thing to a human writing machine" and "a national resource and a natural wonder." A genius whose intellect is incalculable, he is clearly the most prolific writer in the world today. As of this writing, Asimov has written 395 books. Over the past eleven years, he has averaged over twenty books a year.

Born in Petrovichi, Russia, in 1920, Asimov emigrated to New York with his parents at the age of three. He was accepted by Columbia University at the age of fifteen and earned his B.S. degree from there in 1939. The war interrupted his doctoral studies, and he served as a chemist in the United States Navy until 1945. In 1948 he received his Ph.D. in Chemistry from Columbia. He taught biochemistry at Boston University School of Medicine but turned to full-time writing in 1958.

Asimov began writing science fiction at age eleven, and his first book-length work of science fiction, *Pebble in the Sky*, was published in 1950. He branched out into nonfiction with a scientific textbook published in 1952. Since that time, Asimov has written about an incredibly wide range of subjects from math and physics to Shakespeare and music. He has been a successful mystery writer, editor, journalist, biographer, and humorist. He recently wrote his 366th essay for a series in *Fantasy and Science Fiction*—not having missed an issue in over thirty years.

In addition to receiving a special Hugo Award (the Oscar for science fiction writing) honoring his Foundation Trilogy as the Best All-Time Science Fiction Series, Asimov was given another Hugo for *Foundation's Edge*. In 1987, Asimov was the recipient of a special Nebula Award by the Science Fiction Writers of America, designating him a Grandmaster of Science Fiction. He has also received three other Hugos and two additional Nebulas.

As an interviewee, Asimov is friendly but business-like. He had agreed to forty-five minutes and, as if a clock went off in his head, his convivial side switched off and he concluded the interview. A prolific author obviously counts his time as precious.

IRV BROUGHTON: Do you remember writing "Marooned on Vesta," your first published story?

ISAAC ASIMOV: Yes, it was the third story I had written, but the first story I had sold.

IB: Did you have a certain confidence that story would be published?

IA: I can't recall that I actually thought that any of my early stories would be published. I only had hopes, but I recall my surprise and pleasure when it was accepted. I guess I must have really believed.

IB: Wasn't there a librarian who let you work in the library?

IA: I can't recall her very clearly. She was a very small woman, middle-aged, and not extraordinarily good-looking or any-thing—just an ordinary librarian. And I don't know whether she had ever heard of me. But I asked her please if I could stay there during lunch hour and type, and she let me. And she had no cause to regret it because certainly I didn't do anything but type during the lunch hour. I was not the kind of person who struck fear into people. I suppose I always seemed like a mild and gentle person so that they weren't afraid to let me stay somewhere. They weren't afraid I would get them in trouble.

IB: As a young writer did you envy any writers in particular?

IA: No, I can't recall that I did. I didn't have the kind of notion of myself that made me feel I wasn't getting the breaks I deserved. I didn't feel as though I wrote just as well as so-and-so. "Look at so-and-so getting rich and famous." I am extremely—I sup-pose you could say—"self-centered," but I like to think of me as a "self-aware person." However, my universe consists largely of me, so that I'm not particularly concerned about the success of others. It doesn't bother me. I'm concerned with what will happen to me.

IB: What characteristics of your parents do you have? I'm thinking perhaps in terms of the writing and the tremendous work ethic.

IA: My parents had that. They were poor people, and they were brought up in a nation that did not have any sense of caring for poor people. When they came to the United States in the 1920s, it was a United States without welfare, without unemployment insurance, without any of the fixtures of the New Deal, which were later established. They knew and took for granted the fact that if they didn't work, they wouldn't eat. Therefore since they wanted to eat, they were intent on working hard. There was no danger that they would ever stoop to illegal methods of obtaining money because they were brought up in a strictly religious way. Without bringing me up in the rituals of the religion, they brought me up in the ethical content that they allowed. So I grew up expecting to work hard, and I have all my life.

IB: Did they introduce you early to literature?

IA: Not directly. They were unable to. They didn't speak the language. They knew nothing about the English-language literature. What they did do was get me a library card at the age of six and turn me loose in the library, take me there whenever they could. The first time they ever allowed me to take a bus on my own was so that I might go to the library. And all through, from the age of six to the time I got married at twenty-two, I was a library habitué. That was my introduction to literature.

IB: What was your library routine?

IA: The routine would be that I would go to the library, pick out two books or how much ever they would allow me, finish them, and at the first opportunity, return to the library and take out more and read them. I did this over and over. And, of course, my father ran a newsstand, and I eventually discovered science fiction magazines at age nine.

IB: Describe the newsstand and your relationship to it.

IA: The newsstand contained all sorts of magazines. It was the heyday of the pulp fiction magazine where you had weeklies, biweeklies, and monthlies, with every kind of category of fiction: detective stories, love stories, western stories, air stories, jungle stories, hero stories—"The Shadow," "The Spider," "Operator Five," "Secret Agent x," all of which were out-of-bounds for me. My father thought they were not good enough. He insisted that I stick to the books that I got in the library. But then, in August of 1929, I noticed a magazine called *Science Wonder Stories*, and I sold my father on the notion that the stories dealt with science, so he thought I could read that. And then I read other magazines of the same sort, even when "science" was not in the title.

IB: Were there any other ways your parents tried hard to protect you in view of your obvious intelligence and potential?

IA: No, that was the one way. The other thing was that they approved of my doing well in school. And of course it's always nice to obtain approval of your parents. They didn't know the language, and, for that matter, neither my mother nor my father had ever received a secular education. They could read and write both Russian and Yiddish, but except for that my mother had no education at all, and my father only had a Hebrew education.

IB: You mentioned a specific month—August of 1929. Do you remember specific months and days in the way that the average person might not?

IA: I remember everything in the way that the average person might not. It's fading out as I grow older, but, when I was younger, I had a very remarkable memory, and as my wife said it's only now receded to the point where it's slightly better than average.

IB: How did you view that?

IA: I viewed that as though that were perhaps the greatest stroke of luck I ever had. It meant that I could learn quickly because people had to explain things to me only once. It meant that once I learned something I knew it forever. And it also meant I could pack a great deal into my three-pound brain, so that, in the end, I was able to write books of all kinds, on all subjects, and gain a certain amount of admiration therefore. So it's due to a reasonably high intelligence and a remarkable memory.

IB: You've pointed out, haven't you, that memory and intelligence are slightly different things.

IA: Oh, sure, it's possible to be extremely intelligent and yet have a very fallible memory. I've known lots of people like that. And it's also possible to have a photographic memory, a memory which is much better than mine, but which is not linked to any particular intelligence, so that you're merely a parrot, repeating whatever you've heard or read, without really understanding. I remember during the vogue for quiz games in the 1950s there was Teddy Nadler, who was a postal clerk, and who couldn't very well do any work more intricate than that of being a postal clerk. But he had this eidetic memory. He could remember everything he'd ever read, heard, and he could recall so that if you'd ask him questions and if they were quite factual: "What was the middle name of so-and-so?—he would tell you. But you couldn't ask him questions which were qualitative, such as "Explain the significance of American tariff policy after the Civil War." You know, he would draw a complete blank. Nevertheless, he was referred to as a genius. And it struck me at that time that is typical of the way in which people viewed intelligence. I mean, they didn't even know what intelligence was—they mistook it for a trick memory.

IB: How did we finally come to understand intelligence?

IA: I don't know that we—meaning people in general—ever do. Intelligence is an extremely subtle concept. It's a kind of understanding that flourishes if it's combined with a good memory, but exists anyway even in the absence of good memory. It's the ability to draw consequences from causes, to make correct inferences, to foresee what might be the result, to work out logical problems, to be reasonable, rational, to have the ability to understand the solution from perhaps insufficient information. You know when a person is intelligent, but you can be easily fooled if you are not yourself intelligent.

IB: One thinks of a Mozart, who was prolific in his work, and a Beethoven, who wrote little. How does one explain these things?

IA: Well, you're sometimes caught in the grip of whatever it is. I'm not prolific because I choose to be prolific, and I don't imagine that Mozart—with whom I do not for one minute try to compare myself—tried to be prolific either. It's just that in my case, stuff is always bubbling inside me and it bothers me until I get rid of it. And I imagine the same thing was true of Mozart. He had this music continually proceeding inside his brain, and it probably hurt him unless he got it on paper.

IB: Can you describe that hurt—the way you feel when you can't write because something intervenes?

IA: The closest I come is to say that the rest of the world recedes—that, as the thing tightens inside your mind more and more—you become less and less interested in anything else, more and more impatient with everything that's keeping you from the typewriter, less and less happy at not being at the typewriter—

you're staring at your watch more and more. I mean, there have been times when I've hated to go to bed because I didn't want to waste my time. In fact, I suppose that what happens is you become very aware of wasting your time. People say to me that I must be very disciplined in order to stay with the typewriter as much as I do. But that's not it at all. If I were disciplined properly, I could force myself to stay away from the typewriter, live a more normal life. The fact that I'm not disciplined—that I'm a slave to whatever it is that bubbles in me that keeps me at the typewriter—I suppose is the same thing that keeps some people doing nothing, instead of doing something, but it keeps me doing something instead of doing nothing.

IB: What's the most rigorous period of writing you've ever put in? Was there ever forty-eight hours straight?

IA: Oh, no. I've never done anything like that. I just write as I feel like, when I feel like, which is just about most of the time. But I got a lot done—not because I spent an unusually long time at the typewriter, but simply because I write very quickly and I don't revise much. So that, for instance, I have a weekly syndicated science column—each of which is eight hundred words long, and I always sent it in exactly to the line. And I turn it out every Saturday before breakfast, or if I eat a particularly early breakfast, immediately after. It takes me just about one hour from sitting down at the word processor to having the thing in the envelope ready to mail. And this is routine. I can type eight hundred words very quickly, and the editing takes very little time because it's usually fairly correct as I do it the first time. I don't have to brood about it all—it always comes out the same length to the correct line because I automatically pace myself so that if I seem to be coming to an end too soon, I put in another sentence. If I seem to be running too long, I cut out another sentence without even being aware of it.

IB: How fast do you type?

IA: I type ninety words per minute on the typewriter; I type one-hundred words per minute on the word processor. But, of course, I don't keep that up indefinitely—every once in a while I do have to think a few seconds.

IB: Ever had bad days where you have to think for quite a few "few seconds"?

IA: I'm pretty consistent. When I sit down at the typewriter, I write. Someone once asked me if I had a fixed routine before I start, like setting up exercises, sharpening pencils, or having a drink of orange juice. I said, "No, the only thing I do before I start writing is to make sure that I'm close enough to the type-writer to reach the keys."

IB: Baseball players get sore arms. Is there anything comparable for a writer—writer's back or typist's forefinger?

IA: I guess what we do is run the risks—aside from the fact of the sedentary life leading to overweight, flabbiness, which God knows I've suffered from all my life—of piles; hemorrhoids. I don't think I've got them but, you know, sitting down all the time is hard. And I imagine that you also have a chance of lower back pain which I occasionally suffer from. It may seem strange, but you get in cramped positions and you forget to change them. I notice that when I'm working on indexes and am bending over the cards—I do this for hours at a time—that when I try to straighten, I'm in agony. I guess the cure for that is to knock off every once in a while and stretch, walk around and loosen up, but you forget.

IB: How has the word processor affected you and the way you write?

IA: Well, it's cleaned up my manuscripts because I'm a pretty slap-dash typist, and when I type, although I say ninety wpm, it's not ninety wpm by professional standards, because professionals deduct for mistakes. And I don't. I do ninety wpm with lots of mistakes. And then, I'd go over my manuscript and I'd put it through the typewriter twice: first draft, next, go through and make minor changes, then type up final copy, and finally go over and correct the mis-strikes, and all the errors I make. So usually my final manuscripts are not as neat as a professional typist would do. And editors don't like it, but they figure, "Well, it's Isaac Asimov." However, now I do things on the word processor and edit as I go along so that I hand in clean copy. Also, when I do a book or a novel or a long piece, I generally do a first draft on the typewriter because I'm used to that. I work better that way. Then I put it into the word processor and clean it up. Even so, I manage to make a few errors that I don't spot when going over it on the screen, but not many.

IB: Are you a perfectionist?

IA: No, I'm not. You can either be a perfectionist or you can be a prolific writer—you can't be both. If you're going to start polishing and getting rid of every last little difficulty, you might do it, but it's going to take a lot of time. And I never have the time to take a lot of time. I'm much too anxious to get on to the next job.

IB: What was the hardest book to write?

IA: Oh, some I like less than others—some are harder than others. I once wrote a book called *The Human Brain,* which was very difficult to do because I didn't really know enough. I had to educate myself as I went along. And my novels are generally hard to do because my plots are intricate, and I have to think up an awful lot of background, etc. Science fiction is more difficult than mystery fiction; fiction generally is more difficult than nonfiction. Nonfiction is easy if it's on a subject that I know about.

IB: The intricacy of plotting would seem to suggest that you would have to sit down and think it through before you sit down to write.

IA: When I first started, I thought I'd make an outline. But I couldn't stick to the outline because the story wrote itself. The outline was like chains, shackles, so I stopped. What I do is think up a general notion of what it is that I want to do. I think up a nice, snappy ending, figure out where I ought to start, and then make it up as I go along. And so far the intricacy always adds itself, and, when I'm all finished, everyone could swear I worked it out very carefully to begin with—but it's not so. Generally on page x I haven't the faintest idea of what will be ten pages later on.

IB: Do you have a plot that you're proudest of?

IA: The story I've written that I like best is called "The Last Question," but do I like it best because of its central idea or because of the details of its plot? I think it's because of its central idea. When it comes to plots, I'm much fonder of my mystery plots than of my science fiction plots.

IB: Why is that?

IA: Because in the case of the mysteries, the plots are really the whole thing; whereas in science fiction the plots are only one-half—the other half is the futuristic society I've got in the background. That's what makes science fiction particularly hard. I have to juggle a society which is interesting in itself, and I have to describe the society in considerable detail without making the reader feel that I'm slowing up the plot unbearably. And I have to be able to tell the story without too badly obscuring the social background.

IB: Any incubation period helpful when dealing with a lot of research material?

IA: I never do have that—even in my nonfiction. I generally do what research is necessary and it's never very much. I still retain the ability to remember what I know, more or less forever, and to quickly glance over a scientific paper and get what I need and know it. I don't have to go back to it. So that I'm not conscious ever of doing a lot of research. I do it, of course, but it seems to take place fleetingly.

IB: What was the easiest book for you to write?

IA: Well, if you don't consider just short books, a book that took quite a long time but gave the most pleasure was my autobiography because it dealt with something close to my heart. Next to that is something called *Asimov's Guide to Shakespeare* because I really enjoyed the plays and I like to talk about them. Earlier this year I published *Asimov's Annotated Gilbert and Sullivan,* which is a nice, big fat book. It sells for fifty dollars. And I wrote it in two months, in-between novels. And let me tell you, those were a happy two months.

IB: If you could have only one Shakespeare play, what would it be?

IA: Well, I guess it would have to be *Hamlet,* although *King Lear* runs a close second. And when I did the books I was surprised how much I enjoyed *Anthony and Cleopatra.* I wouldn't have thought that would have been one of my favorites.

IB: Talk about the question of longevity. Would you want to live to be a hundred and fifty years old?

IA: Only if I could write. There'd be no purpose of living any longer than I can write. I can imagine an age at which my brain would have sufficiently deteriorated so that I couldn't write— even though I could still live and lead an aware life—I'm not talking about Alzheimer's or anything like that. But, if the time came when I couldn't spend all day writing, there'd be no point in staying alive. So to live a hundred and fifty years, yeah, I would like it provided I retained my mind in its full force.

IB: In its full force? What if you could only write a book a year, but it would be a brilliant book?

IA: I'd be extremely unhappy, extremely. As a matter of fact, when I had my heart attack in 1977, I didn't let it bother me at all—I was alive, I was feeling all right in the hospital, I wasn't in pain. Everything was okay—cracking jokes with the interns and stuff, until it suddenly occurred to me that the doctor was going to insist that I cut down on my output. He'd say, "Come on, Asimov. From now on, if you want to live, turn out only half." And I promptly broke down at that thought. But it was a breakdown for nothing because I never slowed down.

IB: You broke down?

IA: At the thought of having to work at half speed. It made life seem useless. And, as I say, I wasted my time breaking down because that was eleven years ago and, in those eleven years, I have not slowed down. As a matter of fact, at my heart attack I had published approximately one hundred ninety books—maybe a few fewer than that. Right now I've published three hundred ninety-five, which means that since my heart attack eleven years ago, I've put out about two hundred books, which is an average of nearly twenty a year.

IB: Think you could recite the names of all the books you've written?

IA: Oh, I think if I just sat down and thought about it, and just gave you this book, that book, and the other, I could list a good percentage of them. But I bet there'd be several dozen that I'd leave out. I'd probably leave out some of the anthologies—I've edited about one hundred anthologies, and they're not as close to my heart as my own books are. I don't experience them the same way I experience my own books. I wouldn't count them except that when I did my first couple of anthologies, I had no idea there'd be so many of them, and I automatically counted them. Because the number of my books has become a great point about me, people are always asking me how many books I've written. I don't count any book that may have my name in the title but on which I did no work at all. There are a number of books, which sometimes take three of my novels and slap them together. I don't consider that a book because I didn't do anything. But sometimes I put together a collection of stories, which I carefully select, to which I write headnotes, introductions. Every one of those stories may have appeared in earlier collections so they're just a retread, but, on the other hand, I did work on it so I count it. It would be very complicated to figure out which books are completely original, which are re-treads, which are in anthologies, etc. And I figure the hell with it—I'll count them all up and leave it someday to some biographer to make sense of it.

IB: Ever puzzle over putting stories together?

IA: Yes, I did it yesterday and today. There's a fellow who wants to put out a collection out of my books and have me write a special story for it, which has never appeared elsewhere. I'll write an introduction and he would add illustrations. And then I have to choose the stories. I went through the entire list of my stories, and I tried to pick those stories which were not contained in more than one of my collections, did not appear in more than one anthology, and were not so poor—so early written, before I had achieved my maturity as a writer—that I was ashamed to have them included. I ended up with about twenty-seven stories for the book. That took considerable time, going through, making decisions—not the same kind of time as is spent in writing original material, but it takes time.

IB: When do you think your mind amazed you most with its abilities?

IA: Oh, I think my speaking amazes me more than my writing. I command high fees and I've received up to twenty thousand dollars—only once. My general pay is between seventy-five hundred dollars and ten thousand dollars.

IB: I read you didn't like to be referred to as a consultant.

IA: Because I don't consult. But on the other hand, I don't mind being referred to as an after-dinner speaker. In fact, I would describe myself as the best off-the-cuff after-dinner speaker in the whole damn world. I never prepare a talk. I get up and speak without notes, without rehearsal, without anything, and I do well. I simply, again, manage it through my remarkable memory. I remember everything that I want to say, and I think quickly on my feet. Last Saturday I was interviewed on "Open Mind," on the air. It was taped last June and what happened was I walked into the studio, sat down, and he asked me questions, and I answered. I did not know what questions he would ask. Yet, if you watch the interview, you'll see no hesitation on my part. Whatever question he asked, I answered. And that amazes me, frankly, that I can do that. I keep wondering how long I can keep on doing that. But it's much more remarkable than my writing because my writing I'm doing by myself and I can stop and think if I want to. But when I'm speaking on the stage or being interviewed—as for instance, you and me now— I don't have time to think, or at least I don't take time. I don't say, "Well, let me think about this for five or ten minutes, then I'll give you my answer." I generally start talking instantly and coherently. So how I do this I don't know, but it works and people pay me my large sums with smiles on their faces.

IB: At what aspect of your brain are you most amazed—is it memory, perception, reason?

IA: It's always been memory. I'm not continually good at the others. There are other people more perceptive; there are other people who are probably more intelligent, but there are very few people

65

who have my faculties and facilities where memory is concerned. And I'm so aware of how much easier it makes my life.

IB: You mentioned the quiz show a little while ago. Did you ever think of getting on one?

IA: I was asked during the fifties to be on a quiz show. I was strongly tempted. But then, I thought if I get on and win money, it won't get me much. People will say, "Of course." On the other hand, if I get on and make a fool out of myself—which can easily happen in front of a large American audience—I figure I would not like that. In other words, I had too little to gain and too much to lose so I refused to go on a quiz show. As a matter of fact, it turned out to be another one of those decisions I made purely for accidental or adventitious reasons which turned out to be right on the nose because when the scandal broke, I was completely in the clear. I'm perfectly convinced that, if I'd gone on, nothing on earth would have made me agree to fake answers or anything like that, but that doesn't mean that someone else would not believe that I had.

IB: Are there some things you wish you didn't remember?

IA: Oh, many things—wise-guy remarks I made, hurtful answers I couldn't resist making, unkindnesses to my children, to my first or second wife, people around. I mean, everybody does things sometimes in hot blood or out of mistake, because they think its funny when it isn't, and it's embarrassing to look back. And I must admit that I dislike my ability to remember every one of them.

IB: Did a lot of things stem from teasing?

IA: Well, some from teasing and some singly from the thrust or riposte of everyday life. Just to give examples that I remember of where I felt at the time that I was justified, but looking back I figured it wasn't fair. I was growing a mustache. I mean, every young man at one point or another tries to grow a mustache—or at least a great many. I did, and a young woman said to me when she became aware of the fact that my upper lip was bristling, "Are *you* trying to grow a mustache?" Somehow I interpreted it as a slur on my virility—you know, she seemed to doubt that I was capable of it, and so I said, "Why not, you've managed." And she had—that's the point. That was the cruelty of it. I'm sure she was very well aware, too, that she had a few scattered hairs on her upper lip. There was no call to say it except that at the moment I was too annoyed. Well, of course, she burst into tears and after a while I got to feeling very bad about it. It happened over forty years ago. As time went on, I learned not to do these things. But when I was younger, it was difficult.

Also, over forty years ago this happened. I've never had what you might call a trim body—I obviously lead a sedentary life, and it's only with great difficulty that I avoid overeating, so I've always had a kind of potbelly. And in the chem lab during the war, I had a rubber apron on, which kind of sloped down to my abdomen and then went over it and came down so I really looked humorous. I was busily pouring something from one vessel into another, and a young lady in the lab—a thin young lady—came along with a long glass tubing and presented it to me spear-fashion and said, "Isaac, I think I'll let out all that air in your stomach and make you look more like a man." And without looking up from what I was doing I said, "Use it to pump up your chest so that you look more like a woman," which was, again, a true remark, but not one which she appreciated. And she chased me out of the lab, and I didn't dare come back for the rest of the day. That sort of thing I can remember perfectly, and I feel ashamed of it.

IB: Give me another example.

IA: All right. This happened to me about two years ago. I was particularly ashamed of myself because I thought I'd cured myself of it. I was at a table with a bunch of other people. I was reciting limericks that I had written, and I recited one that I thought was pretty good. And the fellow who sat next to me said, "Oh, come on, you can do better than that." And I said, "The point is, old boy, you can't!" And the table burst into laughter. I felt bad immediately. I didn't have to wait and look back on it, but again, it's the sort of thing that I've tried to cure myself of, but it's been a difficult job. However, whereas in my youthful days until my middle twenties, perhaps, I was widely considered as a kind of insufferable, conceited boor; in recent decades I've generally been regarded as a nice guy. Of course, I'm a conceited, insufferable boor inside, but I just don't show it much anymore. (Laughs.)

IB: In a brief bio clip in *Is Anyone There?* you mention that you decided to get a Ph.D. in chemistry and you did; you decided to get married to a specific person and you did. Do you usually approach things that way or was that a little hyperbolic?

IA: No, it did happen precisely that way. It's not unusual. I generally decide to do things I know darn well I can do. I don't decide to become a champion boxer; I don't decide to cross the Niagara Falls on a high wire; I don't decide to enter the Olympics. I know my limitations very well, and when I make a decision, it's something I've got a good chance to do, and it's something that I know my abilities allow me to attain.

IB: What does the future mean to you?

IA: Well, it means something either very bad or something very good, depending on what we do and what the headlines of the moment are. I feel good when there's any sign that we're going to be less belligerent toward others, as nations. I feel bad when the human species shows itself to be unusually stupid. I feel bad, for instance, when there's a race for the presidency, as there is this year, and instead of trying to argue out the future of the nation, you make a big deal over the Pledge of Allegiance of which I can't think of anything more trivial. Now both nominees never make a move without being surrounded by twenty-seven million American flags. I mean, I don't know which is sadder—that the nominees think this is a good thing to do or the fact that the American public would rather cheer twenty-seven million American flags than to consider: What are we going to do about these banks failing in the Southwest? What are we going to do about the balance of payments? What about the national debt? What about the possibility of increasingly hot summers? No one says a word about these things. You'd think they don't exist. What are we electing presidents for—to see who looks better sitting up in the American flags, for goodness sakes. I mean, what value is the Pledge of Allegiance? You take a guy who's ripping the government off in insider trading, in refusing to pay his income tax, in making all sorts of crooked deals. Do you think he's going to hesitate to pledge allegiance? He can put his hand on his heart and say, "I pledge allegiance to the United States . . ."—of course he can say it. It doesn't stop them from being crooks or villains.

IB: If you were forced to trade places with a great scientist, who would it be?

IA: The greatest scientist who ever lived was Isaac Newton, and he and I have the same first name. I might as well be him. Usually, for number two there is Albert Einstein.

IB: Are there any scientists who may be well known, but who repulse you?

IA: Oh, sure. Edward Teller. I mean, there's my idea of a scientific villain. I imagine that there are similar people all through history—not necessarily that everyone would call them villains, but I do. There's a guy called Richard Owen who was an adversary of Darwin, whom I would consider a scientific villain. There are fortunately not many. By and large scientists, no matter how peculiar they might be in private life, usually as scientists are good men. Not always. There were German scientists in the post–World War I era who were violent Nazis.

One was Johannes Stark, and the other—oh, my goodness, my memory! Why can't I remember it? Oh, Philipp Lenard. I always get panicky if I can't remember something. There's a guy called Cyril Burt and there are other scientists also—I'm only talking of scientists of international repute. For instance, Stark and Lenard were both Nobel Prize winners. Burt was knighted.

IB: Is there any scientific discovery you wish you'd made?

IA: Oh, well, who on earth wouldn't have wanted to have been able to write the *Principia Mathematica,* in which Newton worked out the laws of motion and gravitation. By all odds it's the greatest scientific book ever written—or ever will be written, I think. Who with any pretensions to being a scientist could not wish that he had written that book?

IB: Frank Herbert said he believed that eventually we'll leave this earth and live on another planet. Do you see that?

IA: We'll leave the earth and extend our range. That doesn't necessarily mean we'll abandon the earth. Europeans settled America and Australia—it doesn't mean Europe is less crowded.

IB: How important is the ego of the writer?

IA: Extremely important. There's no such thing as a modest writer. Just imagine that a writer thinks that what he writes other people will be willing to pay to read. It's as great an example of conceit as can be imagined, so that before a writer can even be a writer he has to have a healthy ego.

IB: Author John Baxter talked about how many science fiction movies in the past had as preoccupations the loss of individuality and the threat that knowledge creates. Yet, you're a person who creates knowledge.

IA: All through history people have been suspicious of knowledge—even in Adam and Eve's tale. Their great crime was to eat of the fruit of the tree of the knowledge of good and evil. In other words, they wanted to know something more than they should. And people have always felt that this urge to know more than they ought to know is bad. But, naturally, I believe that is just the fear that is aroused on the part of people who are themselves ignorant, and who are afraid of people who know more than they do. I think that knowledge increases individualism, that the more we know the more we understand people as individuals, rather than just as members of a faceless mass. The tendency is always in the direction of recognizing the differences in people that you know more and more about.

IB: What were the origins of the story "Bicentennial Man?"

IA: A young lady wanted to do an anthology of stories, all of them suggested by the phrase "bicentennial man." She wanted to publish it in 1976 at the time of the Bicentennial. She didn't care what the stories would be as long as the words "bicentennial man" would fit somewhere in the story. And so, I wrote one called "Bicentennial Man." I figured if it was going to be a science fiction story, it couldn't be this particular bicentennial, so what bicentennial could it be? I figured it would be someone's personal bicentennial—two hundredth birthday. I didn't think a human being could very well live to be two hundred, so how about a robot? So I wrote a story about a robot reaching his two hundredth birthday and everything else followed. Then it turned out that the anthology didn't work because—of all the stories she got—the only one that was useable was mine, and she herself had a great deal of personal problems, so the anthology never appeared. But the story appeared in another anthology that had nothing to do with the Bicentennial as a whole. But I guess the story was good because it won both the Hugo and the Nebula.

IB: You really predicted the idea of robotics, didn't you, in *I-Robot*?

IA: I was the first one to use the word "robotics." I was the first one to advance the Three Laws of Robotics.

IB: How does that make you feel when you create knowledge?

IA: Well, generally I'm not aware I have until years have passed and then I'm more surprised than anything else.

IB: What's the most fundamental difference between art and science to you?

IA: Science is something that can be confirmed, that human beings can agree upon objectively. Art is something that is purely personal and subjective. One man's art is another man's trash.

IB: What were the watershed periods in your life?

IA: Coming to the United States when I was three years old, discovering science fiction, making up my mind to write science fiction, getting my Ph.D. in chemistry, getting fired from my job in 1958 so I was forced to be a full-time writer, then writing *The Intelligent Man's Guide to Science,* my first book, that attracted the attention of the world outside science fiction, and finally, I suppose, getting my Grandmaster award in 1987, a kind of recognition of my life's work.

ANN DARR

Ann Darr's life as a professional writer developed after the dissolution of her marriage. Her first book was published in 1971, and since then she has gained a following for her clean, tough-minded poems.

Ann is a magna cum laude graduate of the University of Iowa where she attended an undergraduate division of the Iowa Writer's Workshops taught by Eric Knight and Robert Penn Warren. She has taught at the University of Maryland and is currently adjunct professor at The American University.

She is author of *Do You Take This Woman*, *St. Ann's Gut*, *The Myth of a Woman's Fist*, *Cleared for Landing*, and *Riding with the Fireworks*.

A recipient of MacDowell and Yaddo fellowships—and a Bunting Institute Fellow at Radcliffe—she received a Discovery Award from the Poetry Center in New York. She has recorded her own work for the Library of Congress and has served on the Washington Poetry Advisory Committee at the Folger Shakespeare Library.

Ann Darr is a veteran of the Army Air Force and served in World War II. Flight is a major metaphor in her writing. Darr has a theatrical quality—she is animated and speaks with intensity and earnestness. (One of her three daughters is an actress in New York.) She is attentive to others. She is the listener, looking for nuance, the true meaning.

INTERVIEW

IRV BROUGHTON: You write a lot about flight. What does flight mean to you?

ANN DARR: Well, flight is my main metaphor. Flight means running away from, it means a Phoenix rising from the ashes—and it means that marvelous power of flight that one does in the middle of dreams when you take off and fly with your own energy. It also means, practically, flying a plane, because I was in the Woman's Air Force Service Pilots during World War II.

IB: Your group was finally recognized, wasn't it?

AD: Yes, after thirty-three years, we finally won the right to be part of the air force. Before that they didn't recognize that what we did was important. We couldn't have done it without Bruce Arnold's help—he was General Hap Arnold's son. It was Hap Arnold who asked Jacqueline Cochran to go to England to look at what the WAFs were doing over there and start the WASPs here. He expected us to be taken into the air force officially, but the House of Representatives voted us down and we were disbanded. We were told there were many more pilots coming back from overseas than needed, so they didn't need us. They also decided not to recognize the work we had already done, which was a big disappointment to us, because we had performed in army planes under army orders, under all kinds of conditions, and we felt that we really did deserve the recognition and maybe some insurance. We had nothing.

IB: What sort of conditions did you work under?

AD: I towed targets in a gunnery school in Las Vegas. I flew B–26s towing targets that were shot at by the gunners in the B–17s that flew alongside of us. And some of our planes were shot down, actually. Well, that was just part of our job. There were

75

other jobs that were as dangerous—there were women who ferried the planes from the factories to the fields where they were used. Your assignment depended on how tall you were. Because I was 5'6 1/4", I flew bombers—somebody much shorter flew fighters.

IB: Did you ever wish you were shorter?

AD: Oh, every once in a while, yes. But I enjoyed flying the B–26s. I should actually say the TB–26, because it had an extra foot on each wing.

IB: How did the men respond to you?

AD: We had all kinds of experiences—good and bad—but once the men saw that we could actually fly as well as they could, then they would accept us. Until we proved ourselves, they were skeptical. I remember once on a cross-country flight from Texas to California, when I had trouble with an oil leak—I had oil splattering the windshield—and when I landed in El Paso before they'd even look at my plane, they made me tell them what every dial said. They wouldn't have done that to a male pilot. Finally, they went out and saw how bad it was and fixed it. I never would have made the mountains.

IB: Do you still fly?

AD: Only in my dreams. Everything I ever flew is obsolete—that may be the title of my next poetry book—oh no. That would be too easy for the critics.

IB: Why the interest or obsession with flight?

AD: It's a common myth—to fly like a bird. I think it was so strong for me because I came from the Middle West—the Iowa prairie—I didn't have the mountains. I didn't have the oceans. What I had was SKY. As a prairie child this was very important to me. In one poem, I say, "the sky that nurtured me." It was an important point of my psyche someplace, that I could rise up and fly. That's what I wanted to do.

IB: Did you ever come close to death when you were flying?

AD: The risk is always there—there were times I was flying in storms. I remember once a group of us was bringing planes back from California to a Texas factory for wing reinforcement. We were flying solo and great storms appeared over the desert like huge trees. I have a poem on that called "I Remember." We were flying because the planes had wings that would not stand wind damage. So if we were caught in any of those storms, it would be a disaster.

IB: You mention the Phoenix. Have you had occasion to rise from the ashes?

AD: Always. You see, if I had to say a theme of my work, I would say it was "loss." My mother was killed in an auto accident when I was three-and-a-half, and I was with her. This is my first memory and underneath all of my poems is blood and crashing and glass breaking and metal on metal. This is a harshness that I've been criticized by some people for, but it is there and it is as much a part of me as that blue sky is, and rising from this loss is what I'm talking about when I mention the Phoenix. Many poets I know have been writing out of that same basic ground tone. It's astonishing how many poets lost primary nurturing figures early on—a father or a mother or a grandparent. Most poems can only come out of deep emotion, and the emotion of loss is as close to ashes as the human spirit comes to, I think.

IB: Richard Eberhart has a theory that poetry can come from an excess of joy or energy.

AD: As for the joy, when I stumbled onto *J. Alfred Prufrock* at age nine, I didn't know what it meant, but I was so excited I could hardly contain myself. John Malcolm Brinnin said, "When you first come on real literature, it is as if you've found buried treasure." It was like that. I could do no less than try to match what I read.

IB: Little tough to match Eliot?

AD: Yes, the poems that I wrote then were just dreadful. I have the little notebook that I kept from that period until I was about sixteen, and they were miserable poems, but I was trying. I kept trying. For years and years, I thought I was writing poetry for myself. It was only after I had the experience of writing radio scripts in New York, and flying and raising our family—our three daughters—that I really began to know that the poems weren't just for me. That's when I began to publish or try to publish. From the age of nine I was also copying down Edna St. Vincent Millay, Amy Lowell, Dorothy Parker—now those were good poems, but I wasn't matching them.

IB: Remember an example of one of those early poems?

AD: Oh, Irv! You wouldn't want to hear it.

IB: Yes.

AD: They stood together, a boy and a girl.
Yes, hand in hand they stood
And possibly the gods of fate looked
down and said it was good.
But it was not easy for me
to see that curly-headed boy
look down into another's eyes
and her face light up with joy.
And yet, somehow I always knew
I'd lose him to another.

She, you see, was his bride-to-be
and I was just his mother.

I was twelve when I wrote that. That was a dirty trick having me recite that!

IB: Sorry about that. That was a long time ago though.

AD: Yes, once upon a time I had a kind of recording mind and remembered just about everything. I never took a tape recorder with me on a radio interview when I was doing the "Woman of Tomorrow" show. I simply reeled it off in my head when I went back to the office, and I wrote it on the typewriter. That disappeared—that exact memory. It's probably a good thing—it's probably better for the poetry, as a matter of fact, because it makes more space for the words of the poem to come on, and that's where the real joy is.

IB: Do you think this mind set comes from the necessity to open your senses to a number of possibilities?

AD: Well, I'll take it under consideration. I thought it was just plain aging.

IB: You met Marianne Moore.

AD: Marianne Moore was in my father-in-law's congregation when he was the minister of the Spring Street Church in the Village many years ago. She and her brother—a ship captain—and their mother, were part of that congregation, and so my mother- and father-in-law kept track of Marianne Moore for many years—Christmas, that sort of thing—and at some point my mother-in-law sent her some poems of mine and told her about my efforts to write poetry. She was very encouraging and said by all means have me send the work, and I was shy about it and didn't. Finally, once in New York, when she lived on Ninth

Street, after she had moved in from Brooklyn—Brooklyn was becoming too dangerous for her to live there—I got my courage together and went to see her. She had written "do come," although she was ill. She was a beautiful, generous woman. I am awed by her work. She is certainly one of the best poets of the twentieth century. Can I go that far? I don't really want to say "woman" poet, but I admire her work and her courage, and she was generous with her help. She actually saw the first manuscript which eventually became my first book, wrote me a beautiful letter, and only years later did I realize that one of the phrases in it, she really meant for me to use as a blurb for my book. She had just put it in quotes, but I had been so hesitant about sending the manuscript in the first place that I had not really read it correctly. She was surrounded by her exquisite collection of antique furniture. She was still writing. She was frail, but she gave of her time and her spirit in ways that most people in good health don't do. It was as if I had visited the Queen, and I came away from there simply walking on air. That was in 1969. I saw her later and we corresponded after that—her letters are some of my most cherished possessions.

IB: So your visits to her buoyed your spirits?

AD: They certainly did. Although I still knew that part of it was the friendship with my mother- and father-in-law, that she was doing it out of a very strong feeling that she had for them. Well, you know how she did all the footnotes. She simply could not pick up someone else's words and use them, as unfortunately many people today do and do indiscriminately, without any acknowledgments. Marianne perhaps went too far overboard in the other direction, but there are a couple of her poems that have lines straight out of my father-in-law's sermons. And in the footnotes it says, "from the sermon of the Reverend John Darr," and she gives him full credits for the lines. Do you remember her poem called "Poetry?" Wonderful poem of about thirty lines. Written about 1935. In 1967 when she published her *Complete Poems*, she revised it down to three lines. I understand that she did it, in spite of everyone's consternation, because the most quoted line from it was "imaginary gardens with real toads in them." Though she had put the statement in quotes, she had neglected to credit the author, and years later she couldn't remember where the phrase came from. Her chagrin over the error made her delete all but the first three lines, and the author's note at the beginning of that book reads in entirety, "Omissions are not accidents." She was a marvelously determined lady.

IB: Talk about "The Woman of Tomorrow" show. How did your writing benefit from that?

AD: The radio scripts were mostly hack work. The prose that I wrote for "The Woman of Tomorrow" show was not very imaginative. I did the best I could, but it couldn't be poetry and as a result it was rather menial work. What I did learn that was very valuable to me, was to go from my head to my fingers on the typewriter, because in order to write a half-hour's script five days a week, I couldn't possibly do it with a pencil. So, I learned to write on the typewriter and that's been valuable for the poetry, because when the poetry begins to come on, I can't write it fast enough to keep up with the words.

IB: What was "The Woman of Tomorrow" show?

AD: Well, it was what was called a participating radio show. We covered anything in New York that was of interest to women—fashion, clothes, the theatre, book reviews, recipes. It was called participating because there were about five commercials on each show. In those days—that was a long time ago—each program was written up and sent to, euphemistically, the Continuity Department, where they could take out anything they wanted to. "The Woman of Tomorrow" wasn't really one after my heart. It was too limited, just about topics that supposedly interested women. Every time I tried to introduce politics or some controversial issue in New York, the script got cut.

IB: Did you ever try to introduce poetry?

AD: No. That's interesting—I've never thought of that before. I guess I thought that our average listener wasn't interested in poetry. Most people aren't, you know.

IB: Have you become more of a proselytizer for poetry?

AD: I have been trying to push poetry, if that's what you mean. Ever since I realized that I wasn't writing it for myself I have wanted to share it with everybody who would listen.

IB: When did you realize that it wasn't just for yourself?

AD: That was a sudden discovery—almost lightbulb-over-the-head type. We'd had a rocky marriage but at the point where my husband walked out, I was stricken. I remember gathering my two little girls—one-and-a-half and going-on-four—in my arms in the middle of the living room floor, rocking us all back and forth and thinking: They will leave me too, what do I have that is my own? And I *knew*. I had the poetry. From then on, I tried to learn how to make the work better, how to make it really speak to someone else, how to publish it. In other words, I began to take my work seriously, my work, the poetry. Not the volunteer work I was doing for the community. I thought I had dues to pay—to the PTA, Planned Parenthood, Red Cross, the National Symphony, you name it, I did it. I never did volunteer work again except for Arena Stage, because the theatre also had a strong place in my heart. And if I could write what I would most like to, it would be plays in verse. I've tried, and a few one-acts have been produced, but not yet to my satisfaction.

IB: So that is when you began to publish?

AD: Tried to. My first publishing was done for me by a friend who heard my poems being read at a gathering and asked if he could serve as my agent while I was on summer vacation. He said, "I'll bet you are like my wife; you send out the poems, get them back, cry, and put them in a desk drawer until you get the courage to send them out again." I said, "You're right." I gave him a dozen poems, and the first call that came when we returned home was from my "agent" saying he'd sold three poems, now it was up to me. I was delighted! The first poem he sold was to *The Saturday Evening Post*, and I was paid fifty-five dollars for it—with which I bought a hat made of silk cabbage roses. The only time I wore it was in a PTA musical I wrote, in a funny dance with grocery carts, "I've got the course right here," a take off from *Guys and Dolls*.

IB: Then you were able to do the publishing yourself?

AD: Not very well. The return of those folded envelopes in the mailbox was still so devastating that the only way I knew to counteract the fall of my stomach was to keep something going or coming in the mail at all times. I did that for fifteen years. I also think there is a natural progression in the life of every writer. I think that there is a point where you begin to write the words down and it's for you and then you want to show the work to somebody and then to somebody else and then comes the point where you want it published and these points in time may be years apart. The point at which I knew that I was very serious about it—that I really wanted to share it with a wide audience—that was years after I started.

B: How did you sustain yourself when quietly writing these poems? Or was it quietly?

D: Very quietly. No one knew I was writing poems but me, practically. During that particular period, I had no other poets to show anything to. Sustain myself? I guess the way any poet does—by reading other people's poems. The writer who does not read any poetry of any kind he or she likes is not quite in tune with what is happening in the poetry world. I really believe that. I think that any poetry writer should—must—be reading contemporary poets.

IB: Let's talk more about the Women's Air Service Pilots experience.

AD: The first job I had was as a test pilot. After I graduated from the WASP training program, I was a test pilot in Stockton, California, at an advanced trainer base, and I tested the planes that were up for their regular so-many-hour checkups. I tested planes that had been repaired after crashes—any testing that had to be done on a plane, I did. I went from there to Las Vegas where, as I said, I flew B–26s and gunners in B–17s flew alongside and shot their bullets into a sleeve that we towed. They were dipped into a wax—colored wax—the front gunner had his bullets dipped in red, the side gunners in blue, with the tail in yellow, perhaps, and then those targets were dropped, picked up, and after everything had been considered and recorded as to which ones had hit where, we used the cloth targets as bedspreads and curtains with the holes surrounded in color. From there, I went back to Sweetwater, where I was trained as an instrument instructor. I went back to Las Vegas and the program was closed. In December of 1944, the WASPs were disbanded.

IB: Didn't the WASPs finally receive some recognition?

AD: Yes, we made a great push in the late seventies to try to get some benefits. In the spring of 1977, we had Senate hearings, in the fall we had House hearings, and finally we were tacked on to the Veteran's Administration bill and it passed. It was a great fight because the VA did not want it to go through. It was the Department of Defense that finally came to our rescue, and the bill passed both houses and went to the president and he signed it on the eve of Thanksgiving in 1977. And so we were finally recognized. Each WASP's record was gone over to determine whether she was worthy of having VA hospitalization and a burial spot in a military cemetery, but at least we are now legally veterans.

IB: Should we salute?

AD: (Laughs.) If you remember how.

IB: What were your parents like? There is one poem in your first book where your father and the dog are straining at the leash and so on.

AD: After my mother died, my father tried to be mother and father to my brother and me, and my grandmother came to live with us and had a great influence on my life. I have no memory of my mother at all. I've tried and tried to bring back an image of how she looked—when I asked her sisters, they would say, "Look in the mirror." There are pictures, of course, but the clear ones are mother as a girl. I've tried to reconstruct the automobile accident that killed her—no one else was even injured—and I have a theory now that it was an alcohol problem. The last words my mother said were, "There's a corner ahead, you'd better slow down." This was reported by my aunt who was also in the car—it was my uncle who was driving. "That Corner on the Fansler Road" is the working title of my new manuscript.

This is one of the mysteries of writing, how the old traumas rise up through the years and overwhelm you. I thought I had written all of my "mother" poems, and suddenly here is this invading image and feeling—the old Fansler dance hall, where I as a teenager was forbidden to go. It was a dangerous atmosphere—drunken brawls—but the danger that lurked there for me was the terrible tragedy that made my mother disappear forever. The experience left me with a sense of abandonment that could be stirred whenever anyone important to me departed—I would be swept by an enormous sense of disaster, doom. Hard to shake off. This is where the "loss" theme in my poetry comes from, and the writing of the poetry is a kind of healing, a kind of reconstruction of the body of the lost mother, or the nurturing one, and we speak of the body of the work. John Logan pointed out to me some of the scientific writing that has been done on this theory—it helps to explain why so many poets have lost nurturing ones early on. John's mother died in childbirth, in fact, his birth. And when he wanted to know more about his mother, he too was told to look in the mirror.

IB: So, this is where your poetry comes from.

AD: The poetry actually comes from the subconscious. I think the poems are always writing themselves someplace down in the middle and they surface when the right impetus comes—like the "Hangar Nine" poem which ends *St. Ann's Gut.* It was triggered by an invitation to put my name in a time capsule at the dedication of Hangar Nine, an aerospace museum—all those flying images were collecting and mellowing somewhere in me. I knew I was going to write a long flying poem or a collection of short ones at some point, but the invitation . . . well . . . "The morning mail condenses me/into part of the blue I want to become." And I was off—I wrote pages and pages which were then rewritten, compacted, rearranged until I had the poem I wanted. When I started it, I had no idea where it would end, I didn't know I would end putting Freud's name in the capsule instead of mine.

IB: Was that because of your psychiatrist husband?

AD: Not really. It had to do with the placing of my name there seeming grandiose.

IB: Did your husband object to your use of Freud in your poems?

AD: No, but the line where I say, "Freud would have said mine was a death wish/to join the conglomerate blue, that it was heaven

I meant to reach, not Paris." I seem to remember that he thought Freud wouldn't have said any such thing—or how did I know he would have said that. So! From then on when I read the poem, I say, "Freud might have said . . ." I don't put in all those footnotes like Marianne Moore, but I would like not to be scientifically inaccurate.

IB: How does the fact that you were married to a psychiatrist for a long time affect your understanding of dreams, psyche, and the like?

AD: Well, one's spouse's profession does not come through by osmosis, of course, but I've been terribly interested in psychiatry. I have been in therapy myself over various periods of my life and found it extremely useful. I am very much in favor of this approach to emotional problems—and I've had my share. And of course, everything I know, learn, hear about, experience has some effect on my writing. Insights that I wouldn't have had otherwise, different ways to approach the understanding of dreams. (Dreams have been very valuable to me in my writing—for content, for impetus—I keep my journal beside my bed so I can record dreams, so I don't lose them.) All of these things add to the complex recipe for the poems—but not consciously. The poetry is subconscious, working underground. There is an intuitive quality about it, or, as Roland Flint told me once, "You and I are intuitive writers, meaning we have a perceptual dysfunction." I wrote a poem recently using that as an epigraph.

IB: Then do you think the psychiatric approach has been a help or a hindrance?

AD: In itself, neither, and both. I'm fascinated by scientific approaches, discoveries. I read about them with glee. Sometimes something I read in one of the scientific journals surfaces in a poem, but that is not why I do the reading. It delights me, particularly the space investigations, the psychic healing experiments, but I soak up the articles for my own pleasure, not for the poetry's sake—though I think anything can be grist for the poetry mill. I just don't know how the creative process works. I don't really want to know.

IB: For fear you will stop it?

AD: That's right. I don't want to damage whatever it is that makes the poems arrive. There has been much interest lately in the creative process, how it works. I don't want to investigate that area. If you try to analyze them, the poetry vibrations disappear. "It would be like boiling a watch to see how it ticks," as William Stafford says.

IB: But you spoke once about an editor who thought you shouldn't use one poem because of the Freudian concept of the knife . . .

AD: You mean the poem called "The Gift," about the stiletto?

IB: That's the one. How does it go?

AD: Daughter, this small stiletto which I found
sticking in my ribs, I have wiped clean
and given back to you. You will need it.

I had hoped there was some other way.
Some way for you to take yourself from me
without the violence.

The editor who helped me put together my first book, *St. Ann's Gut,* said I couldn't use the poem because the stiletto was a male image. He said that we lived in this Freudian age, and I as a female couldn't use this figure of speech. I decided he was wrong. In fact, that one poem, "The Gift," has had more comments by people of every age—from teenagers, boys and girls, to octogenarians, men and women, who said: "That poem is about me!" They understood the difficulty of breaking away a young person has when leaving home, the hardship on both parent and child. I am glad I put it in. I can't go along entirely with all the psychiatric concepts, but there are some which strike home.

IB: Such as?

AD: The Oedipus Complex, that point where a very young child wants to get rid of the parent of the same sex, so he or she can claim the parent of the opposite sex as a mate. If by some accident the removal of the parent is possible, actually happens, then the child is left with an enormous load of guilt. Because of the car accident that killed my mother, I succeeded in having my father for myself. I didn't do away with my mother, of course, but in my own mind, I did. And the guilt was overwhelming. As I say, anyone could push my guilt button. I've spent a lot of time trying to overcome that burden.

IB: And as your kids left home? Did you turn more to your poetry then?

AD: I was absolutely devastated as each daughter—we have three— left home. There was this great hole that I had to kind of walk around. I had related so closely to each one of them, which was probably not good for them. I did, I turned more to my poetry. The writing filled a need I had for each lovely daughter.

IB: Have you always been looking for serenity?

AD: No. (Laughs.) I may have been. I wanted something more secure than what I was able to do for myself, because I handled things in all kinds of ways that weren't good for me or the people around me.

IB: What has poetry taught you in terms of your everyday life?

AD: I'm not sure except it has taught me something about immediacy of relationships, immediacy of experience, observation

89

that involves me totally. If I am not writing I don't feel very good. It's as if I'm not getting quite enough lettuce—oh, that's a bad word now, because that means money, doesn't it? It has nothing to do with money. It has to do with filling my soul, if you will, my so-called soul. There is something strange about this because most of the things I write are from my dark side. That's where my writing energy comes from. I have tried to turn that around and have not been very successful at it. Once in a while something that is a joke, or light-hearted thought, actually does maneuver itself and become a poem and appears in a book, but for the most part it is the dark and heavy side of me that comes out on the paper. Yehuda Amichai said something at a reading I heard—he, too, writes from his dark side—he said, "I wanted to call this book *Somewhere Near Here a Great Happiness Is Lurking*," and I thought that was a wonderful title for his book. But his publisher did not allow him to use it. He finally called the book *Amen*. This is sort of the way I feel in spite of all these dark things that I write—that somewhere near here a great happiness is lurking, because I don't live in that dark side all the time. The thing that really astonishes me is that I get this extraordinary pleasure out of that first marvelous coming-on of the poem, when the words are coming so fast I have to write fast to keep up with them, and the content may be so sad and sorrowful that I don't quite understand the joy of being able to get it down on paper.

IB: Do you ever feel like a sadist?

AD: No, no, I'm not a sadist. A masochist, maybe. I love people. I can't exist without people around. That's why I never wanted to retire to the country. One season in the winter out there and I'd be gone.

IB: Have you ever regretted writing any given poem?

AD: I regretted publishing a few given poems, but I won't tell you what they are. I will say this: I used to teach poetry in the classroom and I loved to do it. I expended a great deal of energy and I loved teaching the youngsters, but when I did, I came home and wrote dreadful poems about the children, hoping they would never see them. I published a couple of those poems. I hope I have disguised them enough so that they won't know what had really been the exegesis of those poems. Teaching at the American University is quite different—the students are older and more mature.

IB: Do you ever catch yourself coming along with rhythms of a famous poem, maybe something you might have memorized earlier?

AD: I hope not. No, I don't think so. The forms that my poems take are individual to the poem, and although I have written in many different traditional forms, I do not do it well. I feel when I try it that I am boxed in. Claustrophobia has been one of my problems. I get it when I stand in line at a theatre, I get it in particular when I try to box myself in a sonnet, although I did publish one sonnet in one of the books and nobody recognized it as such. (Laughs.)

IB: What does living in proximity to Washington, D.C., do to you? I mean, what is Washington to the poet? Isn't that a kind of claustrophobia?

AD: If you are talking about governmental Washington, one can leave that completely alone. I don't have to know what's going on in the government in Washington any more than anybody else in the country knows. We'll all see it on television news, but what *is* happening in Washington right now is a kind of renaissance of art—the new museums, the new Eastern wing of the National Gallery is one of the most spectacular buildings that has been put up recently, and it is so exciting to go there. If you are open to all kinds of art, which I think any poet should be, or is—just not should be but is—here are all of these inspirations, if you like. The Hirshhorn Gallery, which has been there not very many years now and which we used to call "the doughnut on the mall"—we didn't like the way the building was shaped, though it's a beautiful shape for what is inside. The new Air & Space Museum, because I am interested in air, space, and flying, is one of the most exciting spots in all of Washington to me—and there is a movie called *To Fly*, which I have seen a dozen times and will go back and see again. I hope they never replace it.

Now there are more poetry readings than one can actually go to in the city. Theatre, with the Kennedy Center open and smaller companies sprouting everywhere, has simply flourished in a way that we never thought possible ten or twenty years ago. So there are all the things going on there, plus the fact that Washington is one of the most beautiful cities in the world—the plantings, the buildings—you don't have to get into lawmaking. I don't say that that isn't a place for poetry, exactly, but each poet I think finds the poetic impetus somewhere else and mostly inside himself.

IB: You've published a lot in little magazines. Has that been a good experience, valuable?

AD: It was Ted Weiss, who edited *Quarterly Review of Literature*, along with his wife, Renee, who helped me so much. He wrote notes to me telling me to write deeper, go further down. And that was good advice. He would make actual comments on lines, and this is very personal and important care and feeding of a poet. On the other hand, there was another magazine, a very small one, which when the time came to get back copyright assignments for the first book, this editor absolutely refused. I was dumbfounded—I wrote a second letter and got a second "no." I tried a third time and finally called my editor in New York. He wrote a blistering letter. If I'd received a letter like that, I'd have ended up in the hospital. Within twenty-four hours this editor had the copyright assignment in the mail to me. It depends on the individuals and the sensitivity of the individuals. Small press or big press, it's the individual.

IB: How hard is it for you to change things after they've been written?

AD: It depends. *The Myth of a Woman's Fist* is the title of my second book, and that wasn't what I wanted to call it. I wanted to call it *Yorick Rides Again,* because there's a long poem about death and movies that ends this book, and I was thinking about Yorick's skull—"Alas poor Yorick, I knew him, Horatio," in *Hamlet.* I thought *Yorick Rides Again* was a great title. My editor at William Morrow said "no way." So I said, "How about *The Myth of a Woman's Fist*" and he agreed.

    When the title poem had come out in the *Washington Post,* it was with an article about the poetry around Washington and the editor said, "You know, that final verse doesn't belong there. You ought to end with that "I sing when I'm afraid." I have gone back and forth and I can't decide whether he's right or whether I'm right. Every once in a while I let an editor talk me into taking off the final lines of something and then wish that I hadn't. This is one of the hardest things for me, to know the final version of the poem. And, at least for me, it is very difficult once it is in a book to change it. Now, Stephen Spender said, "You don't worry about having it copyrighted in one style, you must change it if you want to. It is your poem." And I don't know what kind of morality it is that says to me that once it is in print, it's true. Another of my childhood myths? Maybe it has to do with growing up in the little town where there was no library, where books were very sacred things. So that even the idea of writing in a book—I couldn't make notes in a book for years because it was somehow ruining the book. My lines didn't belong in there.

IB: Who was your editor?

AD: Jim Landis was my editor. He's a good editor. He would go through my manuscript and tell me what poems he loved—so those would stay in. Then he would tell me those that were on the borderline, then he would tell me the ones that he hated.

But he also said that I had the final say and even if he hated a poem, it could stay. There are a couple of poems in each book that I insisted stay in. I was glad he let me have the final word, but he was not shy about telling me which ones he didn't like. And he absolutely wouldn't let me use the Yorick title.

About the first book, which was called *St. Ann's Gut*, a poet friend saw the manuscript before I sent it off and said, "Ann, you can't call it *St. Ann's Gut*. If your name were Margaret or Mabel, maybe, but this is sacrilegious somehow." But the fact is it is not about me or St. Ann at all; it is a place in Nova Scotia and "gut" in this instance means a "cleft in the earth." St. Ann's is where we went to hear a Gaelic Mod, a celebration, at St. Ann's College, and the poem is written about a nest of wriggling snakes which I found beneath a stone when we were camping there. The stone and the snakes became metaphors for a relationship. My editor said, "Don't let anyone persuade you to change the title!"

IB: You mentioned something about your biography poem, what was that?

AD: I was tired of writing bio notes for small journals so when the request came, "Send a Biography note . . ." I put a sheet of paper in the typewriter and began, as far fetched as I could, "I have published poems in the Potomac River" and went on from there. The lines seemed to come to me in triplets so I kept writing, two and a half pages or so. And the further I wrote the more I realized that I was hooking into a vein of ore that I wanted to follow. When I rewrote the poem, many of the stanzas were cut out entirely, others were switched around in the positions, but the essential line of the poem was there, the language of the poem was set from the beginning. When the manuscript for *The Myth of a Woman's Fist* was accepted for publication, that poem was the opening of the book. One day I had a telephone call from my editor who said, "Ann, would you change the final line of that poem from 'I am traveling without laughter,' to 'I am traveling *with* laughter'?" Since at one point in the extensive revision, that line had been ". . . by laughter," I was willing to think about it. I said, "Give me the weekend, and I'll get back to you." As I thought about the movement of the poem, I realized that I had tried to make a joke of the biography, and my own words had taken me by the scruff of the neck and turned me around, and made me write it honestly. I was *not* traveling with laughter. My creating, for better or worse, comes from my dark side. Laughter has been important in my life, a saving tactic, but it is not the energy my writing comes from. I couldn't change that poem. Monday morning, I called and told my editor that I couldn't change it, and said, by the way, why did you want me to? Because, he said, the booksellers thought they could sell more books if it started out on an upbeat note. I was glad I had made my decision.

Send a Biographical Note . . .

I have published poems in the Potomac
   River, on Grand Teton Mountain,
      and on the beach at Piraeus.

They were all written
   in an old Indian dialect
      unknown even to Ishi.

I make instant translations
   constantly.
      With everyone.

I alternate between telling
   everything I know, and being
      afraid to speak.

I am made up of everyone
   I have ever encountered.
I am still everywhere
   I have ever been.

I know the wilderness
  is necessary. I do not want
    to live there.

I feel the planet turn away from me.
I am traveling without laughter.

IB: What's your favorite obsession?

AD: Obsession? If you expect me to say "writing," I can't do it. Writing is not an *obsession* to me, it is a *necessity*. Obsession originally meant the act of an evil spirit possessing a person; it still has some of that old aura to me. But writing is a necessity with good, rather than evil connotations. The act of creating is a sustaining act, a buoying up, and that is what the writing is and why it is a joyous act! If I don't write every day, it's as if my blood stagnates, scum collects on the pond of my mind, and if that's too fanciful, well, it's as if I'm mentally constipated. Poetry is what I do, by necessity, by desire, by luck. Maybe it hasn't actually saved my life, but it seems that important to me, whether anyone reads it or not.

ELIZABETH SPENCER

Elizabeth Spencer was born in 1921 and grew up in Carrollton, Mississippi. She received her M.A. degree from Vanderbilt University and received a Guggenheim Fellowship in 1953. She won the $10,000 Fiction Award from McGraw-Hill for *The Light in the Piazza*, the

Henry Bellamann Award, and the Award of Merit medal for the short story from the American Academy of Arts and Letters. She holds an honorary Litt.D. from Southwestern College in Memphis. Her books include *Fire in the Morning, This Crooked Way, The Voice at the Back Door, The Light in the Piazza, Knights and Dragons, No Place for an Angel, Ship Island and Other Stories, The Snare, The Stories of Elizabeth Spencer, Marilee,* and *The Salt Line.*

She is an American expatriate, although she might not call herself that, living in Italy and Canada before settling in North Carolina.

Her voice is mellifluously rich in its Mississippi accent, her manners acute, courteous, and pleasant. But within her finely crafted stories and novels beats the heart of a fierce and powerful writer, and one who is not recognized as fully as she might be.

INTERVIEW

IRV BROUGHTON: What did people say when you were a kid and you said you wanted to be a writer?

ELIZABETH SPENCER: Oh, I don't know. They looked at me like I had a curious fantasy or something.

IB: What was your favorite myth when you were growing up?

ES: I think one of the Greek myths about Pegasus, the winged horse, I guess. There was a pretty picture in my book, *The Wonder Book of Myths and Legends*. It was all about the Greek myths. And next to that was the one about Jason and the Golden Fleece.

IB: What did you like about the book?

ES: It was the way it was written and illustrated. I counted a lot of illustrations in those stories. I also think it was hero worship. Jason was so brave and Orpheus was along on that voyage. I found a lot of heroes in the Greek myths, and they got assembled on that voyage to go and get the Golden Fleece. I remember it was kind of interesting that Orpheus played and the seas opened up; a lot of magical things happened when he played. I would drift away on dreams of this kind of thing. I didn't like so much the story of Daedalus and Icarus because it ended so badly—he fell in the sea.

IB: So you really believed in the heroic?

ES: I loved the heroic in these myths, and I guess the book I had played on my tendencies because it was very much shaped toward the heroes of great myths.

IB: Do you think you told more stories than most of the kids you knew?

ES: Well, I always liked listening to stories. I think I had a tendency to exaggerate and invent things. That was a very neat trick for covering up, because if you could exaggerate one way or another, you could get out of a little trouble. But my parents were very alert to that kind of thing and cautioned me against it. I do think I had a tendency to invent stories and they'd be things that wouldn't be acceptable around the little bunch of kids I knew—not acceptable in the sense that it would type me as a literary sort, which was something I tried early on to avoid.

IB: Were you really secretive about this?

ES: I don't know so much secretive as I just knew it wouldn't go down. I used to write things for my own amusement, but I'd show them to my mother. She was very encouraging about things like that and thought it was wonderful. I wrote a story once and gave it to my parents for Christmas. I remember sitting up late at night, and Mother said, "What are you doing?" You know, it would be cold up there; it gets cold in Mississippi in the winter. She said, "Come to bed. You'll catch your death of cold. What on earth are you doing?" I said I was just working on something, and I wrote all this in a notebook and gave it to them for Christmas. That was the secret of what I was doing.

IB: In what ways were you like your mother?

ES: Oh, I don't know. People always said we looked alike. They still say that, but I think she was very sympathetic to stories. She always liked stories and telling stories. She used to read fairy stories, and she always had a kind of child's delight in things. She was one of those people who never quite lost that. I think it was a wonderful trait to have—the enthusiasm and excitement. And in reading children's stories to me, I thought she was as excited about them as I was. My mother's family was not very literary, in a sense, but they were all great readers. One of my uncles said he found some children's books I would enjoy—they were George McDonald's children's books, things like *The Princess and the Goblin*. They were outside the canon of children's books like *Alice in Wonderland* that we had at home. So, when he got back, he sent them to me and we started reading them. And I remember she seemed thrilled about some of the phrases, and she'd say, "Isn't that a pretty comparison?" She got as excited about these children's things as I did, so we had a great rapport at that age.

IB: In what ways were you like your father?

ES: Oh, my father. That's another question. He had a bad temper and I have a bad temper. I don't know. People have told me that later on in life we clashed a lot because we were so much alike, but I don't think we really were. I never had a very good relationship with him. From the time I was twelve or thirteen, we were great pals, and I was running around with him everywhere. He was a businessman and a very active man. He never liked to read anything imaginative—he thought that was a waste of time. He was proud of accomplishment as long as it could be pointed to as something that people can admire in general, but he was very, very hard on anything about art or artistic effort or anything like that—it was a waste of time. I have to explain, though, that he was brought up when the South was quite poor and his family was rather impoverished and he had to work hard from the time he was a small boy. The work ethic was strong in his thinking.

IB: You seem to understand him.

ES: No, but I think he had many redeeming features, and probably he was nicer to people outside his family than he was to people inside his family.

IB: When you were a child, were there little exercises to try to make you into a lady?

ES: Oh, yeah. You see I was brought up in the summer on my uncle's place—I used to go down to the plantation. My mother's people were plantation owners and her younger brother was running the property. He and his wife didn't have any children so they were very receptive to my brother and me. We used to spend months in the summer. I always rode with my uncle— he was riding a horse all over the place in those years. (That was before the age of jeeps, before the Second World War.) I used to go fishing with Negroes way back in the swamp and climb trees. When it got to be time to go to church or visit with the ladies around home, they dressed me up with these little frilly dresses, white socks, and patent leather shoes. In the winter, I remember I had to wear little kid gloves. There was one lady who had a set of chairs that were covered with horsehair. It's a kind of satin, shiny, handsome fabric, but it prickled me in my little dress. And I was supposed to sit there with my back very straight, not touching the back of the chair with my hands folded, and not speak unless spoken to. And, "Don't scratch!" (Laughs.) And the damn stuff would be stickin' in my legs!

IB: But you wouldn't trade the milieu of the South, would you?

ES: I don't guess I thought it was remarkable at the time. I must have thought everyone was the same, but I know there were distinctions taught me by my mother. I was taught to be very democratic. A lot of the kids out in the country were riding horses and driving buggies in to school and they didn't have anything, and I was taught never to act as though I were better than they were. That was the mark of being the right kind of person. There were a good many people in that little town who prided themselves on their family background and therefore thought they could act superior to other people.

IB: You said once you see the world as a story.

ES: I think story has a lot to do with time and event that we're all involved in. We're involved in circumstance, event, and time, and so those things are indispensable to story. Then the things that are foremost in our minds, that we are living out in a way, are what we long for, and believe in. And those are the foremost things in a story. Then you find the forces that work against those things and you inevitably have a story at every turn of the road.

I was just reading an article in *The New York Review of Books* about certain writers whose characters seem static and characterless without qualities, because the writers are mainly interested in philosophic things—they are beyond events and actions. Well, I guess these may be the great writers of our times, but they don't please me at all. I find them difficult to read. But I guess I shouldn't say that. There's a philosophic point to be reached where you're not interested any longer in qualities, in characters, in events, in nothing but thought process or something. I just do not see that fiction can even exist without the other things.

IB: Some writers talk of the terrible need to communicate their point of view or ideas. Have you ever felt that way?

ES: No, I'm not sure that I have personally any one point of view. I learn so much from my characters. If I'm attracted to a character telling a story, I try to go along as much as possible with their point of view. Sometimes I can see around it—and the character's making a mistake, but I'm not inclined to sit in judgment on that.

The story "The Light in the Piazza" aroused a curiosity in my mind because I was following the main character in the story, the mother, and I thought a lot of times that she may have been deceiving herself. She wanted this marriage so badly for her daughter, she may have fooled herself into thinking—it was a wish fulfillment—"This is going to work out" when maybe it would collapse three days after the wedding. On the other hand, I didn't want to interfere with her in any way. I just let her have it. And a lot of people criticized me. They said, "It's such an ambivalent story. You can't tell where *you* stand." So I say to myself, "Well, they argued that about Shakespeare."

IB: What was the challenge in writing "The Light in the Piazza?"

ES: It wasn't hard enough—I wrote it very fast. I got the idea for the story when we'd left Italy and were living in Canada. The idea sort of came to me about missing the light in Italy very much. Someone said the wonderful thing about Italian painting is the quality of the light there. And I missed that, and it started out of that, but it also started out of an incident of a slightly retarded girl that my husband and I had known somewhere and the relationship she had with her mother. The story really came at me from a lot of directions. Another thing was the Italian attitude toward marriage and the arrangement of marriage. A woman was watching a wedding once and I was standing by her when the procession went by. She said to me, "*Le nozze e una carta che si giocea.*" "It's a card one plays."

IB: Did the Italians take umbrage at the idea of a retarded girl getting together with an Italian man?

ES: Well, some of them did. A friend of mine told me that she had a man friend who objected strenuously to that story. He said, "No father would do that to his son." I said, "I think part of the story might have been that he didn't realize what he was doing." I mean, that was one of the things in it. And several Italians that I knew thought it was perfectly wonderful, that the story had gotten hold of something in the Italian makeup that was just right. They told me that so often that I couldn't believe they were flattering me, but they just really felt that way and weren't offended at all. The preface of the Italian edition of "The Light in the Piazza" had this phrase: The father

"*La capito sulerto*," that is he had understood at once the true state of the girl. And I don't know if he did or not. I couldn't tell that he had understood and I don't think he ever did.

IB: Was there anything that you never quite got used to in Italy?

ES: Well, I had a friend who was Italo-American, who complained about the same things I did after a long time. We both had lived there a long while, and it was like that marriage remark. She said that she had a dress promised for a party and it wasn't ready. She complained to the woman, and the dressmaker said, "Well, I haven't had time." My friend said, "You promised." The woman said, "*Che cosa e un promesso?*" "What's a promise?" This indicates a profound cynicism in the Italian character, and I just think it's bad. It was either there in every Italian I met, or it was recognized by people who didn't see that as being part of the Italian character, and I do think it is. But, of course, they've been there for years—the crossroads of nations. They've seen people come and go; they've been impoverished and seen all kinds of things happen to them, so I guess a certain cynicism has to develop out of that.

IB: Did you feel like an expatriate writing overseas?

ES: I haven't written much overseas except for *The Voice at the Back Door*. I wrote some short stories the rest of the time I was there, but mainly they were about the South. I started writing about Italy when I left Italy. The whole Italian experience meant a great deal to me, and when we left Italy and came to Canada, I had this kind of sense that I was going to lose a lot of that unless I started to write about it. I wanted to get it down. And, honest to gosh, I never did think "The Light in the Piazza" would be published. I just thought of it as a rather crazy story I was writing to get down a lot of impressions. I thought the central idea was exaggerated and that it wouldn't find an audience. It turned out to be the most popular thing I ever wrote, so I guess I'm not a good judge of that. (Laughs.)

IB: Bernard Berenson said Florence was a sunny place for shady people.

ES: Well, the Florentines do have that reputation. There was a lot of that irony, I think, in the story. That she has the experience of the light when she says, "It looks like you can see everything but you can't see anything."

IB: Were you naive when you got to Italy? Also, were there a lot of rude awakenings?

ES: I didn't actually think of moving there. I went there on a Guggenheim for one year. There were rude awakenings everywhere, but I don't think I was so starry-eyed and idealistic that I thought everything was going to be great in Italy. There were many minor things that were always happening, like people giving me the wrong change or promising me something or trying to rip me off in various ways. It got to be a way of life. You got ground down by it, and you just accepted that you had to be on guard all the time. I remember when we first came to Canada there was the tiniest accident—somebody bumped into us at an intersection. The insurance man immediately took the claim, and we called him about six times a week. He said, "Well, I know you people mean well and everything, but it takes awhile to process the claim." And we realized we were in a different country where we weren't going to be lied to, that the insurance was taking care of everything—and the check would arrive. I had this fixed idea when we were in Canada—good old, straight, honest Canada—that people would try things. I used to check things about fifteen times if I sent off a check or an order. It was a habit I had to lose.

IB: In what ways was Italy like the South?

ES: They didn't heat the houses well in the winter. (Laughs.) I think being very socially charming and correct was a point in common. I lived in Florence, but I lived mainly in Rome on that second trip, beginning in 1953, when I was on a Guggenheim. I lived mainly in Rome, but I went up to Florence and found a room in the household of an Italian countess and her family. They had a circle of friends, all of whom were related by old ties, family ties, or actual kinship, and the way their circle moved with each other and the way they talked about each other—they never dreamed of breaking these ties up—was like the South. Close-knit circles bound by long family connections.

IB: Are people sometimes surprised that a gentle lady from Mississippi writes with the kind of intensity and edge that you do?

ES: How do you know I'm a gentle lady? (Laughs.)

IB: Well, you just seem that way. Let me make that assumption.

ES: I think the people who know me well realize all that gentleness is probably a matter of being brought up well and having a certain Mississippi accent. I don't know. Eudora Welty said something like that in a preface she wrote to my stories. It's kind of like when I'm writing it's like being possessed by something else that's not so much me. I think most people who have some talent at times feel the talent possesses them. I think those are probably the times when you're doing your most powerful work—when this force can get ahold of you and make itself felt. It's like being inhabited by a spirit that's not dictating to you, but coming out through the story.

I remember when I wrote "The Finder." That was an old story I heard at home. It's apparently a widespread folk belief, that certain people can find things, a psychic gift. So I went to write that one day in Montreal. I started about nine and I finished at two, and I thought I'd been working about an hour or an hour and one-half. It was all there—it just poured out. But that happens rarely. Usually, I have to hesitate and figure everything out.

IB: What was the hardest plot to develop?

ES: I think I had more trouble because I got involved with something in my own psyche in maybe an unpleasant way during "Knights and Dragons." I had to back up and rewrite over and over and over. I thought, "I'll never get through with this." And I wanted to drop it. It may be, though I didn't think of the woman in it as being myself, that something of her psychic difficulty—it's very internalized experience—may have overlapped with certain psychic difficulties I was having at the time I wrote it. So the overlap was so intense I kept trying to pull back from it and be objective. I was trying to get a distance so that I could at least handle it, but it would pull me back in. It's like the story in Greek myth where somebody made a coat that's beautiful but it stuck to the skin. You couldn't get the coat off without pulling your skin off—it gave me that feeling.

IB: What things in your psyche?

ES: Oh, that's too personal. It just finally got absorbed in one way—I don't know. Some people think of writing as a pouring out of their own troubles. I don't. It was a coincidence that it was that way for me. Robert Penn Warren says somewhere that writing is a purgation of temperament. I think he said that in connection with Conrad. But I didn't do it to do therapy on myself. In fact, it turned out to be a laceration rather than a purgation. I just had to outlive it. I felt I had to go on and finish the story. I had a terrible time because I used to wake up at night and feel I was sinking in the sea. I was holding onto my story as a kind of life raft which was holding me up. But, anyway, this story is separate from me now and a lot of people think it's worthwhile. I'm not sure because it cost me a lot of pain.

IB: Did "Knights and Dragons" change a lot from your original conception?

ES: The original idea of "Knights and Dragons" was that I had already written about the light side of Italy in "The Light in the Piazza"—you know, the charm, the beauty, some dark things too like the runaway carriages, different things that happened. But on the whole it was suffused in light and romance in a way and "Knights and Dragons" was different. A lot of it takes place in the winter in Rome, when it's raining and people get colds. The apartments are not well heated—you know the landlords torment people. Things like that crept in. So I thought I was writing about first the light side of Italy and then the dark side—like the dark side of the moon. I thought the two were companion pieces.

IB: It seems you move in time very well in "Knights and Dragons."

ES: People say that generally I do that well. But it seems to me that there are points in your life, or in stories—what you will—preoccupations, where the past does intrude. It becomes a living present. It's at that point that it's natural to relate it to the present because it is so necessary when living the present.

IB: What's the key to achieving that?

ES: To absorb yourself in the character so when the character has to have the past, through memory or feeling or continuation, that is when it occurs in the story, through dreams or recollections or conversation, or somebody coming. It's the actual pressure of the past on the present. Remember in "Knights and Dragons" when this man comes as a messenger from some property? Then in their conversation he explains what it's all about, and her feelings become very strong toward the past at that time—real misery on her part.

IB: Isn't "Knights and Dragons" kind of a liberation story of Martha?

ES: I think so. She had to destroy her psychic attachment in order to free herself, but in freeing herself she almost destroyed herself because the man she met caught on to this and was very destructive.

IB: What does short story writing owe your novel writing and vice versa?

ES: I look at them as different forms. I think the stories in *Jack of Diamonds* are almost novelistic because in the longer ones I was trying to awaken the resonance of a novel without spelling it out for three hundred pages. They could have been developed that way, but I thought I could do the whole thing in less space. I suppose that's a form in itself. I think of short stories too being sort of like tales that are told. You know, somebody might sit down at one sitting and tell this. I do think novels have to be thought out.

IB: Do you think the short story is the most difficult form as Capote and others have said?

ES: My stories all seem to develop pretty easily. No, I think novels are more difficult because they take so much longer to write. (Laughs.) William Styron said on a program once—it was so funny—writing a novel is like crawling from Vladivostok to Madrid—on your knees.

IB: Give me your three commandments when it comes to short story writing.

ES: Maybe I've got ten of them; what if I've got more than three? Let's see. Don't overwrite description in a story—you haven't got time. Don't bring in scenes that don't pertain to the central story. Don't bring in minor characters that might be nice in a novel to make a diversion, because again, you don't have time. But still try to keep the richness of the thing. Don't strip it down too far. I was never too partial to minimalist fiction for the reason it seems so stripped down that you hardly know where you are. So I think it's got to have some degree of fleshing out.

IB: Peter Taylor said the way to learn writing was to consciously copy the style of the greats. He said if you didn't you would do it unconsciously.

ES: I never have done that. I sometimes make my students do a paraphrase just so they'll be sensitive to prose rhythms—as the writers they admire are sensitive. They'll take a paragraph and do a paraphrase. For instance, in Welty's story, "The Worn Path," there's old Phoenix Jackson who's walking down the road. Well, turn that into a man coming to town for an entirely different purpose, in an entirely different season of the year, with entirely different things on his mind, but still follow the rhythm of the prose. And if Eudora has a simile, you put a simile. Instead of "on a winter afternoon," you say, "On a late summer morning." I thought that was a fun exercise. And, after they'd do a Welty, they'd do a Hemingway paragraph. After that, a James Joyce paragraph. There's one that I use a lot, a Joyce story called "A Little Cloud" where little Chandler is going from his office to meet his old friend. And the thoughts he has along the way are rendered ironically because Joyce is not in step with the characters; he's shoving them. So that's a little difficult for them. But, if they follow, they'll get more sensitive in their writing.

IB: O. Henry felt that if a story was true to the human element, you just had to change the local color so it would fit any town.

ES: That's tending too much toward the formula story to me. I used to know a man who listed all possible stories as formulas. They were fourteen in number, and any story you gave him he could immediately say, "This is the 'Worm-turn' story" or "This is the 'Ain't Love Grand' story" or "This is 'Conflict with Final Success.'" (Laughs.) I don't know, I think that every good story is different. It really never has been written before.

IB: Where'd you meet this fellow?

ES: He was a good friend of mine, actually. He was a mystery story writer who had a seminar in writing in Nashville, Tennessee. And I was having a lean time of it because I had a job at a girls' finishing school in Nashville that I felt I was stifling to death in. It was during the war and I used to go down there to hear him talk—to get out of school, I guess. So I thought he was charming and I thought it was fun to be there, but I didn't believe a whole lot of it.

IB: Did you feel a need to escape the South?

ES: Yes. Part of it was my writing. I felt there were getting to be too many Southern writers and that I didn't know if I was different, but I felt because I lived in the same part of the country as Faulkner did, I was seeing the same sights and knowing the same kind of people all my life. I read Faulkner very late, actually, but I realized when I read him—I already wanted some day to be a writer—that my heart sank because he was dealing already with things: people, landscape, the family, history, and everything that I might some day have to be tapping for my own work. In fact, my first novel, *Fire in the Morning*, people said was Faulknerian—I'm not sure it is. It just seemed to me I was drawing on things I'd known around my home town. Anyway, I thought if I stayed around the South, it was just going to be multiplying and finding varieties of the same sort of thing that other writers are doing in great quantities now. And then, I just wanted another horizon to bring to bear on that—like learning another language sharpens your own language.

Also, I had done a sort of interesting thing. I had a friend who was working for the State Department in Germany. She went over for the Nuremberg Trials right after the war. She had gotten married over there and wanted me to come. It was the summer of 1949. So I took the proceeds of my first book, got a French freighter out of New Orleans, and went to Europe. I visited them for a while and then I left and went down to Italy. And I thought, "Oh, if I could ever get back." Well, that was part of the dream. But the other part was shaking loose from the *single* environment and trying to bring another to bear upon it. Maybe it was partly instinct, but I thought it would be enriching. However, I always meant to come back.

IB: What was the weirdest thing that happened to you on the freighter? That was a daring thing to do, wasn't it?

ES: I didn't realize how daring it was until we were actually at sea. It was a French lend-lease freighter called the *Wisconsin* (pronounce it in French and it sure sounds funny). The passengers were from Mexico, New Orleans, and the United States generally; some got on in Cuba (this was before Castro) loaded with rum and rumba records. It took eighteen days to cross the Atlantic. We changed the port of entry three times and had to send cables. I should have written *Ship of Fools*.

IB: How'd it feel when you finally got back in the states a few years ago?

ES: Oh, I'd been visiting a lot at home. See, I went to Mississippi a lot during my parents' last years of life. I always went back to Mississippi at least once a year all those years except when I was living in Italy that longer stretch. But getting back to Chapel Hill, that was a kind of return too, because I'd been Writer-in-Residence here for a month in 1969, and I'd gotten to know people who didn't go away, in contrast to other places I'd been, people like Max Steele and Louis Rubin, and we really kept up the friendships that we made at that time. Chapel Hill is rather special. My husband says it's Shangri-la.

IB: You definitely use dreams in your work?

ES: Oh, yes, I think I do. "Knights and Dragons" is full of them. There's a little dream in the title story of *Jack of Diamonds* that I thought of cutting out because it certainly goes against my commandments—you know, don't leave anything that embellishes what's been discussed. It's where the girl has a dream about the mother coming from the library.

IB: The librarian promised her a book, which she didn't have . . .

ES: And then she leans down on the pavement and picks up the very book she was looking for. Now I have no idea what that dream means. I didn't dream the dream. I had the girl dream the dream, but somehow I felt like it pertains to the feelings she had for her mother so I left it in. Do you think that was wrong?

IB: No, I think it works.

ES: But why it works you don't know. It's like dreams themselves. Why do they work? You don't know.

IB: Are your dreams vivid?

ES: When you concentrate on remembering your dreams, if you do it the first five minutes after you wake up, you'll remember a whole host of things. And I tried this—I've got notebooks full of stuff. Then the second morning you can remember more. I don't know if you deliver some kind of directive to your subconscious to "start dreaming now because I'm thinking about what you're going to do." Then they come thicker and thicker and, if you try consciously to remember and put them down in the first five minutes, you can resurrect a whole lot of things out of that.

IB: Any persistent type of dreams?

ES: I used to, when I was a child, be very frightened by a dream I

had about running from a fox. (Laughs.) Isn't that silly? I was
never chased by a fox.

IB: What were the watershed periods in your life?

ES: Oh, Lord.

IB: This follows up on the three—or is it ten—commandments of
writing.

ES: Only ten? (Laughs.) I think when I left the Mississippi environment, complete and total Mississippi saturation, and went
off to Vanderbilt to graduate school—that was a watershed.
Then I tried to go back to Mississippi and teach in a small college and I wasn't content. I got a job in Nashville where I was
in graduate school—that new job was confining, too.
     The thing that I didn't like about Mississippi, though I love
it in a sense, was a sense of confinement because I was brought
up by a very strict family, Presbyterian, but the ramifications
of my mother's and father's families extended over the entire
state. There wasn't anything I could do ever to escape. It was
not so much supervision, though there was that in it, but it was
people knowing everything I would do. Every part of my life
was being scrutinized. It's enough to give you paranoia, but it
would be a justified paranoia because it was literally true.
When I got up in Nashville, I had a sense of freedom.
     I won a prize from the National Institute of Arts and Letters
of a thousand dollars, and I went up to New York and got to
live off the thousand dollars some way or another because I
lucked up on a room that was cheap. The lady went off on vacation and left me with the whole apartment. That was a wonderful summer, and that, again, led me to believe that I could
cope with things outside Mississippi and feel freer and happier
by doing so. When I left on the Guggenheim and went to Italy,
that was another watershed. I suppose getting married was another watershed because it changes your lifestyle. You've got to
adjust to another kind of life. And we had to go somewhere

where we could make a living. That turned out to be Canada, and I think that watershed almost put me in a backwater because, though Montreal's a big international city, Canada was so much different from the warm country I'd been brought up to care about—the South and Italy. It seemed to me I stayed up there too long. I was always coming back when I left Europe. This latest move to Chapel Hill is definitely a step I was glad to take. Any more? Have I got ten?

IB: You based *Fire in the Morning* on your grandfather. Didn't he die long before the book came out?

ES: Yes, it was an unsullied relationship because I hadn't reached adolescence when he died. I think adolescence is a time for shaking up and disillusion and all that. I think I was writing about a wonderful man, and I hope I caught that wonderful quality in the book. He was a country sheriff for years before I was born, of course, and all those stories about him as sheriff were real. He had prevented a lynching at one time. And there were several men he had to hang. There were a good many stories about his courage. I made up the conflict over the property. But I got in trouble socially because people thought I was talking about them. It was difficult for my parents to survive all that because it was an irritation in the community, and they were heavily embarrassed and had to go and tell everybody that I really didn't mean them. (Laughs.)

IB: Any specific confrontations they had?

ES: Well, I don't know. My mother was very exercised and unhappy, and she begged me to take certain passages out that had bad language in them, and I gave in to her a few times. But the surprise to me—I guess I was very naive—was that I couldn't see people around home really reading a book or caring if I'd written anything. Instead, it went all over the place, and everybody was reading it. A lot of people in Mississippi were writing at that time and there used to be a game that women played around beauty parlors called "Picking Out the People." And they would sit with these books not giving a damn about the message of the book or what its real literary intent was and say, "Oh, isn't that exactly like so-and-so," "Oh, I know that's so-and-so." And then, I guess people being very fond of my mother and caring about how she felt began to say, "Oh, it's really a wonderful book." So she finally got calmed down. But I don't know what confrontations she had to go through because she was torn—she was always torn, always defending me. In the meantime, probably, she really wished the book was in the creek. (Laughs.)

IB: You heard Civil War stories from your grandfather and others didn't you?

ES: My grandfather tried to volunteer and lied about his age, but they wouldn't take him. He was running the whole plantation, a boy of fourteen, because all his family was in the war. I don't know that he had any Civil War stories to tell because he never saw any combat. Aunt Lucy Breckinridge was my older brother's nurse and the family cook for a while. You see Carrollton wasn't in the regular line of action, even when they made forays through northern Mississippi and burned houses— I don't think Carrollton was in that sweep. So they weren't war stories in the sense of being actual troop engagements near there. But there were any number of reminiscences of hard times after the war. Oh, real fury could be awakened out of people of my mother's generation about the Yankees, and about Reconstruction, and if Lincoln had only lived—and how mad they were at everybody. They'd say, "They take every opportunity to put us down," and "We just don't amount to anything." All that hatred of Yankees, I think, made racial segregation more entrenched in the South because the idea was that the Yankees were trying to force us to do these things. And they hated the Yankees so they hated any sort of attempt of the Yankees to do anything, even though it was probably indicated as right.

There was a story my mother used to tell about an aunt of hers who, when Yankee soldiers came by, they thought they were going to burn the house. She was a very pretty woman, so the soldiers said, "Well, play a tune for us," and she played, "I'll Be a Rebel Still" (laughs) which was a popular song in that time. And they just laughed and said, "You're too pretty for us to take any offense at that." So they left.

IB: You wrote in "The Cousins," "Whatever Southerners are, there are ways they don't change." In what ways haven't you changed?

ES: People in Montreal said, "How did you keep your accent?" And I said, "Well, I never tried to lose it, I never tried to keep it—it just stayed." I don't know. I suppose I have good manners because I was made to sit still in those horsehair chairs. (Laughs.) I can't imagine losing a sense of manners because I think manners are very important to kindness in living. The whole thing that I got from my parents that I am really grateful for is a sense of real democracy. And I wouldn't go back on that part of my upbringing because I think it's right. If that means you're a Southerner . . . I suppose you could learn that in Nebraska, couldn't you?

IB: Have you received any knee-jerk reactions where you were made, as a Southerner, to feel responsible for everything?

ES: I used to get more comments on that than I do now. When I had outlined the book, *The Voice at the Back Door,* people at the American Academy in Rome—it was sort of pre-civil rights era—and a lot of other people out there mocking, made comments. I always felt I had to defend the South, but at the same time I didn't want to seem that I wasn't liberal-minded myself. You can't go to great lengths to explain all that in a social situation where nasty remarks are thrown at you.

IB: Any specific nasty remark you remember?

ES: I met a black man at a party, and I asked this Jewish musician, "What was his name again?" when the black man left. The black man was sort of drunk and flamboyant and threw his arm around me at one time, and then went on somewhere else, and I hadn't taken offense at that, but I asked his name. The musician told me his name and he looked at me and he said, "And he's from a fine old family in Georgia,"—as though this underscored something and took the whole idea of southern family tradition to task. I felt how can I stop all that, so I guess I didn't say anything.

IB: In *The Voice at the Back Door*, Kerney lies about the racial incident and Duncan ruins his career trying to protect the black person.

ES: Oh, I think in politics in the South, in Mississippi, you had to knuckle under. I had a cousin by marriage who was eventually ruined in politics because they smoked him out. He'd been a Congressman under Kennedy, and they sent troops into the University of Mississippi. He had to answer when he was asked point-blank if he agreed with that. He said, "Yes," he did, so he was defeated. Kerney saw the handwriting on the wall if he kept the friendship, so he betrayed the friendship.

IB: What was difficult about writing *A Voice at the Back Door?*

ES: See, for many years, I was a supporter of segregation because I'd never known anything else. I was partially brought up on a plantation where there were descendents of slaves, and there weren't any white people for miles around, except my uncle and aunt. Then I began to place some blame, and, from hearing other ideas, I decided to examine the whole thing in the novel. And the difficult part for me was *I* was maturing in *my* attitudes in writing that novel—it was an evolution and a questioning of my own attitudes from childhood on. So it was a living, evolving experience for me, and that was the hard part— not to be easy on yourself, and to look at it unflinchingly, so I did. In the preface I wrote to that *Time* edition of that book, I tried to recount some of my feelings.

IB: You seem interested in the Southern class structure. You have rednecks, middle class, planters . . .

ES: Well, it's so mixed and so fluid. There were people who have been around in my part of the country for years. My father's family, the Spencers, and my mother's family, the McCains and the Youngs, were there from the earliest times, before the Indians left. But being in the planter class might just mean you had more land than your cousin somewhere who had maybe only two hundred to three hundred acres. So you built a bigger house because you had more money. Then the person with a little land might be married into the family some way. That's what happened to my mother and father. He was an up-and-coming young man who didn't have very much—it was all hard times after the Civil War. My mother's family home burned before she was ever born—it was a big house on a hill overlooking the Delta. They saved very little out of it. Then they built a smaller house on the plantation that eventually got extended and extended until it looked like a planter's house. But they built tack-on rooms for the longest. That's where I spent a lot of time. But the people who made big money after the war were sometimes unscrupulous—it's all in *Fire in the Morning,* how they came up and they gave themselves aristocratic airs—just as in Faulkner, the Snopses ended up buying the biggest house in Jefferson.

IB: It's always seemed to be that the extraordinary people of the South were often even more special because they've frequently had to overcome a lot.

ES: Oh, I know. Everybody's had to fight for their soul in the South, at one time or another. It wasn't that there was just poverty or just losing the war, but also continuing to right things within your own society where people ought to see and appreciate, and people turning against you. You know, that's very hard for people to come out of, I think. It's testing all the time. Maybe it's less now than it used to be because certain things have gotten pretty generally accepted. But in that story in *Jack of Diamonds*, "A Business Venture," that woman is being tested every minute—the one who opened the dry-cleaning establishment—because she's going against the way they thought she should live.

IB: Your stories are reminiscent in some ways of Henry James or Chekhov. Did you read them a lot?

ES: I've read some of James. I enjoyed reading it at the time, but I don't go back to James much. I read some short novels recently that I hadn't read before, and I think the first time you read them, they involve you completely, but then you don't want to work through that again. I think his prose is somewhat labored, but I shouldn't say anything against James. He's really a fine worker. It's really very interesting when he talks about his own work, but I didn't come early to James. I thought *Fire in the Morning* was more like a Thomas Hardy novel than it was like James or Faulkner. I admired Hardy a lot for the way he puts his novel together, but I'm not keen on his philosophy of life. I like Chekhov a lot; I am fond of Turgenev. I don't know, people have been saying that I resemble James. Before, they compared me to Faulkner. I've been compared to everybody. (Laughs.) Sometimes I think it's flattering, in a way. They always pick the very best people to compare me to, but I sort of wish they'd let me be myself. I don't know what's in the way of that—it must be my fault. (Laughs.)

IB: Could you talk about the dramatic elements in your writing?

ES: I've recently written a play! But I think there's been a strong dramatic element in my work all along. I like confrontation and encounter, and I like the sense of nobody being not entirely right about anything—again, situation, desire, event, all colliding and trying to work themselves free. And so I've had a lot of fun with the play, *For Lease or Sale.*

IB: Did it help you to be away from the South?

ES: Well, it does take a lot of pressure off to live abroad for a while. In the South it was a constant daily struggle to maintain your own ideas and beliefs.

A bunch of us from Mississippi were on a trip to Russia last September. The novelist, Ellen Douglas—that's not her real name—and I and several others would all sit around having a drink in our hotel in Moscow, talking about what we went through during different times in our past in Mississippi. And it was just a daily struggle with the people in your own family to keep your sense of humor, not to get your mind poisoned by the things they were saying. I didn't have to live through all that—I was in Canada. But, in many respects before I left, I was feeling that kind of pressure, so I think that that was a strong tide against any creative effort. It was a counter-tide that you were always fighting against. There's an essay that Eudora Welty wrote in *The Eye of the Story* about someone calling her up in the middle of the night. The caller is saying, "What are you going to do about all this, Eudora Welty?" and Eudora asks what a writer owes to current situations. How can you as a writer engage yourself? You don't want to turn out polemic, and yet you want to be on the right side. But, should you devote your fiction to that? I didn't feel that pressure so much when I started writing *The Voice at the Back Door. The Voice at the Back Door* came out coincidentally at the time the civil rights issue came to a head on the national level, but I was just responding to pressures I'd felt all my life. But then, I was able to write that because I was in Italy and I wasn't having to contend—I was just remembering and imagining.

IB: When did you feel you were able to write fully in your own voice?

ES: I've always felt that I wrote in my own voice, but I suppose it was weaker as a personal thing at first, and therefore it was easier to find echoes in it of other writers, like Faulkner and different people I had read and admired. But, in point of fact now, I think my style is pretty much my own instrument. I find that I can lend it very easily to the voices of the women that I've written about—in two instances in the stories in *Jack of Diamonds:* the voice of Ella Mason in "The Cousins" and the voice of Eileen Waybridge in "The Business Venture." They seem to me, though two different women, to generally come from the strata in the South that I know best. And it was easy for me to let them talk and tell their stories. And I could feel their personality operating through the voice, and I think that's really exciting for the writer.

IB: Jack London said that civilization has put a pretty thin veneer over this soft-shelled animal we call man. What do you think?

ES: Oh, I think people are pretty primitive—I really do. I think the primitive nature is just underneath the surface. It's close to all of us, but I don't know why that's surprising. (Laughs.) I think people are pretty much like animals. In fact, I often think about people in a favorable sense, really, as being like animals. I knew this guy in Montreal. I thought for ages that he resembled an antelope and I told him that. I don't know whether he liked it or not. (Laughs.) He even wore little black boots, instead of shoes, and they looked like antelope hooves.

IB: All right. What animal are you?

ES: Oh, Lord, I don't know. One of the cat family. You see, I'm tall and have a rather small head. Somebody told me I looked like a cheetah once. (Laughs.) They can run faster than I can.

IB: What would you like an Elizabeth Spencer story to do?

ES: I had several very pleasant reviews of this last book, and one reviewer said of one of the stories that it would change you a little bit. She said that was what she expected a really great story to do. I think I'd like for the story to be something that is part of the reader's life. I can never look back to a time before I read, for instance, *The Golden Apples* by Eudora Welty—it's become part of my life, part of my experience. It wasn't anything I did except reading it! Like Tolstoy, how can you think back before you read *War and Peace?* It's part of you. Not all of my stories can be that to everyone, but maybe some of my stories can be that to each and every reader.

IB: Novelist William Harrison talks about the writer always having to make choices between the secure and the adventuresome.

ES: Faulkner used to say "Don't do what you can do—try what you can't do." Well, that can be overdone, too, because you can do something wild that you aren't equipped to do at all and fall flat. But I do think much in favor of being adventuresome.

IB: Would you do anything differently, knowing what you know now?

ES: Each step seemed the right one at the time, so given the circumstances I suppose I made choices that were best for me. I think when my first books received favorable reviews, I should have stayed home instead of trying to go around giving "interviews," and attending bookstore "signings." I wasn't ready for doing public things, and being at that time excessively shy I used to feel I said wrong and misleading things and I was in general unhappy about the results.

IB: If you had to be personified as one character in one of your books, who would it be?

ES: I think the character that may be a lot like me is in "Jack of

Diamonds." I don't want to make this sound like I am this person because I'm anything but this person, but I think the character Ella Mason has this sense of remembering without judging too harshly the things she remembers or turns over in her mind. She wonders without making too terribly harsh judgments about anything. I'd like to be sort of like that.

RICHARD WILBUR

Richard Wilbur was born in New York City in 1921 and grew up on a farm in New Jersey. He attended Amherst College, and served in the Thirty-sixth Infantry during World War II. He has taught English at Harvard, Wellesley, Wesleyan, and Smith, is former president of the American Academy of Arts and Letters, and was made a chevalier of the Order des Palmes Academiques in Paris. He is married and is the father of four children.

As a poet, Wilbur's books include *The Beautiful Changes, Ceremony, Things of This World*, which won him a Pulitzer Prize for poetry, *Advice to a Prophet, Walking to Sleep, The Mind-Reader,* and *New and Collected Poems*.

In 1987 he became the second Poet Laureate in the United States, a fitting tribute to one of America's most distinguished men of letters.

Wilbur's major works in translation have involved the plays of the neoclassical French dramatists Racine and Moliére, which he rendered into rhymed couplets. A recent translation of Racine's *Phaedra* (1986) was praised by Louis S. Auchincloss who said, "Richard Wilbur has accomplished, almost magically, what no one else in three centuries has done: he has brought the greatest of French tragedies, in all its beauty, into our tongue." His works translating *The Misanthrope* and *Tartuffe* have won him the Bollingen and PEN translation prizes, and have been produced in London, New York, and in regional theatres across the country.

Mr. Wilbur collaborated with Lillian Hellman and Leonard Bernstein, writing the lyrics for the comic opera *Candide*. This "Renaissance man" has also published a book of essays called *Responses* and has written several children's books including *Loudmouse* and *Opposites*, which he also illustrated.

My interview with Richard Wilbur took place on his farm in rural Massachusetts, interrupted occasionally by the belligerent strains of a cow. Nearby a rustic silo—Wilbur's study—rose into the sky like a huge crown. Before we started, Wilbur wandered over to the fence to exchange a word or two with the animals in his familial, good-natured way. Wilbur seems to be a man at ease with his world. He sat down beside me in the open field and we chatted for a while just before my camera operator settled in to film the proceedings.

INTERVIEW

IRV BROUGHTON: On summer vacations years ago, you toured the United States hobo-style, riding freight cars. I was wondering if you considered yourself an early day "easy rider?"

RICHARD WILBUR: Oh, no, I don't think I was "in search of America," except, perhaps, in some old romantic sense. And I certainly wasn't running away from any aspect of America or trying to find out whether I was courageous. I don't know just what my mission was—part of it, I think, was mere curiosity, restlessness. I had read Hart Crane on the subject of railroads, and I'm sure that I had read some other people. I think there were some good railroad whistles in Muriel Rukeyser, here and there. There was a lot of railroad mysticism in the 1930s, and undoubtedly it was partially that, as well as simply youthful adventure, that set me going. Then, also, I didn't have very much money, Irv, and so I thought that hoboing would be a way to see the forty-eight states; or I guess it was forty-seven of them I saw. I didn't go to Georgia because I had heard they would put me on the chain gang if some yard dick caught me.

IB: You're now on a farm here, and you grew up on a farm. Is this a homecoming with cows and everything?

RW: Yes, I wish they'd make good background noises for us. Actually, the farm I was brought up on in New Jersey was not one which my family worked, and so I had the best of everything. I had the pleasure of riding on the haywagon, but I didn't have to make the load, or get up early in the morning and do all those onerous tasks. And often I had the pleasure of playing tennis against a nice campestral background, against the waving corn tassels. We have about the same thing here. Of course, I do work pretty hard at raising vegetables and herbs.

IB: What are your favorites to raise?

RW: The sensible thing to raise is tomatoes, of course. That's where you really make a difference. But I raise all sorts of other things, rather dumb things. I have some okra plants which are only *that* high and will never get higher. That's my experiment for the year. I raise things like rocket, which you can't buy on the market. I have a perverse taste for hot lettuce.

IB: In 1961 you traveled to Russia on a foreign exchange program. Do you enjoy such things?

RW: I enjoyed that very well. I was given time in which to prepare myself for it. There wasn't time for me to learn the Russian language, but I could read up on Russia, and I could read a good many novels and whatever poetry was available to me in translation—good or bad. And that trip in 1961 was made at a very fortunate time. Peter Viereck and I went over there, as a two-man team, at a time when Russia was anxious to prove that they could be more liberal than we as hosts. We'd been rather foolish to a delegation of Russian writers who came to America. We wouldn't let the novelist Leonov, for example, look through one of our California telescopes, as if the heavens were secret information; and they weren't allowed to look at the Brooklyn Navy Yard, either. Well, the Russians said to Peter and to me that we could see anything or anybody we wanted. We offered them a list of fifty writers we wanted to meet, and not under vodka-toast circumstances, but tête-à-tête and in their homes, if possible. They did play ball with us in forty-nine instances out of fifty. In one case, there was a poet who had behaved badly politically and had been put into the loony bin—a thing they do over there. They didn't give us quite the straight story about him. But we were allowed to go anywhere we liked, and we were not always accompanied by interpreters and Intourist guides. And so I thought it was an extremely fortunate jaunt.

IB: Viereck himself returned to the forms later in his own poetry and so have many others: Borges, Eliot, Pound. Do you think this is an affirmation of the poetic form—when poets return to use of meters and rhymes?

RW: Sonnet forms, that kind of thing. I'm really not militant about that at all. I do think it's perfectly possible to write satisfactory poems in free verse. It does, however, depress me to hear good people like Galway Kinnell say that we're beyond all that formal stuff now . . . we'll have no more use for meters or the trouble of rhyme. It seems to me that traditional means, if you have the ability to use them, can be turned to enormous account; that there are many effects you can get with them that you can't possibly get without them.

IB: Yevtushenko said that there might be one or two unused rhymes somewhere in Argentina. Isn't that a problem?

RW: It is a problem. I can remember talking about cat-rat rhymes at one time with somebody or other—I think it was Jack Sweeney—and saying that nobody again would ever be able to write a poem rhyming "fire" and "desire," and so on. He immediately reminded me of a lyric in one of Eliot's "Four Quartets" which rhymes very freshly on precisely the words I was saying couldn't be used again. It is, I guess, all a matter of how you come up to them, how necessary the words are. Forced rhyme is no good. Unforced rhyme, even if the rhymes have been used a thousand times, can be effective.

IB: If you were a writer in Russia today, do you think your work would be different?

RW: I have no doubt it would be. I think I'd be reacting in some way to the pressure to be edifying, and to encourage the workers in the economy to be orthodox. I imagine nevertheless that my natural inclination to be oblique, and to play, is close to what a lot of the good Russian poets do. They say one thing out of the front of the mouth and another thing, another qualifying thing, out of the corner of the mouth. It makes for poems of great subtlety, sometimes. Also, poems which are awfully hard to translate.

IB: You're doing a good deal of translation now.

RW: Well, I don't do it in bulk really, but whenever I encounter a poem which seems to me an almost-possible utterance for my-self, and which offers me a formal challenge, I feel like taking it on. I like to do sonnets, that kind of thing. I'll take such a poem on, partly for fear that somebody else will take it on and wreck it. Most translation at present doesn't try to preserve the meters and other formal aspects of the original. And I do think that in many cases you simply can't bring across the quality of the poet without trying for some of that. Obviously, everything you do will be at best an approximation. But with certain poets I think it's obligatory to try for a formal equivalence. For ex-ample, nobody in France could translate the Australian poet A. D. Hope into free verse and convey anything that he's about. I don't suppose anybody ever translated Alexander Pope satisfactorily without a rhyme here and there.

IB: Mrs. Osip Mandelstam says that translation is the exact op-posite of verse writing.

RW: Oh, I think they're different, all right. Yes. Because you know how it's going to come out, if you're a translator. You don't if you're a poet. Nevertheless, I think if you take time enough on any job of translation, ask enough hard questions about what every word in the original means, and what relation the rhythm of the original has to the subject matter, and so on, you'll finally end by taking possession of it, which isn't to say it'll sound like you. But it *is* to say that you'll have asked of the original many of the kinds of questions you ask of your own work when it's in process.

IB: She says further that the real poet should avoid translation, that it can prevent the creation of real poetry.

RW: It's undoubtedly true that translation can be a dodge for the lazy poet or the tired poet. It's a way of seeming to have an output when you can't think of any notions of your own. Yet it can have great advantages for your own writing, I think. As I've said, to translate someone is often an act of imposture in which you say something which you're not quite prepared to say in your own person, or take a tone which is not quite your own. Yet you'd like to have that latitude in your own work before you're through. And this gives you a little practice. I'm sure that all of Ezra Pound's translations had some effect upon the central Ezra Pound, wherever that was; sometimes I think it's hard to find.

IB: Do you think verse translations enrich the language in which they are translated?

RW: Oh, very often, yes. Each language does have a particular kind of genius, and it also has its particular individual geniuses. The bringing over of anything that's like the original, into English, is going to make changes, is going to offer people alternative ways of saying it. I suppose the clearest example of this would be the effect of Japanese and Chinese translation on us. The condensation, obliqueness, and impersonality of Japanese poetry has been very suggestive for a lot of our people.

IB: Doesn't it occur that at some point translation corrupts and is detrimental to the original language?

RW: I think we damage the English language, and damage poetry in the English language, by producing bad translation in it. I can't think of an example right now—if I could, perhaps I wouldn't want to give it—but I think there are poets who have done a lot of translations and have fallen into the habit of talking like a book of translation and lost track of their own voices.

It's a little bit like living abroad. Expatriates find themselves using the slang of 1927, or saying "actually" instead of "currently."

IB: Doesn't this sometimes do irreparable damage to our concept of foreign literature?

RW: Certainly so. I believe that when Harvard University began messing around with humanities programs, they rather hoped that students reading the great books in translation would be moved to go into the classics department and read them in the originals or into the modern languages departments. And I don't think that's happened, really. And so, in some cases we've done a kind of public dishonor to some fine book or fine poem by knowing it unnecessarily through bad English versions. I'm sorry about that. Yet, I suppose, in almost every case something is better than nothing. In the case of Goethe, it's hard to say. I don't read Goethe in the original; in such English and American translations as I've read, he sounds awful. I'm not sure it's a favor to anybody that there are English and American translations of Goethe.

IB: What do you think about writing for eternity?

RW: I don't think it's a consideration.

IB: Andrew Sarris considers most film criticism as Puritanical. Do you think this could be said of poetry criticism?

RW: Puritanical. Well, there *are* ways that criticism can be Puritanical. There was a lot of social-minded criticism in the 1930s which imposed political duties on the poet, and for those who were going to perform such duties anyway, I suppose it did no harm. For others, it really may have been harmful for the critics to keep saying to them, "The poet *must*, the poet owes it to his society," and so on. And then there's that "theological" kind of criticism which used to talk about the heresy of this and the fallacy of that. I think that such language is a little strong, a little arm-twisting, and is likely to be damping to the original sort of poet who's out of step with the fashions of his time.

IB: Your poems have been criticized from the standpoint that "How can this artist be so likeable in this horrendous world?" That's a paraphrase of one man's statement.

RW: Thank heavens, I'm not aware of being likeable. If somebody finds me so, I'll pardon him, but I have no desire at all, in my poetry, to be ingratiating. I don't have any consciousness of talking directly to people when I write—as would be required for such an intention. I don't write to please, except to please myself, and to please a group of now nameless people who've established themselves as my superego. Once I've written a poem, of course, I'm very pleased if it pleases.

IB: You talked about carrying a poem around like it was a precious possession and that you didn't show it to anyone until that final moment when it was done.

RW: Yes. Well, I don't want to stop worrying about it. I should hate it if somebody approved of me prematurely, before I really achieved the poem, got through to the last time. And I wouldn't want the contrary to happen either. I did that recently—made the mistake of showing someone a long poem which was in process. I had been working on it for a year and a half, and I suppose I was impatient for a pat on the back. And it didn't make out too well with that critic. Took me some months to work up heart to go on with it. I do think it's foolishness to seek approval before you've pleased yourself.

IB: Louise Bogan feels that you have the exact moment of timing with your poems. She says you let them drop at the exact right time, sort of I suppose, like fruit, out here amongst the apple trees.

RW: Yes, well, I hope so. I do think timing is very important in poetry, as in talk. When you get to the end, you should stop. And your ending, I suppose, is something which, if you have certain effects in mind, you should build toward. Not every discourse, however, need have a crescendo. There are other shapes.

IB: It is possible to write major poetry in two languages?

RW: I suppose that someone like Nabokov, if he put poetry first, would be capable of writing an extremely fine and witty poetry in more than one language. Perhaps more than two. But he's exceptional, isn't he? I doubt that there are many people who could do it, because in poetry especially, you write out of such intimate and, in some degree, unexamined feelings about words. You know the words of your own language as you know your brothers and sisters and your wife and your children— which is to say very deeply, and yet not altogether clearly. However good your feeling is for another language, it's always got to be comparatively superficial, narrowly clear in a dictionary sense.

IB: You wrote the lyrics to the comic opera *Candide*. Could you have written the limericks to *Hair?*

RW: No, no. I'm not attracted to the youth culture or its enthusiasms, and so I don't believe I could have done that. It would have been a technical challenge, I expect, but I'd have flunked it. It's not that I'm "agin" the young, but I really don't care for rock music and I don't care for the kind of language which goes with most rock lyrics. I think it's very good that rock lyric has broken the frame of the old "Musical Comedy" number, and has included a lot of material, a lot of the kind of language, which for a long time was not used. That's the good thing about it. But I really don't feel that anything terribly worth listening to has occurred in the rock lyric so far. I know my children would detest me for saying this, but for my sins, I had to read all the lyrics of Bob Dylan some time ago because some students of mine accepted a challenge of mine, or took advantage of a tolerance of mine, and wrote term papers on him. He may be good with guitar accompaniment, but the words simply aren't much.

IB: Talk about the problems of doing the collaboration on *Candide*. I mean, here you're working with a group of people and hopefully you're working as a unit.

RW: Well, I came into that show, *Candide*, five years after others— that is to say, Bernstein, Lillian Hellman—had started working on it, and there had been five other people working on the lyrics. So I was really asked in to do, initially, a mopping-up action, to rewrite a lot of lyrics which were unsatisfactory, or which, in view of changes in the book, were going to have to be tinkered with. Then we started to change the book so much, and made so many cuts, that there were a number of new lyrics to be done. But, as I think I was going to say, I came into something in which other people had had a longstanding investment, and their imaginations of the project were pretty stubborn. And so I had my times in collaborating with Leonard Bernstein. We tended to butt heads quite a lot. Sometimes I got my way, sometimes he got his way. Once or twice we did it just like Mickey Rooney in the movies, and produced something satisfactory—rapidly, sleeplessly, and in perfect harmony, freely giving in to each other. He would let me knock out a note, and I'd let him knock out a word.

IB: Which poems affect you the most?

RW: Many poems have taken my head off. Oh, I don't think I can go through all my reading experience and say which poems have most excited me. There really are too many. There are a couple of tercets of Dante which overwhelm me with their simplicity every time I come back to them. The exciting poems I like best are the ones which are absolutely inexhaustible. There's a little poem of Coventry Patmore's I keep saying which has as yet shown me no point of weakness. I think I can say it from memory. I don't remember the title of it. It was some dreadful, abstract word. It's better just to start with the first line, in a concrete scene. Coventry Patmore's poem goes:

Here, in this little bay
Full of tumultuous life and great repose,
Where, twice a day,
The purposeless, glad ocean comes and goes,
Under high cliffs, and far from the huge town,
I sit me down.
For want of me the world's course will not fail;
When all its work is done, the lie shall rot.
The truth is great, and shall prevail,
When none cares whether it prevail or not.

The next to last line is from one of the apocryphal books, I think it's *Tobit*, but I forget the context, in any case. It is a Biblical allusion. "The truth is great and shall prevail."

IB: Those words are very close to you, special?

RW: Well, I like the two last lines, taken together. The truth is great and shall prevail, *when* (which I think means *though*) none cares whether it prevail or not. I read that poem at a service at the local church the other day. And I read it as an example of trustfulness in God. It seems to me that Coventry Patmore is saying, with the greatest blitheness, that no matter what he does, no matter what anybody does or does not do, or wish, the truth is great and shall prevail. The world is good and will turn out so.

IB: Are most of the lines that stick with you like that, are they affirmative?

RW: I'm not necessarily stuck on affirmations. I think I simply like the voice to be true. I like, for example, a lot of the real hard nastiness of François Villon, because it seems to me authentic. Limited, perhaps, but genuine.

IB: James Dickey said, "It's not possible to know, nobody will ever know what is poetry."

RW: Well, if you stepped that question down a little and said, "What is a poem?" then you could start to name different kinds of poems, different particular poems. You could start saying whether this or that bit of writing worked as a poem works. Probably that's where to start, where Aristotle starts—saying, "What does it do to you when you are in the presence of a poem?" You discover how what you regard as a poem, what you choose to call a poem, works on you. Then, if something else doesn't, you declare it not to be a poem.

IB: Do you think the reading public is intellectually adolescent?

RW: Well, I don't know. They used to say that about the radio public—that it was really eight years old. I don't know how they went about discovering that. The reading public for poetry is chiefly, I think so far as sales are concerned, a bright student public. I have no objection to that at all. It's very pleasant to think of being read by a lot of such people. It's true that I don't admire all of their excitements, and I suppose that the institution of the poetry reading has led to a certain amount of currying favor with the student audience one way or another. It's a good audience to have. I don't think anybody would write poems, or I think people would write very few poems, if there were not readers. So there has got to be some kind of thought of the reader in the poet's head. And yet, as he writes, no real poet says to himself, "How is my reader going to like this? Is he smiling now?"

IB: Louise Bogan also said of you that Wilbur points to a time when tenderness will not be so rare.

RW: She must have said that about my first book. Well, that's something nobody can know about himself. You can't know if you give a tender impression or not. I'm glad she thought so; I think that's a good quality to have.

IB: Do you read other translations of work you're translating?

RW: Generally not. When I've worked on whole plays of Molière—I've done four of those now—I've sometimes looked at prose translations of plays I was rendering in heroic couplets. But only when I was really stuck for a word. And of course, I would never look at a rhyming translation of anything I was doing into rhyme. That would absolutely cut my thought processes off, I suppose. I would be embarrassed to adopt the rhyme another translator had used.

IB: What happens later when you find you may have used the same rhyme?

RW: Oh, that doesn't matter. If I've arrived at it independently, that's perfectly all right. About that, one can be as self-respecting as that fellow who thought of evolution at the time Darwin did. Curiously enough, the same rhymes don't occur too often—at any rate in translations of Molière. There's a Columbia professor who's done a certain number of translations of Molière into rhymed verse recently, though I guess I was the person who started it. He did one of *The School For Wives*, and he did his before I did mine. I was rather strenuously hopeful that, when I came to look at his version, there wouldn't be too many of the same rhyming solutions. The first two rhymes in his translation and mine were the same, as it turned out. But after that we diverged considerably.

IB: Do you know any poets who use a dictionary, a rhyming dictionary?

RW: No. I guess the only time I've ever used one was in the course of a job of translation, when I felt myself controlled by what the original had to say, and wanted to say that at all costs, in language as close as possible to the original. And so I looked now and then into a rhyming dictionary, almost always in the vain hope of finding a word I hadn't thought of. I work so slowly that, when it comes to rhymes, I usually think of them all. It's very bad to use a rhyming dictionary, in my experience at any rate, because it means that the words you should think of at leisure, and mull over, and discover possibilities in, are given to you too suddenly, too easily, and you experience their possibilities superficially.

IB: Who would you like to be?

RW: I don't think I have ever approached a poem that way—trying to project an ideal self. Partly, I imagine, because from the very beginning, I've thought of poetry as getting one's various selves to quarrel intelligibly in public. And to be ideal, to be an ideal persona, would be to foreclose the possibilities of the poem.

IB: Your sonnet for LBJ was sort of an adventure into the political realm, though you attack him on slightly different grounds.

RW: It's a pretty oblique attack. I'm really angry at him, of course, because of the Vietnam War, but the poem presumes to be attacking him because he refused Peter Hurd's commissioned portrait. I wrote the poem at a time when I hadn't seen Peter Hurd's commissioned portrait. Now that I've seen it, I don't think it is anywhere near as good as most of Hurd's work, in particular, his landscapes.

IB: Would you still damn LBJ on that?

RW: Well, I would certainly object to his reasons for refusing it, and I would object to the churlishness with which he refused it. I think he rejected it because he said (in the painter's presence) that it was the ugliest thing he had ever seen. Whereas he could have found that in a mirror. Enough; I'm being nasty.

IB: Among poets, Elizabeth Bishop wanted to be a painter. You're very concerned and interested in painting. Your father was a painter.

RW: Yes, still is. Well, there is a great deal . . . I don't know whether I can explain it. There must be some poets who have very little visual imagination, even though the eye is the primary sense. Everybody's agreed on that since the Middle Ages, I think. Even D. H. Lawrence, who made out a strong case against the primacy of vision, was a painter. Well, I just can't say. I think I can say why there are more painter poets, or poets who are would-be painters, than there are poets who have to do with music. It strikes me that music is infinitely more abstract than painting or poetry. That you can't make any precise statements as to what music is up to. Poetry simply has to be exact and concrete or it bores us to death. And on the whole, I think—despite some successes in abstract painting—that it's the same with painting.

IB: Brion Gyson made the comment that writing is fifty years behind painting.

RW: What should I do with that? It seems to me that painting is not altogether in good health. There are some fine paintings being done by particular persons, but I should say that the world of the New York galleries was involved in a very sorry way with the fashion world. There's a terrible turnover in styles, and a terrible modishness, falsifying the work of a lot of people who otherwise might be good. I don't think we have any such situation in writing. As for who's ahead in terms of time, I certainly don't know what it's going to be like fifty years from now, and I don't think the writing of poetry is fifty years behind the present. For years, anybody writing an imitation of William Carlos Williams has felt that he was in the avant-garde. I suppose that's been so for thirty or forty years. Funny how "modern" seems to mark time. If a little magazine comes out with a title in lower case, it feels modern. Does your magazine have a title in lower case?

IB: No, it doesn't.

RW: But you know what I mean. That's been modern since 1920. And so much that is regarded as experimental is a repetition of the Imagistic experiments of the teens and twenties. I really think it's much more experimental at the moment to see what you can do with the fresh use of traditional means.

IB: There's nothing new under the sun.

RW: Well, every poem had better be new, but I don't suppose that there are likely to be any new poetic means, new combinations, new ways of handling them. I like the thing that Robert Frost said when someone asked him why he wrote poetry; he gave one of his sassy answers and said, "To see if I can make them all different." Of course, he didn't. Nobody does. But every poet aspires to that and relishes that in other poets. It keeps happening.

IB: Do you feel anything of Frost out here in the countryside? You've got birch trees out there, a wall . . .

RW: Oh, yes, we have a lot of the props here. I don't think I have too many of Robert Frost's attitudes, though I was terribly fond of him personally and think very highly of his poems. I think that Frost is often misunderstood as a nature poet. I recall his saying, one time, that he'd only written one nature poem in his life. I thought about it for a while and realized which one he meant. It was an early poem called "In a Vale," in which he lays claim, in a kind of puckish way, to mystic insights into nature. It's a poem which really denies what it's claiming by the playfulness of its tone. Elsewhere, it seems to me, Frost makes no statements about nature, about what it is, about what it means.

IB: Do you value wit?

RW: Yes, I think that when one is making a serious statement, a little playfulness is, if it's done well, a kind of earnest of one's earnestness. If a poem can't stand to be locally amusing, then I suspect it's really not very serious; not as serious as it thinks it is.

IB: If there was a Richard Wilbur *Hamlet*, what would it be like?

RW: Heavens, I don't know. You mean, what sort of tortured personality would I like to project? I think it'll do, though to tell the truth—I've never thought to a conclusion about *Hamlet*. It's always been to me a puzzling play. I have never known, as Mr. Eliot didn't know, everything that was bothering Hamlet. What was making him so whole-hog disgusted.

IB: Do you like films?

RW: Yes, I like films a good deal, though I must say I treat them badly. I treat them whorishly. I turn on the television and look at the late movie, or I go to a new film without religiously reading all of the critics and seeing whether or not I should. I don't really like to talk about film as an art. Yet I love it, as a medium. I detest, really, a great deal of what's being done now in the films. I made the mistake of seeing *The Godfather* and *The French Connection* within a couple of weeks, and I felt that I'd had enough of that kind of nastiness for a lifetime. I propose to look now and see whether films are labeled "violent." I gather they are proposing to label some films as "violent."

IB: Well, you seem to get something visceral from films. I mean, isn't this fundamental to art?

RW: I simply delight in it. I can sit and watch quite uninteresting films, quite inartistic films, because after all, they're showing me pictures of things. I can watch Antonioni, who seems to me the most boring director in the modern world, simply because when he concentrates irrelevantly on a doorknob it is, after all, a doorknob.

IB: Do you like Bergman?

RW: Very much, very much. I haven't seen a great quantity of Bergman. I haven't seen any of his newer films, but I remember staggering out of his movie, *The Magician*, in tears and I almost never weep over anything. His movie, *The Virgin Spring*, destroyed me.

IB: Isn't that what art should do, set you to weeping?

RW: Nothing wrong with weeping. I'd never cared for the behavior of an old friend of the family, who, when Tchaikovsky's Fifth was put on the what do you call it—what did we call it?—gramophone, used to take out his handkerchief in advance. I suspect that he didn't need to listen to it, that the very thought of it was sufficient to make him cry. I'm just objecting to emotionalism. But true feeling, in response to a fine work of art, should certainly extend to weeping if it's called for.

IB: What do you like about Bergman?

RW: I suppose I like his areas of concern, which are religion, morals, and the arts. I like the fact that he can be thoroughly mysterious without hokum, though I gather he's been charged with hokum in some of his films which I haven't seen.

IB: You talked about "A Baroque Wall Fountain in the Villa Sciarra" saying that this was somehow relating to your Puritanical nature.

RW: That was a very pleasant fountain, but when I lived in Rome and walked past that fountain every day on my way to work, I always felt tempted by it, tempted to linger; and reproached by it, I suppose, because I was driving myself so humorlessly to go and get an eight-hour day done. That statement about Puritanical industry is meant to be a little playful, but it's also true that I had, even in the city of Rome, a tendency to work eight hours a day when I could. That's a rather stupid thing to do with poetry, though not so stupid with translation. I suspect nobody has more than about two or three hours of poetry in him a day.

IB: Do you usually use up those two or three hours?

RW: Not always. I'm awfully capricious, really. At present, I suppose I'm losing some of my Puritanism.

IB: When did you first notice this loss?

RW: Well, I can't tell you. I'm not so introspective as that, so self-noticing. Perhaps when we moved up here to Cummington and I found myself living in an environment so attractive. It's very hard, given those woods out there with the ponds and streams in them, not to go for a walk. And I suppose anyone who uses natural imagery rather frequently, as I do, can feel that he's working when he's out there.

IB: Has there been a change, do you feel a change in the intensity of your poems as you spend more time here in the country?

RW: I can't tell about that. I doubt that there has been. At any rate, I haven't set about intentionally altering myself, either in the mood of my work or in its means. I don't really believe in that kind of manhandling of one's self. Some poets whom I admire greatly have given themselves orders, as it were, have set about to change their styles. And have rather willfully constructed books. W. B. Yeats, I think, was a poet who set out to make each book a constellation, with intelligible relationships between all the poems, and I think very often he wrote poems to fill in the pattern. Well, since Yeats did it so well, it must have been desirable for him, but it's not anything I could do for myself. It would be a violation of myself not to be a little more whimsical, self-indulgent—maybe there's a nice word for it.

IB: If you were living in New York, do you think you'd write different poems?

RW: I'm sure that I would. I have lived in New York, was born there. I've lived there at various times for longer or shorter periods. I'm one of the great majority of ex-New Yorkers who now feel that not under any circumstances could they go back. It's simply too disagreeable a city, at present. I can't consent to Robert Lowell's saying that it's the center of American culture. That doesn't seem to me to be the fact at all. I should say that American culture was remarkably dispersed, and that some of our best writing, some of our best everything, is being done in what, to the New Yorker, would seem faraway and backward places. A theatre person can't think that way, I suppose, but if you're in the writing business you can.

IB: That's getting down to the people, grass roots, then, in America?

RW: Oh, I'm not talking regionalism or anything like that. I suppose I'm simply saying that you don't have to be in New York.

There are certain people you don't have to know, certain connections you don't have to have, certain shows you don't have to see, in order to be fully alive as a writer.

IB: Dan Berrigan said after he had gotten recognition on the strength of his Lamont prize that he knew publishers would accept almost anything and he had to guard against it.

RW: I expect most people find that to be true. There are so few editors who have any taste about poetry. Most of our major magazines, I think, don't even have poetry editors. And your chances of getting published, and in some sense published well, are very good, once you've been approved of once or twice. That's too bad, of course. You don't get whatever kind of criticism a rejection slip amounts to. For the other kind of criticism, you have to depend not on editors, but on your friends. On a few friends who, without malice, can be quite honest and tell you, "Don't publish that," or "Do fix that."

IB: Who have been your friends in that regard?

RW: One of my best friendly critics is William Meredith. I show him about everything I write, and he's one of the few people on whose say-so I've made changes. He feels that my diction is a little bit intolerably antique. And so when I say, "yet," he wants me to say "still." Sometimes I say "still" just to please him. And there are a number of other people. One of the best pieces of friendly criticism I ever had was from Archibald MacLeish. Again, that was a matter of one word. He looked at a poem I had sent him, and said, "The poem buckles a little at precisely this point. Can't you find a better word for that?" Happily, I could. I call that terribly good criticism, when someone can put his finger on *the* weak word in a poem which otherwise is not too bad.

IB: William Jay Smith spoke of seeing one of your poems early in its life.

RW: Oh yes, yes. I've often shown poems to Bill Smith, and as a matter of fact, he took my disorderly sheaf of poems, the poems which made up my book, *Walking to Sleep,* and put them into order, and I thought very artfully. That's the kind of thing I can't begin to do. When I organize a book, since the poems are all—as I say—one-shots, and don't amount to variations on a theme, I use the crudest possible methods of organization. I'll say, well, that was a long poem; let's rest it with a short one. Or, that was a heavy poem; let's have something trivial. Those really are the principles on which I've put all books together except the last one which, as I say, was delivered into Bill Smith's hands.

IB: You refer to the baroque wall fountain as the very symbol or concretion of pleasure. Can you explain that?

RW: Well, we all have a general sense of what pleasure is, before somebody asks us to define it. One way to define it would be to decide on certain words. Another way would be simply to point. And if I could point, I'd point at that fountain with all its marvelous splashing water, and its scallop shells, and its geese, and its fauns.

IB: You once said that one does not use poetry for its major purpose as a means of organizing one's self in the world until one's world gets out of hand. When did your world get out of hand?

RW: Well, I think what I was referring to was World War II. Of course, everybody's world gets out of hand in peacetime, but mine spectacularly did in wartime for all sorts of external reasons and, I think, on account of a corresponding internal confusion. Out of that shakeup, poetry is likely to come as a means of achieving some kind of security.

IB: You've written several poems about war.

RW: Well, I didn't write as many poems—as many printable, usable, bearable poems—out of the war as I thought I might. Even now I think of turning back and using some of my experiences in World War II, but I don't know whether I could manage to do it. I don't know whether I could recover the experiences authentically.

IB: How long does it take to translate an experience into a poem ordinarily? Is there a waiting period or something?

RW: I should think so. The large poem called "The Mind-Reader" is based on an experience I had in the fall of 1954 in Rome, and I'd been thinking about that experience for seventeen years. And making occasional notes about it on the backs of envelopes, or in one or another little scribbling-book I have. But it wasn't, I suppose, until three years ago that I got around to setting down a few lines and it took me, on and off, three years to get it done. That's a longer period of waiting than has generally been the case with me, and I must say I *can* recall occasions in which something happened to me, and I sat plump down and wrote about it.

IB: Which of your "plump down and wrote about it" poems has become most recognized?

RW: There's one called "The Death of a Toad," which I wrote immediately after killing a toad with a power mower. I suppose what happened was that the experience jelled a lot of feelings I'd already had, because the poem isn't in fact, simply about a toad. I was ready for something like that to happen, to which I might instantly respond by writing.

IB: Would you say that's responding out of inspiration, or do you believe in that word?

RW: Well, inspiration is a word forever out of fashion. I think everybody's always embarrassed by it though I can't think of a better word. Yes, I think you have to be somehow mysteriously ready to go, things have to fall into place, and there's no willing that to happen.

IB: No conditions that would help?

RW: None that I can think of. That is, there's no right room in which to write, no correct time of day, no proper meal to have had, no drink to have avoided. I really can't think of any sure-fire arrangements, and I try not to worry too much about such things. If you do, of course, you can find all kinds of handsome excuses for not writing.

IB: Do you sometimes have a drought—a few weeks or months?

RW: Oh, yes. I have long ones—and, as a matter of fact, what happens during such periods is that I lose the habit of converting things as they come into poems. It's hard to get that habit started again. I wish my dry periods were briefer, so that the habit would be more readily recovered.

IB: Then, do you discover oases in your writing, also?

RW: Oh, spates, spates! I never have much of one, because to write two poems in a couple of weeks would be going pretty fast for me. One reason for that, I think, is that I've never had the habit some people have of writing in poem sequences. That sort of note poem that Bill Williams used to write could become a very long poem, accomplished in a series of fragmentary inspirations. Wallace Stevens, in a somewhat more formal way, did the same kind of thing. What I seem to do when I have a hunch or a notion for a poem, is to collect ideas and images that belong to it and write about them very slowly and try to kill the subject once and for all in one poem. Once you've done that you have to pause awhile before you go on to something else.

IB: Say you had a time machine. What period of history would you pick to visit?

RW: I'd like to visit—not for all reasons, I assure you, but for some—Italy during the age of Leonardo or Alberti. The period when the sense of human possibility was enormous. What other periods, I wonder? I don't do much longing for other periods, actually. Maybe that's the only one I can come up with at this moment.

IB: What's the most poetic experience you've ever had?

RW: I don't really think of experiences as being poetic. I suppose that's an evasive and half-true thing to say. A poem amounts to rendering an experience, and other ideas and experiences which you associate with it, as fully-stated as possible. Very seldom, I think, do you accomplish in life that kind of fullness of consciousness. Life isn't that concentrated. Mostly it's "splendid waste," as Henry James said. I suppose if I thought of "poetic" as signifying intensely emotional, I could give all sorts of answers, but that really isn't the way I think about it. Poetry is, to be sure, emotional, but it's emotion at its most precise and understanding. Nothing to which you would say "Wow!" in ordinary experience seems to me to resemble a poem.

IB: Did you notice any different treatment after becoming America's poet laureate?

RW: That certainly wasn't the case in the world of friends and neighbors, or of poets and readers of poetry. But one's relation to the world of "media" certainly did alter. I found that I was continually giving interviews when I was down in Washington, and indeed elsewhere. I was allowed to sound off about such matters as the state of the language in a way that hadn't been so readily permitted before. I think that when they name you poet laureate the press figures that you probably have a certain amount of guaranteed wisdom and are to be indulged in a little more blather than previously. I wasn't really full of things I wanted to talk about. I think there's a limit on what a poet can say by way of interviews to a public that isn't steeped in his work or in poetry in general.

IB: What sort of questions did the media ask?

RW: I found that a lot of their questions were curious questions— questions about where you get your ideas, how often a day you write, how many books you sell. There's a lot of curiosity about poets, perhaps more curiosity about poets than there is about poetry.

IB: Why is that the state of poetry?

RW: I don't suppose that poets are any more distant from the public than they have been in most periods of human history, but at present there are a lot of competing art forms—to put it politely—and I think there are many people who read the newspapers and feel conversant with the world, but haven't in-cluded poetry in their view of things. For them, the poet's a curious animal.

IB: Did you ever get asked where your sandals are?

RW: I wasn't asked about sandals, although I must say I wear a lot of sandals these days, living as I do in Key West for part of the year. I *was* asked whether the baby needed a new pair of shoes—that is to say, whether you make any money in poetry.

IB: In "Cottage Street, 1953" you write about a meeting with Sylvia Plath.

RW: Well, as I said in a note on that poem, I think I may have com-bined a couple of occasions. What I am sure of is this: my wife's mother, Edna Ward, back in '53, invited us over to her nearby house in Wellesley to talk with Mrs. Plath and her daughter, Sylvia, who had rather recently tried to take her own life. My wife doesn't remember going, and I'm a little troubled by her failure to remember the occasion. Mrs. Ward was forever having us over to Wellesley to meet this or that mother or daughter, often a Wellesley college mother and daughter. It may be that I've combined Mrs. Ward's invitation with some other meeting I had with Sylvia Plath. I did meet her several times—once when she was an undergraduate at Smith. She came and interviewed me for, I think, the magazine *Mademoiselle*. My image of her in that poem may be derived from that occasion rather than tea time at Mrs. Ward's—I can't be sure. But certainly my reactions to her were the reactions that I record in the poem.

IB: Do you remember the interview with her?

RW: Not very clearly. I know that Sylvia Plath was interviewing Tony Hecht and maybe three or four others and me about the teaching of poetry in the colleges. What I carried away is in the poem—the feeling that she was shy and pale and not altogether a happy person at the time, and that she needed encouraging and was not the sort of brisk, businesslike interviewer you encounter when talking to a professional. She needed to be prompted, I remember. I had to do some of the interviewing for her.

IB: How did you feel when she killed herself?

RW: I felt very distressed. My poem suggests that I was in some degree responsible for cheering her up—giving her at least one day's good cheer about the life of the poet. And, of course, that's why Mrs. Ward wanted me to come over. I can't feel guilty about not changing the course of her life, but I did feel sorry that someone of so much talent should not have been able to make it as an ordinary person.

IB: Let's talk about your younger days. What do you owe your parents in terms of your writing?

RW: I'm indebted to my parents for many things. They were very indulgent toward everything I did, in the way of trying to play the guitar or the banjo, drawing, painting pictures, and writing in all sorts of forms. I don't mean to make any of this sound impressive. I'm talking about childish efforts in all of these domains, but my parents were very encouraging always.

IB: They did have artistic skills?

RW: Yes, my father was a painter. Initially, he was a commercial artist and then he moved into doing portrait work. He was a very good portrait painter. And my mother was what used to be called a housewife. She was a marvelous user of words, and she came out of a family of distinguished journalists; articulateness was not a rarity in our house. And my mother was a great appreciator of any verbal good licks that I could get off.

IB: Puns and riddles?

RW: Well, anything. Anything that was felicitous in the way of words. Certainly there were riddles to be encountered, including those in *Mother Goose,* which was one of my first exposures to poetry. I don't remember that the household specialized in the asking of riddles, but there were lots of word games. We played many evenings of charades, for example. As I got a little older, I played a great deal of the old Victorian game of anagrams with my parents and with my godmother and her mother—who were part of the same strange English-colonial community in which I grew up. I remember feeling very proud when I stumped Aunt Helen once with the word "flylfot"— and she challenged. She simply didn't believe that such an odd word existed, and because she was so clever, I remember the moment with triumph.

IB: You mentioned Key West. Has that found its way into your poems?

RW: So far I have not put anything about Key West into my poems, and that's very funny, because I've been going down there—for longer and longer periods each year—for more than twenty years. Somehow I've not come to be able to say anything through jasmines and palm trees and crotons. It will come, I think, but it hasn't happened yet. If poetry were about beautiful sunsets, I would long since have written about Key West; it has simply the best sunsets around if sunsets are what you want.

IB: Writing the text for "On Freedom's Ground" must have been a challenge.

RW: At first it seemed impossible. When Bill Schuman, the composer, had been given a commission from a consortium of symphony orchestras to do something about the Statue of Liberty, he phoned me and asked me to write him a text. I initially said, "Good heavens, Bill, it can't be done without simply stringing a lot of old cliches together. It's all been said too often." But he persuaded me to sleep on the idea and to see if I could not find some approach to it which would be acceptable to patriotic America and at the same time be fresh. And I hope that's what happened. At any rate, I woke up feeling that a general attack on the subject was coming to me, which would prevent me from being altogether tiresome about Miss Liberty, and so I got hooked in. I'm glad I did because I'm satisfied with a good bit of what came out in the way of words. William Schuman set them very beautifully, I think. Every time I listen to the tape of "On Freedom's Ground" I learn more and more about music.

IB: What are you most happy about in terms of the text?

RW: I like the fact that we start with New York harbor before the Europeans got there and see it as a natural scene in which everything is under compulsion from so-called natural law, and then return to it at the close, seeing it now with the eyes of free people, reading our own freedom into it. I like that idea, and I like the jolly little section in which various ethnic dances are evoked and jumbled. That's handled very boldly in Schuman's musical setting. He shifts into the major for that and it is a glorious romp of interwoven dance tunes of all kinds.

IB: What is your favorite poetical device?

RW: Well, I suppose that what I like most of all is the likening of things—metaphor. That's where I get my chief excitements, when I find the figure in which to say something and in which to connect one thing to another. It seems to me whatever else we're doing in poetry, we're always knitting the world together in a way that reveals its actual fabric.

IB: What was the metaphor that gave you the most trouble?

RW: Irv, I don't think I can answer that question. Whatever else in poetry is laborious and achieved by will, good metaphors come in a burst. They come to me, at any rate, as happy surprises, not that I won't have been waiting for them. But they do seem like something given.

IB: Do you use dreams in your work?

RW: I think that I use dreams a great deal. For a very short time, when I was sixteen or so, I kept a book in which I recorded all of my dreams. Now I don't think I directly mine the particular dreams of particular nights as much as I might have done at that time—though the very first poem in my *New and Selected Poems* is called "The Ride," and that's a quite straightforward recording of a dream, and how I felt when I awakened from it.

IB: Can you talk about that?

RW: It's a hard one to talk about because it has, for me, still a quality of mystery. I felt that it was an important dream so I put it down as it occurred. But precisely to say what it means is beyond me at the moment.

IB: Any frequent theme to your dreams?

RW: One thing that happens to me is that I sometimes dream in intense color. I remember discussing dreaming once with I. A. Richards. I mentioned having had a dream of intense blue, and he said, "Oh, well, people don't dream in color." (Laughs.) By which he meant that he'd never dreamt in color himself. Obviously, that's not universal. For some people color is very important in dreams, and other people dream in black and white. I know that, as my poem, "Walking to Sleep" might suggest, my dreams for me often involve perambulations, explorations, wanderings through infinitely complex buildings—that kind of thing. And I've talked with other people for whom that is a frequent experience.

IB: Can you assess a change in subject matter? I was thinking of "Prisoner of Zenda" and I wondered if you would have done that years ago.

RW: Well, that's one of my latest and maddest poems. I think that a poem like that, however silly, should feel quite at home in one's *New and Collected Poems* or in any collection. One doesn't always have to be straightfaced and weighty. Mostly, my light verse is written for people's birthday parties, or it's written for children. I've written a certain number of light poems for children. But through all my work, even at its most serious, there are jokes and puns. And every now and then, I feel entitled to offer a whole poem that has no particular gravity whatever. I shouldn't like to become altogether a light verse writer, but I do not look down on the form.

IB: Do you have one poem that was more difficult to write than the others?

RW: I don't think I could name the hardest because very few of my poems have happened in an altogether easy way. I take a long time about it and am often stalled for a day, for a week, for a month, for a year. I know that in the new poems the poem about which I nearly despaired was the one called "Lying." That, I think, is one of my very best poems and it's also one of the densest. It's a poem in which every word is working pretty hard. I wrote it very slowly, and, at times, I wondered if I wasn't writing something altogether too rich and strange. Given the slowness with which I was going about it, I naturally had times of discouragement in which I said, "Let's put this fruitcake aside and write something transparent and easy." But it just happened to gel and come out in a way that satisfied me.

IB: Ever have an historic day where three or four difficult poems are solved?

RW: I've had such days. I don't think I've ever finished three poems in a day. But I've had days in which suddenly it was possible to finish off a difficult poem and be satisfied with it. I've also had days, as I can see in retrospect, when a number of poetic conceptions were beginning. I observe this in the dreadful, smudged worksheets which I send from time to time to the Amherst College Library. On one sheet which I was filing away just the other day, I noticed the first scribbles of three poems, which ultimately did work out. So, at *that* end of poetry, at the beginning end, I sometimes seem to be in luck.

IB: Has the translation of Russian poetry had an effect on your own poetry?

RW: The people who've asked me to translate Russian poems— people like Patricia Blake, Max Haywood, and Olga Carlisle— have been people who knew my own work pretty well, and who had an idea of what in Akhmatova or Voznesensky would appeal to me. They detected affinities between my work and this or that Russian poem. I know therefore that I've been specially attuned to some of these poems, but perhaps through the sensitivity of my linguistic advisors. To say what I've learned from them would be pretty hard. I certainly admired two poems of Joseph Brodsky on which I worked for a long period of time. And it's quite possible that something in them has touched me and turned up in my own work. I can't be sure. I *can* be sure, I think, if I talk about Molière. I feel an affinity with Molière's comedy. I know that I've enjoyed putting his rather conversational dramas into rather conversational English, and I think that they've had the effect of inclining me to be a little more colloquially dramatic in some of my own poems, to write lines of my verse as if they were going to be spoken on stage.

IB: What is your muse like?

RW: My muse. Well, she's a she and I have not gone so far as to visualize her, but of course she'd be terribly good-looking. She's not Greek, I'll tell you that. I simply don't imagine her in flowing robes, looking like the conventional Erato.

IB: What about favorite lines? Have any favorite lines from your poems?

RW: I have no doubt that there are such lines. I know I like some of the lines in the one you just referred to, the light verse poem about the Prisoner of Zenda. I like the way the last line comes out as a well-timed gag line, worthy of a stand-up comedian.

IB: You wrote a sweet poem, "The Writer," to your daughter, and I wondered if you had forgotten as you said in the poem that writing is a matter of life or death?

RW: In the poem I wanted it to seem that my wishing her well in her writing was initially a little perfunctory, a little shallow. In the early part of the poem, I'm not aware of how vitally necessary it is for her—as for any writer—to find words for things. Poetry is a matter of life and death, I think, simply because there's no more miserable situation than muteness—being unable to find words for one's sufferings and one's happiness—and so, being inadequate to one's experience.

IB: How would you like to be remembered?

RW: As I think any poet would like to be remembered, for a finite number of good poems which, as Robert Frost said, "the world can't easily get rid of." I don't think he said it quite that way, but that's what he meant.

IB: What about the future—your future efforts?

RW: I think that poets always write with a certain amount of obliquity—that is, they create situations in their poems which are not precisely true of themselves and yet which render themselves, which allow them to get their own experience off their chests. And that's what I shall be doing, I trust, in the poems I shall write from now on. I'm having to cope now as a man who's retired from teaching and who's sensibly older than he was before. These things I register as a person, but I haven't yet begun to write out of a sense of age. That will come, I trust. I hope that I shall measure up to it. Helen Vendler talks about the necessity for poets to "finish well."

JAMES DICKEY

I met James Dickey in the late sixties when he inscribed "at the beginning" in my copy of *Buckdancer's Choice*. Dickey is a man concerned with beginnings, endings, and going deep into the self for his art. He has said, "My way is to go deep, not wide, to look deeply into a subject and find meaning there. And I have written what I have, gone deep, and in my own way, I have carried my small sword."

Dickey was born in Atlanta, Georgia, in 1923. He studied at Clemson University but was interrupted by the onset of World War II. During the war he was a night-fighter pilot in the Pacific and flew more than one hundred missions. He later received his B.A. and M.A. degrees from Vanderbilt University, where he graduated magna cum laude and was a member of Phi Beta Kappa.

An advertising career in New York followed, but based on his desire to write and spurred by a disparaging remark his boss made about his literary endeavors, he left to pursue a career as a poet. A Guggenheim fellow in 1962–63, Mr. Dickey won the National Book Award for Poetry for *Buckdancer's Choice.*

He has taught at Rice, Reed College, the University of Wisconsin, the University of Florida, George Washington University, and is presently poet-in-residence and First Carolina Professor at the University of South Carolina. He holds honorary degrees from a number of institutions including Hamilton College, Wesleyan College, Northwestern, the College of Charleston, Moravian College, and the University of Idaho. He is a fellow of the American Academy of Arts and Sciences and a member of the American Academy and Institute of Arts and Letters.

He is author of numerous books of poems including *Buckdancer's Choice; The Early Motion: Drowning with Others, and Helmets; Falling, May Day Sermon and Other Poems; The Central Motion: Poems 1968–1979; Poems Nineteen Fifty-Seven to Nineteen Sixty-Seven.* His succession of work also includes a children's book *Bronwen, the Traw, and the Shape Shifter;* a book of criticism, *Babel to Byzantium;* and two novels, *Deliverance* and *Alnilam.*

An older but still impassioned Dickey spoke and answered my questions with the kind of openness and teeth-clinching intensity present when we first talked some years before.

INTERVIEW

IRV BROUGHTON: The Buckhead Boys seem to mean an awful lot to you—they even have a symbolism that can bring back youth.

JAMES DICKEY: Well, I think anyone has certain areas of experience, especially in youth, where things and people one knew in that time, in one's imagination, constitute a special experience. You have moments when you're taken by surprise—sometimes when you're much older and for a brief flash of time, you feel that time has never happened, that you are really seventeen, you've never been anything else. And the fact that you're sixty or sixty-five, whatever old age you may be, is something that never really happened. It's like a kind of dream. "The Buckhead Boys" poem is a sort of deliberate attempt to recapture that feeling of never having aged.

IB: So you feel you'll never die if you succeed in discovering the Buckhead Boys—they're a sort of fountain of youth.

JD: In a way. It's an illusion, of course, but maybe one of the necessary illusions.

IB: Your dad was a lawyer. Do you have that lawyer-type mind, that steel trap?

JD: I suppose in some ways I do but not strictly that. No, too much of my imagination has not to do with facts and evidence, but with an invented kind of world, an invented experience and, I suppose, a make-believe or fantasy. I don't know who it was that said this; it might have been Nietzsche. Someone said no real artist would ever accept for one moment the world as it is. The artist wants to make it his way. And I have something of that attitude, I think.

IB: Is it hard fighting the world as it is?

JD: No, I can cope with that fairly well. It's creating the other world which is hard for me, but also it seems more or less natural. I just think that way.

IB: What do you owe your father?

JD: I think there's a love of rhetoric—of words, of the ability of words to alter a situation. In his case it was the courtroom situation. But it's possible to extend the same thing to many other areas besides the courtroom, where words make a lot of difference. Politics is one example. But the ability of words to alter a situation or shed a different kind of light on it, I owe my father.

IB: What do you owe your mother in that regard?

JD: Well, my mother was a rather sensitive, rather dreamy sort of person—extremely sensitive. I think to her I owe the great emphasis on feeling, emotion. She always put that first, and my father was very largely reason and logic.

IB: Are you a Romantic?

JD: I think in putting so much emphasis on feeling and emotion and intuition and spontaneity—all of those things are very strong with me. I think any act of imaginative writing is a vindication of the supreme importance of the individual and the irreplaceability of every person who's ever existed. I also like some of the classical doctrines, too. However, my essential mind is more romantic than classical. I like the classical concision and the ability to say a lot in a very small compass. I also like the classical poets' emphasis on parsimony and on balance and on the harmoniousness of statement—all that's fine and I admire it. I admire Horace very much; I admire Alexander Pope very much—a neoclassicist like him; I like an American classical poet like Richard Wilbur very much. And I even admire some of the doctrines of Dr. Yvor Winters out of Palo

Alto, who was such a vociferous advocate of the classical or neoclassical virtues. I can read him with a great deal of instruction, though I don't always agree with him.

IB: In *The Eyebeaters* you have a poem, "Diabetes."

JD: Diabetes, our family has been full of that. And we were always very weary of it. I had a sort of pre-diabetic condition myself for a while. It seems to have disappeared, thank God. But we were always very conscious of it.

IB: There's something very real but also metaphoric about the disease diabetes.

JD: I think so too. As a person in one of my poems says after he's been diagnosed as a diabetic, "a liveable death at last."

IB: Any other fears like that?

JD: I have many. I'm essentially a product of the war-time generation of the early and mid-forties. I was in the Pacific a good long time with the 418 Nightfighter Squadron. My viewpoint on existence is essentially that of a survivor, a sort of perennial convalescence. I'm always very happy to see the sun come up in the morning, you know. I feel very lucky.

IB: Has that attitude helped you adjust to old age a little more?

JD: Well, I think so. Not that I am old officially. I am at the age where you count half birthdays. I'm officially senile. But as far as I can tell, despite the fact that I've spent some time in hospitals in the last ten years—some crucial time—I feel pretty good right now and I feel like I can go on a ways. None of us gets out of this thing alive. I not only feel pretty good physically, but fairly lucky. I've got a lot of projects going and I want to carry as many through to completion as I can.

IB: How does the vigorous man feel when a few of his powers start to decline?

JD: There are a lot of things I can't do. I sure can't run as fast as I used to be able to do, and I'm not quite as strong in my arms and shoulders as I used to be, but almost. I can't play tennis quite as well. On the other hand, I have gained some. I have been in and out of music all my life, but I've never in my life been able to play the guitar as well as I can play it right now—today. I think it's giving yourself one of the necessary kinds of presents when you cultivate some kind of discipline in which you are better later on in life than you could ever have been earlier. I think this is a good way to grow old.

IB: Could you have been a musician? If you could be as good a musician as you are a writer, would you switch?

JD: No, I wouldn't, although I love music. Language attracts me more than music does because of the scope it gives the imagination. That's the point of the art of language and especially poetry that I like most, the enlargement of the imagination and the enrichment of that part of the personality. I respond to that in a way I never could respond to music—as much as I love music. The other reason is that I don't like the musician's life, especially with the kind of music I play: bluegrass, blues, and variations on one sort of jazz and another. I'm essentially a day person. This business of staying up all night playing clubs and dates, not to mention the general atmosphere that musicians live in, is distasteful to me. I had far rather listen to Doc Watson play on a record than I would go to hear him play in some dingy nightclub.

IB: Where'd you get that day personality?

JD: When night comes I say, "Thank God. I can shut things off now and get into the great sleep world." As Gerard de Nerval says somewhere, "The dream is a second life," and I always welcome that no matter if the dreams are bad. I always look forward every night to going there, and, of course, the night is the time you do it—or at least the time I do it, I prefer to do it. I can't see how anybody could exist very well or even very long if he had to do most of his sleeping in the daytime. When I was in Nightfighters we had to do that but it always seemed to me to be profoundly out of sync with the way things ought to be, in the biological part of human life.

IB: Dreams are important to your writing, then?

JD: Very. I've read around in an unsystematic way a good deal about dream imagery and the relation of dreams to the creative writer's actual productions. Very few of my poems are recountings of dreams that I've actually had, but a few of them are. The ones that are called "False Youth," two or three of them are. I also have a new one which is a nightmare about the worst thing that can happen to a person in this day and age which is to be stranded down in the Bowery, in the slums of New York, at about three in the morning and not be able to get a cab. (Laughs.) I had a recurring dream about that. That happened to me a couple of times actually, but the dream is far worse than the actuality, and I tried to get some of that into the poem.

IB: Is the dream usually far worse than the actual experience?

JD: Yes, it is. Or it seems at the time to be. That is, in your consciousness, inside the dream, in the emotions you feel when you're in the dream, they seem much more terrifying. I've never been frightened in actuality ever as much as I have in certain dreams.

IB: What sort of recurring themes are the frightening ones?

JD: Pursuit or being pursued by something you never see. And trying to escape in the teeth of some tremendous wind in which you can't move forward. That quite often comes to the night hours.

IB: Do you wake up in a cold sweat?

JD: Sometimes and sometimes in a warm sweat. (Laughs.)

IB: Can you put yourself in a kind of daydreaming trance?

JD: I think writers do that often, even if they are not writers. The kind of person who does write, the kind of temperament that produces writers, will tend to do that.

Gore Vidal is a very good essayist, I think. He talks about his adolescent fantasies and he says he once had three serials going at one time.

IB: You like Herman Melville, don't you?

JD: Well, I did my graduate work on Melville and he's an interesting writer in certain ways. He's also one of the biggest bores on earth. No writer that comes to my mind is a better example of someone who built it better than he knew. Nine-tenths of Melville is extremely pretentious, humorless, would-be intellectual. He has all the self-assertiveness that a self-educated writer often has—someone like him, Jack London, Kenneth Rexroth, or Charles Olson or anyone you want to name who has those characteristics. There is though, some kind of way that he tapped into his unconscious without knowing it. And I have always had a special affinity for special things in Melville, although his language is very hard to take. Edgar Allan Poe is another of these self-educated writers who have these long-winded perorations in an attempt to prove that they're just as educated as an educated man, or maybe more. But Melville has some kind of visceral quality that I haven't found in anybody else.

IB: What about Alfred Lord Tennyson?

JD: Tennyson is an example of a craftsman who can bring off cer-
      tain effects better than anyone else. There's something about
      him that's extremely seductive. I know he's good because he
      seduces me with qualities that I do not normally like in writ-
      ing, and one of them is that soft soporific kind of honied dic-
      tion that he uses—that sweet, soft, sort of feminine sound of
      Tennyson is so wonderful. I feel about Tennyson the way I feel
      about the novels of Frederic Prokosch, who is another one who
      gets to me against my will because he gets to me with qualities
      that I don't like in other writers.

IB: Any ideas or theories on the line in poetry?

JD: One of the things that does poetry the most credit is its ability
      to make use of a linear arrangement. I remember the dialogue
      that Gordon wrote about Yeats. He cast the whole thing as a
      trial—the public versus the late W. B. Yeats. He's the pros-
      ecuting attorney, the one that's trying to prove that Yeats is not
      a great poet, and he asks the jury to reflect a moment and then
      ask themselves how many of his lines they remember. Now the
      fact that the line is referred to is itself a measure of the effec-
      tiveness of poetry because we do remember poetry or great po-
      etry or even poetry that's memorable to me personally, whether
      it's great or not, because it's in a line. It's not a statement, it's
      not something in a paragraph, it's not a sentence. It's a line of
      poetry, which means it has in some way with its component of
      rhythm contributed to what is being said. And when we get
      that line that's perfect, we are quite cognizant of that quality;
      we adore that it's a line of poetry and not a statement. It's fit-
      ting that it be a line of poetry because the linear form contrib-
      utes to the effectiveness of it.

IB: Let's talk about your work in advertising. Did you learn any-
      thing for your prose or poetry from that experience?

JD: I learned one thing from the ad business and only one: Get into the subject quicker.

IB: What did you do there?

JD: I wrote jingles, I wrote television commercials, I wrote radio.

IB: Why'd you leave? That money's pretty tempting.

JD: I remember we were going out on a presentation. I was making part of the presentation to a bank group, and my boss was introducing me to the business executives from the firm, whatever it was, and he said, "Jim is our Copy Director of Radio, Television, Media"—you know how ad men love their titles. Anyway, I was introduced and he said, "Jim writes poetry as a hobby; a lot of his poems are in *The New Yorker*." That gave it to me as more or less nothing else could. I'm either going to have to have poetry as a hobby, at which point I'll probably phase it out, or I'm going to have to go with it all the way, leave the business world, and go with what I really want to do. After a splendid conversation with my wife, that's what I did. I left the company, took a Guggenheim Fellowship, and went to live in Italy.

IB: Did writing *Deliverance* overseas afford you any emotional or aesthetic distance?

JD: No, I don't think so. I only did some notes. Then when I was teaching at Reed College, I began to expand the notes I'd written in Italy and wrote ninety or a hundred pages. Houghton-Mifflin bought it on the strength of that. After I took an advance—a very modest advance, but a lot more than I'd ever gotten from poetry—I was then stuck with having to finish it. So I cast around this way and that way and did the novel two or three different ways before I found the one that suited me best.

IB: What ways did you first write it?

JD: I did it in third person first and I did it with a whole lot of
       Proustian reflections and a great deal of description. It took me
       a long time, a number of years, to see that the best thing the
       story had going for it was the narrative thrust—the forward
       motion of it or what I call "the ongo." Then I began to change
       to first person and concentrated on that aspect.

IB: Was there something else that was especially hard about writ-
       ing *Deliverance?*

JD: The hardest thing was the first part of it. I wrote the climb off
       the cliff first and wrote the part after that up to the end. Then I
       went back and invented the guy's life and work and lifestyle,
       his family, his relationship with Lewis Medlock and the others
       before they get on the river. That was hard. I recast that several
       times and it all fitted together in the end.

IB: Was the character of Lewis hard to write?

JD: The character of Lewis was hard for me to realize at first. I
       tried him two or three different ways. At first he was more
       overbearing than he is in the novel. And then we come along
       and make the movie, and Burt Reynolds comes along and
       makes him overbearing again. (Laughs.) So that's life!

IB: If you had to live in another age, what would it be?

JD: This is my age. I'm not one of these people who wants to have
       another time. Gee, I really don't know. It would be way back
       somewhere, though. I mean it would be back when magic was
       a real and tangible thing and when people thought that every-
       thing was inhabited by spirits—the animals, even the rocks,
       the artifacts and the objects and things were imbued with un-
       seen presences. I kind of like that. I wouldn't have minded

living when people really believed those things—not when they wanted to believe them, but when they did believe them.

IB: What would you be in that society?

JD: Oh, I don't know. Just one of the hunters, I guess.

IB: You frequently write about animals.

JD: I've always liked them, and birds, too. They just fascinate me as the other form of life—things that think differently than me and more than me and have different styles of existence than I do. I enjoy thinking along those lines. I would love to be able to fly without any airplane.

IB: Your favorite animal and bird?

JD: A kind of totem animal. I side with the wolverine. They're sort of the ultimate wild animal, at least in North America. And the other one would be some sort of migratory sea bird, like a wandering albatross, that makes those thousands-of-miles voyages every year and then comes back to nest at some little island in the Galapagos somewhere. They can go celestial navigation by some instinct that I don't think anybody will ever fathom.

IB: You write a lot about celestial navigation in *Alnilam*.

JD: I did it because I was fascinated with the subject to the extent that I went through a school and graduated—not so I could write about it and use that material but because I liked it itself. It just came into the novel naturally because I did know about it and because it did seem to have some sort of mystical significance that has never been noted, at least not noted in the same way.

IB: The title, *Alnilam*, comes from a constellation, I understand.

JD: It's the middle star of the belt of Orion.

IB: Why is that significant?

JD: If I wanted to be pretentious, which sometimes I do, I would say that the notion of centrality of the star in that huge, spectacular constellation was suggested to me, at least in part, by the philosopher Heidegger's notions about the mystical properties of centrality. I wouldn't insist on that at all. I would say that it was suggested to me by something I was reading of Heidegger's where he was discussing at great length what it means to be the center of something. And it occurred to me that the centrality of the constellation Orion was marked by that star, Alnilam, and the notion from there that it seemed to radiate out into the whole notion of the group of young flyers, the cadets that are led by Joel Cahill, the young pilot, who calls it the Alnilam Group—he himself being the center of them.

IB: How do you start a book like that? What is the motivating factor—an idea, a phrase?

JD: I started it with an image. I started *Deliverance* with an image too. With *Deliverance* I had a sort of half-waking, half-asleep image of a man standing on top of a cliff in a forest. After I woke up a little, I began to wonder what he was doing there and what was down below the cliff and how he had gotten to the top of the cliff. Did he climb through the woods on the high side of the cliff or did he climb the cliff? Originally, it was just a guy standing on a cliff with some trees and it all came out of that.

    With *Alnilam* it was something that I heard several times when I was in the service to the effect that if you look through a turning propellor, and on the other side there was another aircraft that had a propeller going—if you looked through both of the spinning propellers at the same time, one back of the other one, they would seem to form a figure of a man. That impressed me very much when I first heard it, and I remembered it all those years, probably mostly in my subconscious, which was fine, but I did remember it. The thing that appeared to me was the sort of ghost in the machine aspect of it.

IB: What did you learn from writing *Deliverance?*

JD: Well, I learned that I could write a narrative and keep it going, which I was never sure I could do before that. I learned to think about certain aspects of human behavior in a slightly different way, I think, than I had before.

IB: What character are you most like in the novel?

JD: Well, in a way all of them. That's sort of evading the question, I guess. I suppose at one stage of my life I was more like Lewis because I used to have—and still do to some extent—all these mystiques, like archery, astrology, poetry, folk music, one thing and another. I was not as fanatical as Lewis, but I could see that if I had pushed it a little more in any of those directions, I could easily have become fanatical. But then, I worked in the advertising business like Ed did, and the description of Ed's house is pretty much a description of the house I lived in Atlanta when I was working in the advertising business. Of course, Ed does not work in the advertising business per se. He works in a sort of commercial art studio that works with the agencies. Of course, the description of the office is pretty much my office and so on. So that character I had a good deal of affinity with too. And the guitar I shifted over to Drew. And, of course, I like a good time like Bobby, although I don't like to say I identify a lot with him.

IB: Bobby didn't have a very good time, did he?

JD: No, not that time. I liked the actor who played him though— Ned Beatty. I thought he was very good, maybe the best of the four, although he had the least rewarding part, the least sympathetic part.

IB: I've always considered the screenplay of *Deliverance* a wonderful adaptation.

JD: The hardest part is that any screen venture is an exercise in group think. If you write a poem or a novel, all you need is a piece of paper and a pencil and you go off in a corner and try to work out an interesting piece of work. But, when you make a movie, a lot of people are involved in it: the producer, the director, the cameramen, the sound people, etc. Everybody and his brother is in on it. And the writer very frequently finds himself in the position if he pleases one, he displeases everybody else. He's supposed to solve all the problems but some of them are not solvable so it's a relatively frustrating thing to do.

IB: Can you describe one of the specific frustrations you had in writing the screenplay for *Deliverance?*

JD: Yeah, I can. I asked the director, John Boorman, if I could have five minutes to show the lives that these people came from—you know, to show them being picked up at their homes and apartments, just a little bit. I wanted to show the life that they go out of and the life that they come back to so the story would have a sort of circular movement to it. They start out from a certain environment, they go into the wilderness, and they end up in their original environment. But he said, "We've got to get them on the river sooner—we've only got 110 minutes of running time." And also the director wanted to build up the music scene. He thought it was a very big factor in the movie, which indeed it was. So I lost that battle and some others, but I think we won the war, which was to get the original story line preserved intact. I think if you want the movie the way you want it to be, you ought to get in there and fight for it. I would say this: there can be very few movies made from novels in which the movie version is as close to the original as that one is, and that is much. And that was the thing that was most satisfactory to me about it.

IB: You write well about relationships between men, for one thing.

JD: Well, thank you. I like to think so.

IB: Do you think men trust men completely?

JD: No, I don't. If you'd been in the military as long as I have, you'd see a lot of times that there'll be a certain type of person who'll let others down. I came out of being in the military service with two terms of duty—one was in the second war, the other in the Korean War. I came out of the experience with two fundamental beliefs that I've never had cause to doubt. One of them is that too much discipline imposed on someone from the outside is bad for him and the other is that responsibility is good for him, is good for a man. Those are very broad principles such as they are, but they seem to me to be very serviceable and in most cases true.

IB: If you had to divide your life into watershed periods, what would they be?

JD: I started out as an athlete. I was not really awfully good, but I was dedicated and I was pretty good—I had my moments. (Laughs.) Sports was pretty much my whole life until I went into the service and then flying was a watershed period. When I got out of the service and went to Vanderbilt, the struggle to learn something about literature and philosophy became the most important thing. And after that it was writing and attempting to earn a living as a teacher and support my family. And since that time, everything has centered around what I've tried to write.

IB: On the athletic front, did you have any great, famous athletic moments?

JD: Well, famous for me, remember, but not any great shakes. I was a fairly good football player for Clemson for one season— I played freshman ball there part of the season of '42 and I started. My best claim to fame there was that I scored the only touchdown in the intrasquad game. I started the last game against the University of Georgia, which we lost. (Laughs.) And then I won the conference high hurdles championship when I was in high school. I also won the high hurdles at the annual "Cotton Carnival Games" in Memphis in 1947. My younger brother was a really great track athlete—he just missed the '48 Olympic team by about six or eight inches. He died of cancer last Christmas.

IB: What is the key to using the past?

JD: I think by giving yourself to your own past—giving yourself to it. The emphasis is on *giving*, letting go and not having any resistance to reentering your own past. It's that act of surrender to it. That's the means by which you reenter it and recreate it so you can use it as material for what you write. This is what I tell my students here—to commit yourself one hundred percent to your own vision of the way something is or the way it feels or the reality of the situation and the people that you're writing about and don't try to hold them off and be objective about it—get into the characters and into the situation and into the setting and, if you need to, get into your own former or previous self any way you can.

IB: What are the Puritan traits of James Dickey?

JD: I don't know. I would never put it that way. Except that I think commitment and responsibility are important, and anybody that doesn't have them I can't find in favor of. I think that the worst human trait is deliberate cruelty, and I can't find any good in anybody who exhibits even a slight bit of that—and there's a lot of it around.

IB: "The Sheep Child" is one of your very powerful poems. Could you talk about the origins of that?

JD: That comes out of my former life and that's one I did commit to one hundred percent. Some of them I don't. Despite my own best advice, I can't quite make the connection and give everything away to the situation. But I did with that one, I think.

IB: In what respect?

JD: Somebody told me years ago, just as the poem says, when I was a young impressionable kid, that a man and sheep could conceive progeny and I just went all the way with that and tried to imagine what the creature would think and also what he would mean. Goodness, you should see the faces of the audience when I read that poem in New Zealand. (Laughs.) Australia, too—to say nothing of Scotland and Wales. But I don't think there's anything blasphemous about it, although some people do think that. It's essentially a poem about the universal need for contact—love, even—which doesn't recognize any barriers and which will be served if in the end it creates monsters that themselves have no place.

IB: You've written a fair amount about sex.

JD: I don't think in the way a Norman Mailer writes about it. But I think if you are honest about all the implications, it's good—it can be good.

IB: Is sex a metaphor to you?

JD: Creativity. I think there's a profound connection between the two. I don't think if you become impotent, you'll cease to become creative. That's not quite it, but there's a certain thing about the coming of an image or a good line of poetry or just a conjunction of two words together that you like that definitely has a kind of orgasmic feel about it. It's impossible to explain it but once you feel it, you would recognize the connection immediately.

IB: Growing up, what was it like being a sensitive kid in a big frame?

JD: That's one of the hardest things there is. I did have a lot of friends, but when I began to display a certain amount of athletic prowess, that helped. I was always among people whose company I enjoyed, and I seemed to have my place among them. I was one of the Buckhead Boys, myself, and I never really felt isolated, although there were in myself things I really wouldn't talk about to anybody else. I knew that my preoccupations were not those of these other fellows that I had as friends. I knew that I had feelings that they didn't have.

IB: For example?

JD: The relationship to words and the way things were said were different. Things would make an impression on me, say, in a classroom—things that we would read, and the other fellers would just let it go right by. But they stayed with me. I knew this was something peculiar—maybe akin to some kind of vice.

IB: What sort of things would stick with you?

JD: Oh, things that I would read in literature sections of the books in English classes. I remember reading "Birches" by Frost. It was in some book and I kind of liked that. I thought it was nice that someone should have those observations and write them down. But then I read that poem of Carl Sandburg's about the fog coming in "on little cat's feet," and I knew even that early— even when I was fourteen or fifteen years old—it ain't that way.

It ain't so. That's just the way them poetry fellers write, I guess. But I knew there was a difference between that and what Frost was trying to get over on the opposite page. There was a story of Hemingway's in there—I forget which one, one of his early stories. I had never read anything like it, and I remember reading the biographical material about Hemingway and the disillusionment that he represented. And I thought, "Gee, there's a possibility to get these secret thoughts down on paper in some way, in other words, there *are* people who do it." (Laughs.) I realized it wasn't just me who thought these things and never said anything about them to anybody—there were people who put them down on paper and that was remarkable to me.

IB: Did you realize that you were born with a sort of poetic temperament?

JD: No, I didn't. I recognize it now with the divine gift of hindsight. I could see that my relationship to language and to different ways of saying things was unusual—that my preoccupation with it was unusual. But early on my whole life was taken up with sports and later with the military life, and it just developed with fits and starts—just a little bit here and a little bit there.

IB: Did you ever wish you weren't such a participant?

JD: No, I like to do it. If I like music, it's not enough for me to listen to music. I want to play music at no matter how humble a level. I like to get in and do it. I love to watch tennis matches on television, but I'd much rather get out and play tennis.

IB: What Biblical passage haunts you?

JD: Absalom—the revolt against the father and the father's grief when his son is killed. My mother was an invalid and she used to read things to me. And she would say, "Oh, Absalom, my son, my son, would God I had died for thee." She said, "I thought you'd know Jim when you get older how much that father meant that when his son was killed, and you can't bring him back." Well, my mother was right—I do know it. And I know how the father felt, how David felt. And it's one of the things that makes the Bible or some parts of it as memorable as it is, because it's got that universal, it touches that universal nerve, you know—everybody has those feelings.

IB: If you were a preacher, do you think there'd be any recurring theme to your sermons?

JD: Well, the thing about Christianity that's the most appealing is that of forgiveness, and the part of it that's the most unappealing is sin and especially original sin. But forgiveness and rebirth are the important things—I would stress those.

IB: Oscar Wilde said, "Nothing succeeds like excess." You believe in excess.

JD: Maybe. I suppose that stamps me as much as any other quality does as a Romantic rather than a classicist.

IB: When you were younger would you have preferred to be known as a man's man or a ladies' man?

JD: Well, I don't know. I never tried very hard to be an man's man, but I tried plenty hard to be a ladies' man. Those types of questions are too close a focus on myself to be able to say. Somebody else would have to say that. I love women. I love sex and all that stuff. I'm not really all that much of a Casanova or Byron type of a person with women—I never thought I was, anyway.

IB: It seems many people can't accommodate the heart and the mind, the guts and the heart. You've been able to include both sides.

JD: I sure hope so.

IB: Hasn't that been a dichotomy in your life?

JD: Maybe so, but I'm a great believer in chance and in seizing something when it comes—when the tide and the wave crests, the emotional wave or the imaginative wave. And it's going to crest in different ways and in different times, and different parts of the personality get into the poem. Aristotle, it was, who said that man contains both an angel and a monster. But I think you should give the monster a chance to speak as well. That's why I write poems like "The Fiend," which is about a sex murderer. You should try to get the whole personality into it and not neglect any of it.

IB: Let's designate some favorite poems. Let me give you the criterion.

JD: Fine.

IB: Your favorite in terms of the pride you have in the poem?

JD: I don't know. Being asked a question like that is almost like being asked which one of your children is your favorite. You have one, but you ain't sayin'. I don't know. I would go with some of the longer things because I like to have a kind of narrative build-up be part of the effectiveness of it. I think a poem like "Falling" or "May Day Sermon" or "The Eyebeaters" or "Shark's Parlor"—those are the ones that I thought are probably the best.

IB: Your favorite in terms of the meaning it had to you when you wrote it?

JD: Maybe "The Performance."

IB: Favorite in terms of its ending?

JD: "Them Crying."

IB: Your favorite in terms of honesty, you revealing yourself, or directness?

JD: "Adultery."

IB: Your favorite in terms of its affirmative quality or philosophy?

JD: One called "False Youth: Autumn: Clothes of the Age" where a middle-aged man with a fox hat turns around to the redneck barbershop and shows them the back of his denim jacket on which there's an eagle. It bears a banner—it says "Poetry."

IB: I think it was Stevenson who said if you begin a sentence, you must end it in a pleasing or ironic way.

JD: I don't know what he means exactly, but I'm very high on Stevenson. I've loved Stevenson. Stevenson, among other things, is one of the best literary critics I ever read. He didn't set up shop as a critic, but he's a damn good one. He doesn't like Whitman and he says the most damning thing that's ever been said about Whitman. He says a man and an honest poet is going to have good moods and he's going to be affirmative some of the time and he's going to be negative some of the time. Whitman is immediately suspect, he says, because he is "affirmative as per contract." Isn't that great—"as per contract"?

IB: How have your views on form in poetry changed over the years?

JD: I have my own attitude, which is not something that I would codify in any way. But it's something that I'd be using in a sort of work in practice—it comes out in a practical way in the actual writing rather than in statements about the writing that I make. I don't think I could make a blanket statement or even a series of them that would cover what I actually do and what comes into the poems largely from instinct. I'd just prefer to let it operate rather than intellectualize about it.

IB: What's the longest and the shortest time it's taken to write a poem?

JD: The longest would be two poems I'm working on now that I've been working on for six years, called "Two Poems on the Survival of the Male Body." They're going to be the best things I've ever done, if I get those finished. If I had to, I'd be willing to throw in the jock on the basis of those two—if they're as good as I think they're going to be. The shortest time would be some of the very short poems in *The Collected Poems,* poems like "The Flash" or "A Burr." I can write those in a day or maybe a couple of days.

IB: Have you ever written an epitaph?

JD: No, I enjoy the form, though. I have my students write them. No, I might write my own epitaph on my own gravestone, but I wouldn't quote myself; I'd quote somebody else. I've been thinking about having put on my gravestone something from the German, "the pure spirit rises and wanders"—I'm not sure where I got that from. I just noted it down somewhere. Another one is also from the German: "From earth I shall not fall." And there's one from Ezra Pound—that is, if I'm buried on a hillside, "By this door I enter the hill."

IB: Let's talk about your novel, *Alnilam.* You do an interesting thing in dividing the point of view on the page—it's kind of Joyceian—trying to do more than one thing at a time.

JD: I'd certainly like to be in that guy's class. To my knowledge no one has ever attempted anything like that in fiction before, but it seemed to give another dimension to those parts of the novel where it's used, where you have the blind man's attempt to interpret his world from his position of darkness on the one side of the page and right exactly opposite it physically, is what's actually there. Sometimes the blind man, Cahill, is right, sometimes he's close to being right, sometimes he's totally wrong. The idea just came to me at one time, and I started to experiment with it. Then I got so interested in the possibilities in it that I kept doing it and used it. But I saw immediately that I couldn't write the whole novel that way, especially as long as it seemed to promise to be. But I thought in certain key sections I could bring it in, sort of like changing gears or changing the pitch on the propellor.

IB: Talk about the evolution of *Alnilam*, which you worked on for a long time.

JD: The hardest thing was to decide what the *Alnilam* plot was going to lead to, what Joel told them they were doing all these destructive things in order to achieve. I read a good many works on utopias, and at one time, I had him lead his followers or disciples with a long detailed schemata of the new society that they were going to try to found, that they were going to bring into being, but I realized that it would never have been that detailed. It was more compelling to leave the ultimate goal of the *Alnilam* plot in a kind of mystical vagueness so that they don't really know where they're going, but they're convinced through the charismatic character of their leader that he's going to create a new heaven and new earth. If they'll just follow him, they'll get there—everything's going to be different.

IB: Ever almost give up after so many years?

JD: I hadn't any idea. The deeper I got into it the more implications there were and I felt I wouldn't be able to realize a lot of things, that it would take somebody with more ability and more experience than I had. But again I kept coming back to the idea that it was my story and my notion and it was up to me to try to fight it out to the end no matter what it took. I kept putting it to the side and I kept picking it back up, changing this thing or that thing. Different things began to evolve and change of themselves and the characters began to develop and the situations came out of the characters. I kept thinking of more things, inventing more things that would go with what I had. And I kept trying to balance one thing against another and eventually it came out like it did. I wouldn't change a word now.

IB: Did Cahill change a lot?

JD: Not a lot. He became a little less likeable at the beginning. I mean, I don't want the audience to like him at the first—they might feel sorry for him, but they won't like him. I wanted the liking of him—if the reader would come to that—I wanted the reader to feel that almost against his will and overcome the previous prejudice against the character. The hardest thing for me to do was to present Cahill's own dialogue. He's almost illiterate, but he's a person—as is Hanna in the book—who can feel more than they can say, so that their language is never adequate to express what they can feel. I felt if I could get that quality into what they said—especially into the dialogue between the two of them—then there would be a degree of believability about it, about what they say and about their characters that's unusual in a novel.

IB: Who's your main novelist hero?

JD: Oddly enough, the ones I like the best are ones I can't argue that cogently for as artists, but I like, you can say, the writing personality of them. James Agee is one. He's a very seriously flawed writer as an artist, but his sensibility is so overwhelmingly original and it seems so close to the sort of thing that I do. Not anything of mine sounds like his, but I just feel a very close spiritual and creative affinity with that guy. I discovered him when I picked up *Let Us Now Praise Famous Men* on a remainder table in some department store somewhere. I bought it for nineteen cents.

IB: What about meanings? Do people ask you a lot about what this and that means?

JD: I keep coming back to Hemingway's retort to his critics when they found all those Christian symbolisms in *The Old Man and the Sea*. He said he didn't have any notion of that when he wrote it and it was his job to make a real sea and real sharks and a real boat, et cetera, and if he made them real, to use Hemingway's favorite word "shrewdly" enough, then all the other things could be implied if people wanted to imply them.

IB: You work on a lot of projects at once. Most writers I've talked with can't juggle that many projects at once.

JD: I like to do it. As I say, different parts of my personality get into different kinds of works, but they also cross-fertilize one another in the strangest ways, and I want to take advantage of that.

IB: A specific example of that cross-fertilization?

JD: In my poem, "On the Coosawattee," there was an episode about the chicken processing plant and all the feathers in the river which I had seen on a trip there that I took once. And it was such a powerful image it seemed to work well in the poem, but I felt it needn't be limited to that. So I used it again in *Deliverance* in the first part where the fellers first get on the river. So the way I work on several projects at once sometimes does seem to cross-pollinate themselves in a way that I would sometimes be the last to understand.

IB: How would James Dickey like to be remembered?

JD: Just put on my tombstone—instead of any of those other statements—"James Dickey. American Poet, 1923–1995" whatever it is. That's all. Not as a novelist or a literary critic. The poetry is the main thrust. Out of that everything else comes and to it everything else returns.

RICHARD HUGO

Richard Hugo grew up in White Center, Washington. He attended West Seattle High School and the University of Washington, where he was inspired by Theodore Roethke's boisterous presence and poetic genius. He worked at Boeing for several years. His first book, *A Run of Jacks,* was published in 1961. The book brought his love of place into view with poems like "Snoqualmie," "Duwamish," "Alki Beach," and "Graves at Mukilteo." In the work that followed, Hugo rooted his imagination in the small northwest towns and the people who inhabited them. He published more than a dozen books and chapbooks before his premature death in 1982. Another book, *Making Certain It*

Goes On: Collected Poems, was published posthumously in 1984. Richard Hugo received the Theodore Roethke Memorial Prize for his poetry and was a finalist for the National Book Award.

The interview with Richard Hugo took place on a Missoula afternoon in 1974. Hugo was teaching at the University of Montana, and things were bright for him. He was writing, and he had fallen wonderfully in love; the object of that love, Ripley, would soon become his wife. Ripley listened attentively as Richard spoke animatedly through much of our discussion. He was warm, charming, gentle, and outrageous. His was the kind of interview that is a joy to do.

William Stafford wrote of Hugo, "Whatever your trouble, whatever your fear, Hugo has been there, and his poems will not let you feel forsaken any more." As I look back on this interview, his presence was that way too. He will be remembered for his poetry but also for his uncommon kindness and generosity.

INTERVIEW

IRV BROUGHTON: You used to work at the Boeing Company.

RICHARD HUGO: Yes, for thirteen years.

IB: What's it like to come out of the world of industry into the world of poetry?

RH: I am a person who depends on familiarity for my stability, and I'm not at ease with new people or new situations. I take teaching very seriously. I guess I took it very seriously from the opening moment. Teaching is much more informal, of course, than working in an industry. In industry it's comforting having hours. You go to work at a certain time, and you get off at a certain time, and there's a comfort to a quotidian existence. However, there's a psychological trap about it. There is a tendency, I think, if you're punching the clock, that the ring of the clock as you punch your card on your way out of the factory is a kind of signal that your obligation to the world is finished for that day, and sometimes this becomes a license to goof off and not work on your writing at night. When I came to work at Montana I was more established. I had one book published and another one coming out, so most of my growth and certainly my reputation has come about since I've been in the academic world. Part of that is due to the academic world. A poet in the academic world simply meets more poets, editors, publishers' representatives, et cetera. A poet who works in industry is on his own, and it's harder to find people to take up your cause. In a country this big and this diffuse, it's just hard to know who the poets are, and I think I would have started to make the anthologies a lot sooner had I been in the academic world. If you're working in a place like Boeing, it's much easier to be overlooked. Somehow when you work in an English department you just get around more. Also it's much easier to take time off to give readings because schools feel generally that this reflects well on them. If you give good readings and the people like your poems and so forth . . . It would be rather absurd to ask Boeing if you could have two weeks off to go on a reading tour. They would think that a very strange request.

IB: You told a story about, or I read about, the fellows at Boeing and how they responded to the Kennedy assassination.

RH: Oh, yes. I wasn't there at the time. I was in Rome when President Kennedy was assassinated. That was a story told to me by a friend of mine, Rick Demarinis, who was a mathematician at Boeing and who now teaches creative writing down at San Diego State. Incidentally, he is a very good writer, and an excellent writing teacher. In fact, if I was given enough money to build up a writing program, he's one of the people I would look for to be on my faculty. I think he's an excellent teacher, especially for beginners. He's kind, intelligent, has a lot of feeling and observation. Also, he's tough-minded but not in a harsh or brutal way. He sees things. And he's sensitive to other people. Rick told me he was in this office with these technicians, engineers, and so forth. When the announcement of the assassination came over the company intercom, he said that there was complete silence and that all the men on the drafting boards did was to lean closer and concentrate more on their work. There was no reaction. There was a deliberate attempt to avoid having any reaction. I felt it was kind of a scary story. But I can well imagine it happening at Boeing. I met a lot of men there, engineers, who kept their humanity hidden. Perhaps they didn't have any. I remember when I was going to quit, I had been there thirteen years, and I was going to Italy. A man I had worked in the same offices with on and off, an engineer, a group supervisor, who I never thought had any real feelings—he seemed so quiet and kind of grim and sort of attentive to his work—suddenly became very articulate and was genuinely moved that I was going to do this, and he talked about how he would have liked to have done it. I was terribly touched, just overwhelmed. The one thing I did learn at Boeing is that people keep their humanity hidden in industry, and they presume it is necessary to do that in order to make a living. This is the frightening thing about it. There were really a lot of very decent and feeling people there who simply assumed that for at least the time you were in the plant you never showed this. Naturally, I was more attracted to the people who had a sense of humor and were warm and friendly.

IB: Isn't there any advantage for the poet who works in a different environment?

RH: I suppose you have to have something to do. That hasn't been a problem with me because I like to do nothing. I like to stare moodily out of the windows.

IB: What's your favorite obsession?

RH: I think I'll skip that, it's dirty.

IB: Tell me about the old days. You lived in West Seattle?

RH: Actually, in White Center. I went to West Seattle High School. The kids who lived outside the city limits went to Highline, and the kids who lived inside the city limits went to West Seattle. Roxbury was the city limits. It split White Center right in two. We lived a block and a half inside the city limits.

IB: I've heard that you kind of delight in going back there. Bill Kittridge says you drove through that area, and you were all full of reminiscences.

RH: Yes, that's quite true. I used to be considered a person who was very immediate minded, but I think as I got older I tended to dwell more and more on the past. It's not the reminiscences themselves I like; I've just never been able to separate the scene from what happens there. It's a peculiar trait of mine. If I walked the beaches of Normandy, say, had I been a soldier in the invasion, I would not be able to separate the beaches from what happened, nor would I be able to say the event of the invasion was any more important than where it happened. This is a quirk of mine, and it makes no sense, but I actually do feel that way. It's a mysterious way that I think about things, mysterious to me anyway. I don't understand it. I actually cannot separate place from event and consider them both to be of equal importance.

IB: There is a terrific concern for placeness in your work. When you go into another town or into one of these small villages or taverns or old houses, what do you feel? Do you feel at home?

RH: Not necessarily, though I think in the case of bars that's true. When I was a heavy drinker, which I was for thirty years, there were certain bars I used as homes. They became places of refuge, the way men used to use churches for sanctuaries. My best poems come out of places I've seen just very briefly. Oddly enough, a lot of people who come from these places tell me my poems are extremely accurate. This really bewilders me because usually I know nothing about the place, I just imagine the whole thing. Somebody told me when I was a young man that I had an uncanny intuitive ability to walk into a small town and to know what it was like to have lived all your life there. I couldn't do that with cities at all. Something where you could see the limits and walk through it in a few minutes, a place like LaPush or, say, Wilkinson, although that's the bane of my existence. I've never written a good poem about Wilkinson, Washington, and it's just rich, but I've never made it. But that kind of place. In other words, I could at least formulate possibilities in the poem, somehow. Possibilities as to what it would be like to live your whole life there would come out in the poems. If I ever had that gift, I don't have it anymore.

JB: Is that kind of existential? Is it kind of an empathy with the people, and do you actually feel how the people in these very small towns suffer and lead their very lonely, desperate lives?

RH: Yes, I suppose I did imagine that. But I don't think I thought of that as the people but just as one individual, usually, and I think in most of my poems the speaker is alone, and if he has relations with anybody it's usually somebody already dead. I think you'll find that theme running through my books quite a bit. Edgar Allan Poe said all good poems are about "beautiful women who have died."

IB: What's the strangest, darkest town you've been in?

RH: Well, I would say Browning, Montana, is a pretty grim place. I'm trying to think. I've been so many places. I was recently in the deep South, and I saw some areas in some of the towns in Alabama. I saw shacks where black people were living. I'd never seen those before. They kind of shook me up, mainly because of the smallness of them. How tiny they were. The idea of not being able to afford space the way people can't afford it in New York, say, yet this was . . .

IB: In the plains?

RH: Yes, a rural area. Here in Montana, space is very easy to come by. I rented a house for a hundred dollars a month that would have cost at least seven hundred and fifty to eight hundred dollars a month in Manhattan. That's what I mean. But in rural areas in the South, you have these little houses and black families living in them, and although there was space in terms of countryside, the houses were small, indicative of the poverty and degradation. That shook me. But Browning is such a despairing place you can almost smell it in the air as you drive in. You're not surprised when you hear the suicide statistics are four times the national average and all teenagers. It's very bad.

On another place on the reservation, I think it was Wolfpoint, last year an Indian who teaches there told me there were one hundred forty attempts at suicide. I think about one-third of them made it, and they were all teenagers. This is pretty grim business. This is desolation. This is something the imagination can't work very well with, or perhaps doesn't want to. I think the imagination always requires a bit of play, and that's something you don't feel much like playing around with.

IB: What else about this place?

RH: Well, there was this policeman who came in and said to the Indian, "Your children have been out in the car, locked in for about four hours. Finish up your drink and get out, drive home." That kind of thing, people so discouraged, so without hope, that they just ignore their responsibilities to their children, to anything. It's a broken society, a crack never to be repaired again. The attitude always comes back one way, there is no hope, there never was, and there's none in sight. It is almost shot in the air, in the ambience of the place. If you went there, a sensitive man like you, you would know right away what I mean a couple of minutes after you drove into the place.

IB: Is it also a kind of loss of tradition to see these decaying ghost towns, these great immortal pasts fading away?

RH: I think there is a kind of myth that poets live, that things used to be better. Stafford wrote a poem about that, I think, it's called "A Starred Story," that once things were much more ordered and defined. He paints a picture of benevolent facism in some deep, dark past. We always feel our present is chaos and undefined. It's easier to define the past when we're not there. Maybe things were chaotic then. I suppose there's something to the notion that once the Indians were happy on the plains and had a sense of spiritual fulfillment. But literally we don't know that this is true. I'll say it's most likely the Indian teenagers were not committing suicide one hundred or two hundred years ago at the rates they are now. And it's quite likely they weren't committing suicide at all.

IB: Your life has changed recently, could you talk about that?

RH: Yes, I've met a woman with two children, and I'm in hopes we can get married. I think we'll be able to. She has to get a divorce, and it's certainly a big jump for me. I've been living alone for ten years with the exception of one summer when a twenty-year-old girl lived with me. The trouble with any existence, except for the most brutalizing kind of existence, is that it always has its compensations, and there're a lot of good things about living alone. People say it isn't good for you, and I suppose that's true because your mind does play too many tricks upon you ultimately in that kind of void.

IB: What kind of tricks?

RH: Well, it's very easy to convince yourself over a prolonged period of loneliness, especially if you don't have any girlfriends, that women have always been disdainful of you, and so you remember all the women who didn't like you and rejected you. You generalize this to mean all women don't like you. But you don't remember the ones who loved you. That kind of trick. It cuts off part of existence. You amplify some aspects of existence and completely ignore others. All men have been rejected by women. We're not all so good and wonderful that every woman we see is going to like us.

IB: Where do you go for roots?

RH: Oh I don't think about roots.

IB: You don't find them in the little towns, little kind of transient stopovers in these towns?

RH: Roots is a funny word. There is something about me which is drawn to what I assume is ignored. I don't think it's so much the town is dying, as that it's ignored. I guess it's almost a perverseness about me. I don't like what's in the public arena usually, and I tend to think mass attention destroys things. Social critics such as Lesley Fiedler and Benjamin DeMott, for instance, at the basis of anything they do is the presumption that what the world pays attention to is of great importance, no matter what it is. My attitude is just the opposite. What the world is paying attention to is never important, and what it is ignoring is of extreme importance. I think both attitudes are a little ridiculous at times, but I think there's more to be said for their position than mine. Mine is almost indefensible, but I can't help it. It's the way I feel about things. And it doesn't bother me if I'm being illogical. That's a risk a poet takes. He has to accommodate the silly areas of his mind.

IB: How do you mean that?

RH: Well, I mean if one feels that it is bad luck to drop a potato on the floor, and the only way one can counter this bad luck is by cutting the potato in ten equal pieces and burying each in a separate hole, this would be a silly area. But if this is what the poet does and he doesn't know why he does this, he must still accept it about himself. He *is* this silly person, and he plants ten different pieces of potato into different holes just to get rid of bad luck. In other words, it is necessary to accommodate all areas of the mind, the superstitious as well as the logical.

IB: Do you write to find yourself?

RH: I don't know what I do. I think I wrote at one time to create a more interesting life than I thought I had. I created a person I considered more worthy of acceptance, more worthy of your affections and the world's affections, and more worthy of finding stability and of finding a home than I felt that I was in real life. Unfortunately, this sort of turned out to be a tough-minded guy, a Humphrey Bogart, who looked the world straight in the face unflinchingly and who talked tough and hard, very manly, said exactly what he meant, and called things by their right names. In real life I was sort of weak and spongy and rather accommodating and flexible. I'm quite a flexible person. Certainly I'm not a tough man.

IB: What events caused this change?

RH: Oh, it's just that I got tired of writing in that language. I suppose if there were any key thing that changed it, it was my return to Italy almost twenty years after World War II. Seeing the country again, somehow seeing Italy, and seeing the way Italians behave, especially the southern Italians, I felt I could risk letting my feelings show more in the poems. I think the Italian book, though it's not a very good book in some ways, has more unity than any book I'll probably ever write, and I think that my emotions are closer to the surface in the poems. I risk sentimentality. That's a trick I picked up from Bill Stafford who knows when he's risking sentimentality, and when you think he's going to slop over he pulls out of it. This tough guy act was not necessary. If you see a beggar and feel like crying over the human condition there's nothing wrong with that. You still have to write it well, of course, if you can. And Bill's poems were of some help to me. I find his best poems extremely attractive and moving. I knew I could never write like that because I don't have that subtlety in the ear for the rhythms and so forth. My ear is more obvious, and my techniques are more obvious than Bill's.

IB: When you went back to Italy and realized this interior self, did you find there was this war experience, a measure of guilt, staring you in the face?

RH: No, no, I never felt guilty about the war. I nearly got killed in the war, and the war was not my making. I don't have any guilt about it. If anybody should have guilt about it, it's the people who started the goddamn thing and caused me to be there. That's their guilt, not mine.

IB: Are there any tragic images that come back to you from that experience?

RH: From the war? I saw a couple of bombers explode which was terrifying. They didn't seem to explode exactly. They vanished. Suddenly, they weren't there, and you realized ten guys had been obliterated in each bomber. I saw some sad things. There was this bombardier named Mills. He was made a head of the Officers' Club, and they gave him five hundred dollars in lire and said we needed some booze. He had to go down to the town of Barletta which is on the Adriatic coast, north of Bari. He had a jeep and asked me to go along with him. We carried guns, forty-fives. I even had an army trenchcoat which I had a forty-five stuffed in the pocket of like Humphrey Bogart. And we went down to Barletta, pulled into the town, and as we got out of the jeep, great soldier that I was, my gun fell out of the pocket. This forty-five automatic fell out of my pocket onto the sidewalk. Now the children had been running towards us as they always did in the Italian towns, begging for cigarettes, food, candy. I bent down to pick up the gun, and when I raised up the street was empty and silent. The kids had simply vanished. I thought what it would be like in America which had never been touched by the war, if you dropped a gun like that. The children would be curious and flock around and ask questions—"What's that, Mister? Can you show us how that works?" I realized the kids knew terror. The British Eighth Army had been through there fighting their way up the east coast of Italy against the Germans. I don't know what happened, but it was a terrible fear that children shouldn't have. A man who worked in the gunnery shed, I didn't see him, happily, but my co-pilot did, he shot himself in the stomach with a forty-five. He had had a "Dear John" letter from his wife, and he was very depressed about it, that she wouldn't be there when he came back. The Army forty-five is a very powerful weapon. If you hit a man in the hand from twenty feet with a forty-five it would spin him around and flatten him, that much impact. Now he put this thing in his stomach and pulled the trigger. My co-pilot was assigned to fly him down to Bari, and he said the man's face was absolutely green, dark green like a fir tree, you know, a cedar. These things, like girls who, had they had the breaks, wouldn't have been prostitutes. They didn't want to be prostitutes but were reduced to it by circumstances. The displaced people. Today, when you get into a taxi in Naples, you say to the driver in Italian, "It seems like a nice town. I like Naples," and he says "*Troppo miserere*," too much misery. They're not talking just about Naples, they're talking about the world, and that's right—*troppo miserere*. And that sums up a lot of the human condition.

IB: You feel all this sympathy. I was wondering, do friends and people you meet come to you with their woes? I would think you would be a person who listened.

RH: Well, sometimes. I'm not very good at handling it. I get more strangers. Often I get people who come to my office who have been in mental hospitals and who don't even know me, but for some reason they'll go to a poet's office. Madeleine DeFrees, my colleague, has this happen. And so you just get a certain number of disturbed and overwrought people, people with problems. And as they talk to you, almost everything they say is a sort of cry for help. And you always feel a little helpless because you don't know what to do. I'm not a doctor. I don't understand mental diseases or nervous afflictions. I suppose all I do is try to pacify them, try to assure them or maybe suggest. One thing I *do* do is that I find that when I tell them that I spent three and a half years in psychoanalysis and had many problems myself, then I find I'm more in a position to suggest to them that there's nothing wrong with seeking out help from a doctor. Whereas, if I just sat there and said "Well, you ought to go to a doctor, Jack," it would sound like I was judging them. But when I do it that way I'm saying, "I'm like you, and I don't see anything wrong with this." That's what I want to tell them, that it is not admitting defeat or admitting anything when you try and find some help, and the best help you can. And I know that psychiatry is a very inexact and fairly recent science. But it's all we have. Certainly it's better than what they had in centuries past.

IB: Were you able to write during that period of depression, while you were seeing analysts?

RH: Yes, and I wrote better at a certain point of analysis, and poems seemed to explode out of me, just came rolling out. Some of the strongest poems of my first book were written during analysis.

IB: Why?

RH: It was a kind of getting rid of fears, certain blocks. It seemed to give me the license to write. I had a better mastery of technique than I realized early on as a writer, a better ear. I struggled a lot with my poems, but there came a time when all of a sudden I realized I could do it and do it very fast. Poems just came out. Ways I felt about people in my past came out, and the poems just almost exploded on the page. One poem, I think it was one of the strongest in my first book, called "The Way a Ghost Dissolves," the last poem in the book, was sort of modeled on my grandmother, not an accurate picture of her, more accurately about the feeling I had about her. But that poem I wrote at Boeing, and I wrote it very rapidly. I just started putting stanzas down. I think I might have written that poem in a couple of hours. It came, and I couldn't stop it. I just had to write it. So that I think certain blocks were removed. A lot more energy was released, and it came out in the poems.

IB: You wouldn't advise young poets to see an analyst to help their poems?

RH: Oh, no, that's just silly. But I also wouldn't advise them to stay away from one if they need help because they think analysis is going to stop creativity. That is nonsense. Creativity is the one area of the human mind that we know nothing about, and any psychoanalyst or psychiatrist that's worth his salt is going to tell you that they know nothing about creativity. They don't know what causes it, they don't know how to start it, and they don't know how to stop it. It's the area of the human mind we know the least about.

IB: You talked about the senses: how you can read a book and not remember everything that happened, but you're very keen on remembering sights and sounds and smells.

RH: I just don't remember what I read as clearly as what I see and hear. That's just because as a boy I didn't read much. There were just a couple of books—four books to be exact—in my house. My grandfather had gone through eight grades of grammar school, and he could read. He had a subscription to the *Saturday Evening Post* as long as I can remember. It usually was a gift somebody would give him for Christmas or his birthday. My grandmother had only gone through four years of grammar school. She could read, but she had to move her lips to do it. She didn't make the sounds, but she did move her lips as she read, and she wrote almost illiterately, that is, very weird spellings—even weird by my standards, and I'm a lousy speller—and no punctuation. It was very difficult to tell where the sentence began and ended. And very simple words, the most basic kind of vocabulary. I just wasn't literary.

IB: Did your family tell you stories or anything? You're a great storyteller.

RH: No, they didn't tell me stories.

IB: How did you get that ability to tell stories?

RH: I suppose maybe I used to tell myself stories for entertainment, because of the boredom, the drabness of the house.

IB: Do you remember any of the stories that you told yourself?

RH: No, I don't remember any of that kind of thing. I used to make up games. I made up a game of dominoes, and these were games of conflict, war games actually. And certain patterns on the dominoes I considered very heroic, usually the five over the six. That seemed to me a very beautiful one. Ones like the blank where there were no dots on it, or one over two, I thought were ugly. Two over three was lovely. But I made the ones that I considered beautiful the good guys, and then the ones I didn't like—the blanks, one and zero, usually the lower numbers, sometimes the upper numbers—I put in the enemy camp. And then I would arrange the dominoes on the table and kind of have a war with them. The good guys would sort of wipe out the bad guys. I would just push the dominoes together.

IB: Did they force you to go to church?

RH: Yes, they did every Sunday from the time I was three until I was thirteen, and I was forced to take Confirmation. When I was a little boy I had to go because they threatened to beat me if I didn't. I was frightened and I went. And when I was older I had to take Confirmation, and I was threatened to be turned out of the house if I didn't. And so everything was done under a kind of threat. And this is not the way to have a good taste for religion in your mouth. I've not been religious for many years.

IB: What were your childhood poems like?

RH: When I was nine or ten? I don't remember. One thing I remember, and I remember this very vividly, when I was twelve,

I was in the eighth grade, and there was a teacher named Miss Aiken who was one of those marvelous teachers, a great big fat woman who had taught grammar school her whole life. She was an educator. She educated young people, and she took no crap. She was a big fleshy woman, and, boy, she ruled the class. But she wasn't a bad woman, and one day she read Tennyson's "Brook" aloud. That's the one with the refrain, "For men they come and men they go, but I go on forever." I remember I thought that was just beautiful, and I thought someday, someday I'm going to write a poem that beautiful about a stream because I just love streams. I fished in a couple of streams as a little boy, and I just loved flowing water and the sound of it and the dazzle of it, the foam, everything about it. And I thought someday I'd write a poem that beautiful about a stream. Well, I don't think I made that, but I've written more poems about streams than Tennyson did, so in sheer numbers I think I've outdone him. But I remember also that in those days that wasn't the kind of thing that you told anybody in the schoolyard, especially if you weren't tougher than I was, couldn't fight any better than I could. You didn't tell the boys that you thought poetry was beautiful. But I did think it was a very lovely poem. I was very touched by the rhythms, sounds, the way she read it. It was important, it's funny, but it really was a very important time in my life. And looking back on it now I can't say that it wouldn't have all happened the same way anyway. That's silly to think that one thing changed things, but whether it changed anything or not isn't important. It was important in itself. I don't care about causes. I just loved poetry that day, and I've never stopped.

IB: The poems in one of your books are mostly given to people. That seems very rare. Do you like to give things to people?

RH: Yes, I do, as a matter of fact. I like to do it in an impromptu way. For example, if I'm out driving in the country with a woman and we come to a gift shop, I'm quite apt to stop and take her in and let her pick out a pendant or some earrings or something she likes and buy it for her right on the spot. But I cannot stand to go shopping for gifts for people. My way of shopping is to go into a store and get it over with just as soon as possible.

IB: Are you a good receiver as well as giver?

RH: No, I'd say I'm a phony when I receive things because I don't like to be given gifts, and I pretend I like them more than I actually do.

IB: Are you impulsive like this in other ways?

RH: Please understand I do that out of politeness not to hurt the other person's feelings, but I don't like to receive gifts.

IB: Is there a poem that it hurts you to read?

RH: Well, it's hard for me to read Yeats' "Easter, 1916," aloud. In fact I've never done it in a class. Roethke used to read it so beautifully, and it's a favorite of mine. I think it's a great moment in poetry.

IB: Why does it touch you so?

RH: It's a very moving poem, and it has an enormous emotional depth. I think it's a great poem, and I'm most touched by the depth of his feeling and by the rhythms, rhymes, everything about it. It's serious, very serious business. It does pain me to read that. I read it aloud at home sometimes because I don't mind tears welling up in my eyes. But a class, especially a freshman or sophomore class, doesn't like to see a big fat blubbering instructor. They prefer someone a little more in control of himself, and so I don't usually do that poem. In fact, I don't even read that poem to poetry writing classes because I cannot read it in front of people without crying.

IB: As a student of Roethke, what was the biggest thing you remember him for? What did he most contribute to your . . .

RH: He was such an outrageous, and at times insufferable, person
that I sort of got the impression that since I was outrageous and
insufferable, too, that if this man with all the things that were
plaguing him, all the terrible troubles he had, the agonies that
he went through, that if he could like himself well enough to
create something beautiful out of this that there was hope for
me. That was mostly what I learned from him. Also, I learned
from him what I should have known, that I really love the
sound of my own language. But he was a master of teaching, as
I say in the *Review* article.

IB: Did Roethke let you know him?

RH: Not me so much, other people. I don't think he trusted me
very much. I think he liked me quite a bit, but I don't think he
trusted me very much.

IB: Why?

RH: Because I obviously had problems that would perhaps give him
problems. He liked me, I think, probably as much as or better
than I liked him. I found myself being very angry at him sometimes. But when he died and I was walking into the Boeing
Company out at Renton and I read about his death in the paper,
I literally fell against the fence. I realized that he had meant a
lot more to me than I had ever admitted to myself. I remember
there were some funny things. Just a week before he died we
were shooting baskets together, playing basketball, an outdoor
hoop. Ted was a terrible shot, and I was really quite good. Not
in a game. If somebody was checking me, I wasn't any good,
but if I just had plenty of time I was pretty good at one-handed
push shots. And we were playing twenty-one or some game
like that, and every time he'd shoot and not come close to the
basket, "You know, I threw my shoulder out about ten years

ago and it's never come back," he'd say. There was something very childish about the guy all the time. I remember that day I called him up and asked him if he wanted to shoot baskets, and he had to walk up a flight of stairs to the hoop, and I had to walk a block and a half, and he wouldn't come up to play unless I came down to his house to get him. So I had to walk all the way down those stairs and get him so that we could come back up the stairs. So it was this kind of childish quality about him. But then no adult would dream of writing a poem.

IB: How does your size influence your poetry? For example—this sounds a little far-fetched but—Galway Kinnell said something about wondering how Robert Mezy, a heavy-set fellow, could write all those slim poems.

RH: Well, I kind of think it's better if you write poems that look like you. And J. D. Reed, who's just a monster, when he came out here and was in my class, I suggested to him very strongly that he was writing little thin poems, and he was a great big fat guy and he ought to write big fat poems. I kind of believe that, in a way, there is something to that, the poem looking like the poet. So J. D. did start to write big fat poems, and I think he was writing better. But that's kind of a mysterious thing. I wouldn't put too much trust in that as a general rule. You might be scratching the mask.

IB: Do you think you have difficulty reading novels because the writers have tin ears?

RH: No, not at all, some novelists have marvelous ears, John Hawkes for example. But it's just that there is something in me that wants to always hear something better, to improve the sound of it, and so quite often with a novel, especially with a good novel, I'll tend to rewrite every sentence in my own mind. It took me nine months to read *Ulysses*. In fact it took me longer than that because it was assigned in a class by Jim Hall of Washington, and I finished it nine months after the quarter had ended. And I went to him and said I finally finished the book. So it's very slow going. In fact I refuse to read novels for the most part. Except for mystery novels.

IB: What do you like about mystery novels?

RH: Well, I don't do that for some reason. It's just kind of fun.

IB: Do you think they captivate your mind more, keep your mind more preoccupied?

RH: No, just the opposite. When I read a mystery novel, I do more reading and less thinking. When I read a more serious work, I start thinking all the time. I tend to do this in conversation. People think of me as kind of a remote figure, because if you and I are talking about something, you'll say something that will set off a whole chain of things in me, remembrances or things from the past, something that happened. And I don't hear the next thing you say, and I don't pay attention to it, and people think I'm rather rude and that I'm bored by them. But that's not true, I'm not bored by them; what has happened is that they've stimulated me once, and then my mind starts going this way, and so I stop being a very good listener. I'm an excellent listener for just a moment sometimes but then I'm off. And I think that happens when I read, too. That is to say, the author will say something, like John Hawkes, I think, would be very difficult for me to read, almost every sentence starts me thinking instead of reading. I've never been a good reader. In fact, I don't like to read.

IB: What sounds do you hear in nature? Is there a primary sound that you hear?

RH: No, I don't think so, I'm not aware of hearing things in nature, except for streams. I'm very aware of streams. For example, there is a lovely creek out here and perhaps you've heard it already. It's called Rattlesnake Creek, and it's making some fine music out there.

IB: How important is the physical landscape? You wrote a poem "In Stafford Country" where the "words are far apart." Do you think that the terrain affects poetry that much?

RH: It does for me, or at least it seems to. I notice that my early poems that take place in Seattle are rather jammed up and make surprising jumps. They are full of surprises because Seattle is like that. There are steep hills, a lot of groves, so that there is always something between you and beyond, and quite often you come around a corner and all of a sudden there's a great big mountain. Kind of a country of sudden surprises. And the views are limited by fog, by haze, and things seem to change distance as you look at them. You know how many clouds will pour across the Seattle skies. And I think a lot of my early poems are kind of jammed up. Bly remarked on this once in a review, that my poems seemed rather crabbed and jammed. I notice that in my Montana poems things can be seen coming a little farther off. This is a more panoramic vista here. The surprises are a little slower in coming.

IB: Do you think this is less frightening or more frightening? One could argue the plains are more frightening because you see these things. They're so imminent, and they're, after all, finally going to arrive.

RH: Less frightening for me. I'm a little claustrophobic.

IB: Do you use dreams in your work?

RH: Well, I have a whole series of dream poems that I'm going to combine with the letter poems in a manuscript. But most of them are dreams I made up. In a couple of them, one or two lines are portions of dreams I had. The majority of them are not. Maybe one of them is a complete dream. I'd have to go back and look at them. I could tell which one was real and which wasn't. But you wouldn't be able to tell the difference because I happen to be an expert on dreams. I got to be an expert on dreams and dream interpretation in psychoanalysis. So much so that the doctor told me I was every bit as good as he was. That was at interpreting my own. So he used to let me interpret them for him.

IB: Couldn't that get in the way of good writing? You interpret your dreams beforehand and decide you don't want to write down some unfavorable story.

RH: No, that doesn't bother me. I'm shameless. At least about certain things. As I say, you have to be a bit of a show-off to be a poet. You have to kind of enjoy saying "Look how awful I am. Look how bizarre I am." There is that quality in a lot of poets. Also there is a technical show-off quality in poets—like, "God, watch this next rhythm, or listen to this next stanza, I'm really going to blow your mind." That kind of hammy, childish attitude.

IB: Were you a ham as a child?

RH: Yeah, and I think it was because I was rather ignored by my grandparents, not given any responsibility nor any direction, which caused me a lot of trouble. And because my mother had left me there, I always felt this need for many, many years to prove myself worthy, worth paying attention to. So I did all kinds of attention-getting things.

IB: Like what? Were they mischievous?

RH: Sometimes. I tell you one form it took. Whenever I saw someone, since I considered almost everyone I met stronger and more in control than I was, I used to imitate them and actually say what they had said because it would impress me. So that when I first started swearing I didn't even know what the words meant, but I'd heard older boys use them and this impressed me. I used to repeat jokes or anything. And at one time in my life I even just imitated voices, ways of speaking that I'd assume, ways of pronouncing words.

IB: Could that have helped you in your poetry, listening to different voices, different people? Do you do that now?

RH: All the months that I lived in London and the trips I took to Ireland and Scotland, I didn't once drop my American accent. There is something they tend to do that I find has a very comic effect. I do it myself sometimes, and that is to ask something obvious, and then follow with the phrase "Isn't it?" "Well, that's hardly the way we feel about something, isn't it?" Have you ever heard English people say that? I think it's unconsciously very comical, and it always charges me when I hear it.

IB: Could you be a comedian?

RH: As a matter of fact I almost became a humor writer, and I seriously at one time wanted to be a stand-up comedian.

IB: Why?

RH: I don't know, I like comedy and I like to laugh. Partly the show-off in me. And I like to make people laugh and entertain people. I like comedians. I'm a marvelous audience for comedians. A comedian has to be really very bad before I won't laugh at him. If there's a comedian I won't laugh at, he's terrible, because I'm a big sucker.

IB: What sort of comedy really gets you? You mentioned the English . . .

RH: Well, I like almost all kinds, but I prefer a sort of zany quality or else a certain amount of madness. I like Jonathan Winters

very much, especially when he first appeared on the scene, because of the bizarre quality to his humor. But I like W. C.
Fields very much. He's inherently funny. He had a sense of the
absurdity of life and revealed it so many times. But I would say
the Marx Brothers movies were the funniest ever made.

IB: What scenes?

RH: Well, I think some of Groucho's remarks in *Night at the Opera.*
But I didn't like the stateroom scene as well as some people,
where those people were caught in the stateroom. I didn't find
that as funny as other people did. But I just liked the way
Groucho rattled off "Margaret Dumont" a lot in the thing.
And there was a sequence between Groucho and Chico in *Animal Crackers* that's terribly funny where they're having this
conversation, and they're not in rapport at all. Chico is being
crazier than even Groucho ever could be, and Groucho's playing the force of sanity but he's destroying Chico with just looks
when they're talking. Very funny. Also the end of *Animal
Crackers*, Harpo has a very funny scene where a policeman is
lecturing him on his responsibilities to other people, the community, and so forth, and Harpo has many stolen things under
his coat, and they keep falling on the floor while he's listening
to this lecture and nodding his head. These things keep crashing on the floor. This doesn't stop the cop at all. He just goes
right on with this pompous lecture. And *Duck Soup*. I like the
sequences with Harpo and Chico and the old slow-burn comedian, Edgar Kennedy. But I always remember great lines from
Groucho: "Either this man is dead or my watch is stopped," or
"Send Mrs. Upjohn a dozen roses and write 'I love you, Emily'
on the back of the bill."

IB: Do you think you'll be tempted in your wonderful new relationship to write love poems?

RH: Well, I don't do that, but I do tell students this, and I'm gonna
take my own advice—"Don't write love poems when you're in

love." Write them when you're not in love. And right now I'm in love so I can't write love poems.

IB: Why? Do you think love is a blinding force?

RH: Not necessarily. I think love poems are just very hard to write. It's a very difficult kind of poem to write, and the reason is because love is a very poor subject for art. Art is a demonstration of love, so when you write a love poem it's hard to avoid sounding like you're discussing the meanings of your own poem in the poem. A poem is an act of love. Dylan Thomas's "In My Craft and Sullen Art" takes up this very problem—writing a poem is making love to language. It can be, and that the putting of words on paper, in loving, caring ways is an act of love in itself. So if the poem is about love your problem is compounded. I have always thought that love is a very lousy subject for art, though sex and passion are good subjects.

IB: I heard the poet James Wright say once, "Poetry is the art of kindness."

RH: Yes, I suppose it is, no matter how harsh the poems seem. It's an act of kindness, and it's also an act of generosity, if the poet is being honest. Any work of art is an act of generosity because all any artist is saying is, "Here." You mentioned giving a gift. That is what the artist is giving. He is saying, "Here." He is presenting, and hopefully somebody will accept—although quite often people who write seem rather ungenerous in other areas.

IB: Do you start a poem with an idea, or how do you start a poem?

RH: No, never with an idea. I start a poem usually with a cluster or phrase, a cluster of sounds, some rhythm, something I like, and quite often a poem will be triggered by some experience, something I see or sometimes a person, usually something I feel is kind of ignored. This new book of Philip Levine's is just gorgeous, that's one thing that Ripley was pointing out to me. But the one thing that makes it so moving is that he's writing with such passion and compassion for people. And one reason it's so powerful is that these people obviously are people the world ignored, people that you would never know, that only he knows. That gives it a kind of power. I think that's a beautiful book. I think it's possibly the most beautiful book of poems that's been published in this country in many, many years. And Stafford has never put out what you'd call a good, total book. You have to look around in Bill and find the best poems and judge him by those. And they're remarkable. They really are moving and touching and affecting. But this, almost the whole book is just a sock. I think it's better than *They Feed They Lion*, though I understand that Philip Levine does not.

IB: How do you block a book of poems? Do you have difficulties doing it?

RH: Sometimes. I find usually I can fit sections and lump poems in sections of the book. I don't think it's a very profound problem for me because my poems tend to be boring and repetitious, and at any large setting I become boring in a great hurry because my poems are a great deal alike.

IB: Does that bother you at all?

RH: No. I think that if I had my choice between having tremendous variety and being repetitious, I would prefer to be repetitious. But now of course, we're more turned into ourselves, and our art is personal. That's why John Donne seems more modern to us than Shakespeare. Donne seems more like a modern poet because he was involved in his own passions and thoughts. And his writing was a lot harder for him. But I think if you have a choice between being Shakespeare or being Donne, that is to say being flashy, brilliant, eclectic, a master of a lot of different styles, or having your own style and risk being boring or monotonous, I would risk being boring, because I'm not sure that modern poets have too much choice in that matter. The real poets in our time are boring and monotonous, not within the single poem but when a lot of poems are put together.

IB: Who would those be?

RH: I think Levine. I think it's a good thing that *1933* is a short book though even at that when you go through it, it just seems enormous, if you have the emotional reactions that I had to it. I think Stafford is very much a real poet. He still isn't a perfectionist at all until he gets on the trail of what he really feels is a good one, and then he's apt to go at it and write it and rewrite it more than some of the others. But Bill is quite content with most of them. But at his best he's a marvelous poet. I think Jim Wright is a good poet because his obsessions always come through in his poems. I think of the honest poets as being the ones who are dealing with their obsessions. Most good poems come out of obsession, and I think one's obsessions are limited. We can't go out and find new obsessions. Our obsessions choose us and are limited. That's why I think good poets are limited and tend to be monotonous, read very long at any one sitting. Levine certainly is. My God, you can hardly read that *1933* at one sitting. You'd be worn out. It took me about three to get through it. I must have spent a total of about an hour or two each time—four to six hours. That was the first time.

IB: Have you ever done any volunteer work in agencies for the poor? Do you think you could stand to do it?

RH: No, I don't. I think I would become frustrated very easily. I wouldn't have the patience. I'm kind of fascistic in nature. I just want to shout at people, "Shape up!" and I want to shout at society, too, the thing that's causing these problems, this poverty. I want to shout at everything "Shape up!" and just have it done. I'm very impatient.

IB: Do your long, poetic lines suggest your impatience?

RH: Well, I don't know that my line lengths suggest my impatience. I think the fact that I jump rather rapidly in the poem—now that's a part of my own fear of being boring within the poem. Most minds, like mine, if they stay on one subject for any length of time and try to develop it become less and less interesting. My colleague Sister Madeleine—I take that back, she's left the order—Madeleine DeFrees, has almost the opposite kind of mind. She can stay and milk and develop things and become more interesting as she goes along, and just all kinds of things happen. She's more like Bach in that respect than I could ever be. I find that if I stay on any one thing for any length of time in a poem I become boring. I teach people to jump. I teach them to keep getting off the subject.

IB: How do you do it that way? Is it hard?

RH: It's not too hard for me. Actually, the way I started doing it when I first started writing, and I do it second nature now, is I let the tonalities, the rhythms, the voice of the poem act as the adhesive force. And actually, although I think sound, the reason why one thing follows another in a poem is kind of mysterious, I suppose. Basing the relationship on sound is not an infallible method, yet it may be the least fallible. The most fallible is logic, to try to connect things up logically in a poem. In fact, one of the problems in my poems is I'm not crazy enough at times. I am too logical, too sane. And that bothers me a bit, but I don't try to force the issue. I don't try to feign madness. But I'm not as wild sometimes as I'd like to be.

IB: In this recent year you started to get some acceptance that's long overdue. What does this mean to you?

RH: It was going to my head and in a very negative way because I was just terrified of being accepted, success. And I think if I was still on the booze I'd still find it hard to handle. Since I have had to stop drinking I find I do very well. The other thing is that enormous demands are made on my time by a lot of people, and I just don't have the energy. I think I'm going to have to become more insistent on my own time, on having my own time.

IB: Is your God a fierce God?

RH: Well, I'm not really religious. Would he be fierce? At one time he would have been, but I think now he'd be rather a pleasant fellow.

IB: Where would you meet him?

RH: Where would I meet him now? Fishing. That's a good romantic answer.

IB: You're a dynamic reader of your own poetry. In the kind of dynamism you put in your reading, can you be so involved that you are more or less unable to gain audience feedback?

RH: No, as a matter of fact, I'm rather sensitive to the audience, and I do get the feedback all the time. It's important to me, because I'm performing, and it has nothing to do with writing. It's satisfying some kind of infantile impulses and desires. It's wonderful, and I love it, and it doesn't last over half an hour after the reading is over. It's all gone. But the way you feel about your own poems which is a much more durable feeling, and the way you feel about your writing when you're writing, these are important matters. I always feel best when I'm writing. I tend to be more easily annoyed with people when I'm not writing at all. When I don't have anything in front of me, anything I have to write, I tend to get a little irritable. I tend to be more impatient and unsympathetic. And when I'm writing I find I accept everybody as they are. I find it much easier to accept the world when I'm writing. When I'm not writing I get madder at Nixon, and I get madder at Watergate people. When I am writing it's very easy to be pleasant and gracious.

IB: Have you ever been frightened in the wilderness—been lost or anything?

RH: Yes, and it was very odd, too, because I shouldn't have been lost. It was, of all places, on the Bumping River. There was a highway very close above the river. It's a heavily fished river, and there are a lot of people. What happened was there was a section of the river where part of it branched off, and I crossed this on a log, an old log, that had fallen and been there for a long time. And I was kind of fishing on an island in the river, and then this branch was coming down. When I fished down the length of the stretch of the river and was down the other end of this island, I started back, and I forgot that there was this water that I crossed, and so I kept coming to this stream and then going back and turning back to the river and turning around and going back. It was just that I forgot, and for about thirty minutes I was very disoriented. I mean, it was absolutely silly because I wasn't very far. In fact there was a big campground where I crossed that stream—a great big campground with a bunch of people in it. But all of a sudden I panicked for a minute. That's very unusual. I just got terribly disoriented for a minute. Then I finally thought, "Well, I got here and there must be some way I got here," and so I walked back up the river, because I knew I'd fished down. And when I came to that log it all came clear to me, of course, I'd crossed this little branch.

IB: Is that like the poetic process?

RH: (Laughs.) No, I don't want to tangle with that!

JULIA RANDALL

Julia Randall sits answering questions with her arm in a sling from a canoeing accident. She has just moved to Bennington, Vermont, having given up on her native Baltimore. As she explains in the interview, this lover of nature and the environment is fed up with the city, the lack of concern for the environment, the poor or nonexistent planning. She feels more comfortable back in Bennington where she is ensconced in a natural setting.

Julia Randall was born in Baltimore in 1923, educated at the Calvert School, the Bryn Mawr School, and Bennington College, class of 1945. She received her M.A. from Johns Hopkins in 1950. She has taught air force personnel overseas for the University of Maryland. She has also taught at Towson State University and Hollins College. She has received two NEA grants, one award from the American Academy of Arts and Institute of Arts and Letters, the Shelley Prize, and an award from the Poetry Society of America in 1980.

In addition to two—what she refers to as—"preliminary books" of poems, she is author of *The Puritan Carpenter, Adam's Dream, The Farewells,* and *Moving in Memory.* Despite her relatively restrained poetic output, Julia Randall is a poet's poet; there is craft and assurance in every line.

I was curious about the move, about her leaving friends and relatives at the age of sixty-five to find herself starting anew in an old, new place.

IRV BROUGHTON: How do you remember the Baltimore of your youth?

JULIA RANDALL: I remember the Baltimore of my youth as a town that you could get to in twenty minutes and walk through in twenty minutes and everybody went downtown to shop. That has drastically changed—which is why I have left Baltimore and moved to Vermont. I mean, the Baltimore of my youth is all gone. It is all Mr. Rouse's waterfront, and actually I don't care about the city. I care very much about the county and that appears a lot in my poetry because it's my native place. It has been absolutely ruined and leveled in all-American malls, condominiums, highways, and polluted streams. And I couldn't stand it so I moved away much to my sorrow, in a way. I just woke up one day and I said, "I don't have to live here."

IB: It's not often a sixty-five-year-old woman picks up and leaves home, friends, and family.

JR: Well, I have friends here. I know the place and you can't much change mountains. And the population of the whole state of Vermont is less than the population of Baltimore County. I loved my little house and my little place. But it's happening all over America—and I want no part of it. For my last twenty years, I want to live here.

IB: You were outspoken as an environmentalist there, weren't you?

JR: Yes, I got my district on the Historic Register and I worked very hard, but everybody in Maryland laughs at environmentalists and up here they don't. They are really concerned with conserving their state. It has nothing much to do with poetry except that it's a preoccupation of mine. It's the loss of a great thing—the leveling of America, which may be a good thing, and it may be bad. It's just that I don't want to live in Anywhere, America. I want to live in a place.

IB: You need that place in your poetry?

JR: I need that place, yes. It's very important to me to have a specific place—it's a physical thing. I need to have room to breathe and something individual that doesn't look like, as we say in a cliché, New Jersey. We use New Jersey or Los Angeles as the signature of no place anymore. I think we need roots. I'm not sentimental about it, but I think mobility of people— of people of all classes and the lack of any sense of belonging anywhere, either to a church or a place or a school—is seriously affecting us. We've got to go ahead and get through it and I don't see the way, so since I'm sixty-five I begin to mourn what we have lost.

IB: In a sense *Moving In Memory* is an environmental book of poems. It's more than that, but it is environmental.

JR: Yes, it is. Elegiac thing. Partly it's because of old age. One does look back and perhaps sentimentalize what was, but I don't really think I'm sentimental. I do regret our lack of foresight and our ruining everything instead of saving something. Both my last two books are that way.

IB: Any environmental battle stories—things you fought over that illustrate the point?

JR: They plunked a Grumman Aerospace plant down in the middle of our cornfield in the Long Green Valley in Maryland and everybody fought and fought. They had eleven thousand acres, zoned commercial, but they put this down in the middle of a cornfield in the middle of a tiny village in the middle of the county. And nothing the citizens could say would prevent them from doing it. And nothing the citizens can say prevents them from doing it anywhere they want to. I worked very hard for—loosely speaking—the environment, for saving nature and streams and woods and wildlife, and also for historic houses. They can't all be saved, but what's awful is spot development. They don't say we will save this area and develop that one. I realize that people have to have houses and businesses, but they do not plan. They grab anything they can get and they think the tax base is so important. The real thing is that development never pays for itself—it just ruins everything and for the county it means much more expense when they develop than when they don't develop. Even up here I'm fighting the battle of the dirt roads. We're trying to save a few of the dirt roads. Nobody can fight the developers—they've got the money. They're selling ninety thousand acres of upstate New Hampshire and Maine, which has been put on the market by a lumber company. Ninety thousand acres they're selling to a developer. So there ain't no place to go. I went to college here so I decided to spend my life in a village context where everyone knows everyone else and where I can walk to the store, the bank, the post office, and the library.

IB: Louis Simpson said that "we need the Earth for all our metaphors."

JR: Well, I do. I need a place because I really work out of the back window. Most of my poems are what I call backyard poems. It's looking at this or that or another thing and making a poem that might turn into something quite different, but it starts right there in the place, the circumstances. I'm the old lady in tennis shoes, the bird watcher, the gardener. God knows, I always loathed gardening when I was young, but I don't anymore.

IB: Your poem "A Valediction" kind of puts the cap on it.

JR: Naturally, when you reach your sixties, you tend to look back

and reassess things not in a terribly personal way. But I think
it's natural to look back and remember. Memory becomes
more vivid, I think, when you get older and it becomes important to you. I think going ahead is important too. I'm not really
a pessimist. I think we'll get through this. We're at the moment
in terrible transition, and I think it's very difficult for both the
old and the young to have anything to latch onto. If I were
young, I don't know what I'd do.

A Valediction

In the great shade of August, under the sycamores,
if it is hard to imagine Piedmont without trees,
think of Sahara, or the Hebrides.

Yet they are coming down,
the German woods, and templed Oregon;
deep in the Gros Ventre, and the Amazon,
the chainsaws buzz like locusts all day long.

Where did pollution enter: acid rain,
base power? Caryatids cannot keep;
the Law and Prophets smoulder on the heap
like California. We are left
whatever tinder memory can heft.
The very stuff of cells
forgets the fire, the glacier, the sea-swells,
sweet-breathing air, and finally ripe earth.
Nature and Liberty uphold a weight
like chastity—too grave, too great.

So poets enter, and forbid to mourn,
since by division we grew
into ourselves, and growing die,
still wanting our reunion
with earth or sea or sky. What planetary dust
made Cain the first contender for our meat,
saw Babylon and Rome fall out,
saw Donatello and Mozart? saw trees?

I shy at purposes,
and shrivelling, like the branch of Noah's dove,
praise passengers like leaves of love.

IB: Did you love nature as a child?

JR: I went to camp in New Hampshire, spent summers in Maine, and then we moved to Baltimore County and we had dogs, horses, and walks. There's no explanation why I like it. I just like it, which is why I like Wordsworth. My family were not hikers or campers. I just responded to nature. I can't tell you why.

IB: What were your parents like?

JR: My father was a businessman. He worked for Proctor and Gamble. His great hobby was sailing on the Chesapeake Bay. My mother was a housewife—not well educated but intelligent and in her older age got very interested in music and art.

IB: Did they stimulate you to write?

JR: They stimulated nothing. They provided everything. If I said, "I want to go to the opera," they sent me with the maid. (Laughs.) If I said, "I want a Victrola and records," I got a Victrola and records. They were very good. And we had a lot of books—mostly from my grandparents—a Victorian library—Dickens, Tennyson, Browning, Stevenson, and Shakespeare. And we went to excellent schools. And I will say that my parents who were not themselves intellectual were very supportive. When I said, "I want to study ballet," I studied ballet.

IB: Did you have a kind of classical education?

JR: Very much so. I went to something called the Bryn Mawr School in Baltimore, a private girl's school, founded as a preparatory school for Bryn Mawr College and it was very classical—Latin and all of that, a very excellent school. I didn't like it very much, but I got an excellent education.

IB: What didn't you like about it?

JR: Well, I left home at 8:10 A.M. and got home at 6:00 P.M. You had to have athletics all afternoon—that was the main part I didn't like. And I didn't have any time. We had four hours of homework—we didn't have much freedom. No electives. It was a love-hate relationship. I always did very well, of course. I won the scholarship to Bryn Mawr College which I turned down. But the longer I live, the more I appreciate the education I got. We had to write, we had to read. We had a whole course of English literature, starting with Chaucer which we had to read—in seventh grade—in Middle English. And it never occurred to anybody we couldn't read it. We started with Chaucer and we came straight all the way up. We had excellent science, we had languages—I had French. It was a wonderful school—I just didn't like hockey, basketball, and lacrosse. It was very disciplined. I mean, no man was allowed on the campus. We had uniforms—it was all very *comme il faut*.

IB: How did you look in your uniform?

JR: I thought it was wonderful. You never had to think of what to put on—you always put on your blue jumper and your white blouse and your sneakers and off to school.

IB: Who was the most memorable teacher to you there?

JR: Her name was Grace Branham and I had her for English nearly all my years and she was a spoiled nun—that is, she had entered the convent and quit. She had wild hair and wild purple clothes, and she was one of the most intelligent women I have ever known in my life. She was absolutely wonderful, though she always gave me horrible grades. I was obviously the brightest person in class, and she said, "You could do better than this." When she died she was translating the Psalms out of Hebrew.

IB: Do you think you wanted to be like her when you grew up?

JR: As a schoolgirl I never thought of becoming a teacher. I wanted to be a microbe hunter or a ballet dancer—or a writer. But when I started to teach my models were some of my high school and college teachers.

IB: Were you ever a bit of an intellectual snob after that schooling?

JR: I think I was. In fact, at age fifteen or sixteen, I announced to my family that I was quitting school, because I had learned everything I needed to learn and I wanted to write. Well, you can imagine a conventional bourgeois family's response—they immediately took me to a shrink. And I said, "I have learned everything I need to learn and I want to write." And of course, the shrink said, "Oh, my dear child, what do you know to write about?" I knew a lot more than she did, I can tell you. Well, after four months, I went back to school because I didn't want to hurt my parent's feelings, but actually, I'm sorry I didn't stick out my rebellion, because I *had* learned everything I needed to learn and I was perfectly self-motivated and I could have done all the rest by myself, which is what would have happened in the nineteenth century, but it didn't happen now. So, I went back to school, and when I graduated the only way I got back at them was by picking the wildest college in the country—to spite them.

IB: So then you went to Bennington.

JR: Which was a very happy choice. It was very scary at first, because they didn't tell you to read pages twenty to forty tomorrow. They said, "Well, next week we will discuss *Madame Bovary.*" Period. I had great teachers—I loved it. And partly I loved the landscape. My mother took me around to Wellesley, Bryn Mawr, et cetera, and we drove in the gates and drove out. And we drove into Bennington and it's a wonderful setting. It's a five-minute walk from me now.

IB: Any ideal place in the world, or can you live anywhere?

JR: I adore the Rocky Mountains. I adore Scotland and Wales. But I can't live anywhere except in the United States, on the east coast, between Virginia and Maine. That's where I know the names of the birds, the names of the trees, the quality of light. I just know it and I couldn't live anywhere else, really.

IB: What things in nature startle you the most?

JR: Well, everything startles me. I love the seasons which is another reason I like the east coast, because it does have four seasons. I am very fond of trees, and I love animals, though I don't know a lot about them, but it is exciting to see a deer or a turkey in the woods. And I'm fond of birds. And I love flowers—wildflowers and cultivated flowers. I mean, just the whole scene. I love mountains, I love the sea, but I've chosen the mountains.

IB: What plant would you like to be turned into?

JR: I don't know—something common like a daisy or a daffodil. I like all flowers, especially the blue and yellow and white flowers. I love the wildflowers.

IB: Is there anything in nature that confirms for you a religious faith every time you see it?

JR: I just think day and night. Day and night and the growth of trees and the age of rocks. It's the whole scene, and it has to do with my sense of place that we are, as a people, losing any grasp of the things which have furnished the metaphors for poetry, for all of our literate history. There are indeed children who have never seen cows or never seen forests, and really never seen the sun go down or the moon rise, or the sea or the mountains. And I shudder to think what effect this has on their psyches. It must have some effect. We cannot go back to the Garden of Eden, it's obvious. I'm a complete believer in evolution, and I think we will adapt to whatever. But I think that's one of the things that's wrong with poetry—that we have lost our contact, the *ground* of our symbols, and there are many poets who are desperately trying to grasp it, again, or re-invent it. That may be an atavistic gesture; it may be passé. It's what I've got to do. I can't do anything else. You can only do what you are given to do.

IB: Your great-uncle Burton found a clovis point, the poem says.

JR: I don't know anything about it. The clovis point is from one of the earliest Indian civilizations—there's still a mystery. They're earlier than anything that we really know. My Randall family came from Annapolis—well, they came originally from Virginia and then they all came up to Annapolis, and they were all sort of amateur historians. They poked around and dug things up and I was told that Uncle Burton, whom I never knew, found a clovis point.

   I mean, a poem is a wonderful thing. Things you thought you would never use or remember suddenly cohere and turn up in a poem. It never occurred to me that I would use Uncle Burton—or lots of other things in a poem. They just suddenly come when you're intensely working—things come up, fit in, and cohere. That's the mystery of writing a poem. You don't know why they come up at that particular time or you don't know what's going to come up.

   When I'm starting a poem, I often start from a musical phrase or maybe a look out the back window at a bird or a plant or something or the playground next door—what have you.

Or sometimes a more human thing like a death. And then as Pound said, "It's that rose in the steel dust." Things just fling themselves around your center of concentration and they come up from God knows where. They may come out of literature, they may come out of music, they may come out of nature, or they may come out of family history. I think the poet's job is to make them into a whole.

IB: You wrote several poems in your latest book dealing with poetry and poets. It really seems in those poems that the act of poetry is kind of a puzzling one to you.

JR: I think it's very puzzling. People say why do you write poetry? There's just no answer. The only answer I give to that is because I've always done it and it's something I can do. And being a Puritan, I figure if it's something I can do, then I better damn sight do it. But it is a very puzzling act. It's like dreaming, it's very strange and it's fascinating. What does come up? It's not entirely unconscious—you have to shape it consciously, as I say, with your ear as well as your mind. But I cannot speak for what comes up. It just appears and fits in.

IB: You do have two dream poems in *Adam's Dream*.

JR: Yes, and they're quite literal. Yes, I do use striking dreams if I happen to have them. Ninety-nine percent of your dreams are about getting up and going to the store tomorrow. But occasionally you do have—I would not say Freudian because I take that with a grain of salt—but something that seems to be quite significant in some way. I've used those. And I think that the way images come up when you are really writing, really into it, is very analogous to dreaming—something where the surface consciousness is shut off, and images, whatever you wish to say, come up. They're not in your control. This sounds like Coleridge, but I think it's very true. I think Coleridge knew a great deal about composition and where it came from and it scared him to death. We know where all the images from the

"Ancient Mariner" came from. The scholars know every book Coleridge ever read, and they found practically all the images in his travel books, when he was writing the poems. But he didn't think, "Oh well, I'll use the image from so and so." They just boiled up within him. The same with "Kubla Khan."

IB: Do you find the act of writing poetry disquieting?

JR: Well, I find it difficult and I don't particularly enjoy it. But, no, I'm really happy when I'm producing poems. It's hard work—you have to concentrate a lot and cut off other things. When I'm working hard, I just can't accept engagements or have things on my mind. It's like an athlete being in shape. You have to keep at it, keep at it, and keep at it. You can't do all of the other distracting things you'd like to do.

IB: What is the perfect environment for your writing?

JR: I think where I am now, or where I was in Baltimore. Simply in the country. Having a lot of time to myself is important, although I did produce two volumes while I was still teaching.

IB: Did you find teaching rewarding?

JR: Oh, very much so. Learning by doing the homework and contact with the students. The trouble is when you're getting to be a senior member of the faculty you're spending practically your whole time on committees. Also, after twenty-five years I got bored. The first ten years you're learning just as much as the students so you're not bored, but then it does get a bit tiresome to teach the same books over and over.

IB: You like music. Who's your favorite composer?

JR: Well, that's a hard question. When I was in college, my favorite composer was Bach. Then I guess in my middle years my favorite was Mozart, and of course, he ranks still very high, but as I get older I really enjoy Handel, Haydn, and Gilbert and Sullivan. (Laughs.) I like Benjamin Britten very much.

IB: How did Gilbert and Sullivan slip in there?

JR: Well, they come in like the hymnals. In the nineteenth century I like the Beethoven Quartets and Schubert Lieder and Italian opera—I like Verdi. But I don't listen to music as much as I used to, or don't depend on it as much as I used to. I love early British songwriters from Purcell and early ballads. I like real American folk music.

IB: You say depend on it?

JR: Well, I used to have to listen to it every day, but now I very seldom put on my records. I turn on the FM now and then, but I don't listen much.

IB: What do you owe music?

JR: I think that music itself helps my ear. I mean, I used to play the piano—I did music all the way through college. Whether my ear attracted me to music or music helped my ear, I can't say, but I think that music functions in a physical sense, and I hear cadences and rhythms that I've probably gotten from music. The Elizabethan lyricists that I much admire were always writing for music. And so there's a very intimate relationship there which I cannot deny, but I think any poet who doesn't like music is only half a poet.

IB: Could you be a recluse poet?

JR: Could I be or am I? I could be, but I don't think I am. I have a lot of friends. I like to cook and I entertain and I go out. I'm not particularly interested in cloning up with other poets. Some of my friends are poets, but most of my friends are not. I am reclusive in the sense that I don't go out to seek publicity. I can't go on the circuit—I've been offered a couple of writers-in-residence things. It doesn't suit my lifestyle. I have a garden—I have two dogs. I can't go and spend four weeks at X University. And I don't go out to make friends and influence people. It's very nice to be published, it's very nice to have readings, but what really satisfies me is writing a good poem.

IB: Do you think this has influenced your fame and fortunes in the area of poetry?

JR: Yes, I do. I think the people who are best known make an effort to be known and some of them are very good, I'm not saying they aren't. But they are mostly single people who live in New York or someplace and can shut the door and move around. Or they have a wife to mind the home fires. I like to have my place, my home, and I just can't up and leave it.

IB: You're a friend of poet Howard Nemerov. Do you ever trade poetic messages or poems?

JR: Oh, yes. But most scurrilous. Not to be quoted. We write jingles, as I do with several of my friends, but those are not for publication.

IB: What books were pivotal in your life?

JR: When I was in college, I discovered Henry James and Plato, and Kant who was very influential, though I haven't touched him since, and Shakespeare and Dante and the usual things. But the people I love best are mostly the people I taught for years. They're mostly nineteenth-century novelists: George Eliot, Dickens and Hardy, then Lawrence and Conrad and James. I would say Virginia Woolf is very important, a favorite of mine. I admire Thomas Mann's "Joseph" novels. I read philosophy and aesthetics, for instance Susanne Langer, and Gombrich and Voegelin. In the poets I've always loved Herbert, whom I discovered myself—I don't think I've ever had a course in seventeenth century. And for years I taught Romantics. So, I'm very fond of Wordsworth; I am independently fond of Emily Dickinson. I love Gerard Manley Hopkins. And Stevens and Yeats and Rilke. And the 1940 Hymnal and a lot of the things I read in elementary school that are just the old standard stuff that was given to children—ballads and poets like Longfellow, Thomas Campbell, or Thomas Moore—I mean, all of these third-rate poets that still echo in my mind.

IB: Do you remember a lot of lines from those third-rate poets?

JR: Oh, I remember a great deal.

IB: Give me a couple of lines.

JR: I remember, I remember the house where I was born

or

Molly, come and call the cattle home across the sands of Dean

or

Linden when the sun was low
all bloodless lay in the untroddened snow
and dark as winter was the flow
of Iser rolling rapidly

or

Horatius at the Bridge

Lars Porsena of Clusium
By the nine gods he swore

Those things keep going around and around in my head because I've known them since I was eight or nine years old. And there are the people that I admire greatly like Milton and T. S. Eliot, but they are intellectual affinities rather than poetical influences. I mean, I love Yeats because it's the ear. But I do not like Yeats', I hate to dignify it with the word, philosophy—I think it's half-ass. But he is a marvelous poet, and I respond to the cadence of the verse rather than what is behind it. So there are different things. I respond to Eliot and Milton and of course, I have lots of their phrases in the back of my head, but I do not imitate them or derive from them. Whereas I find myself very often speaking like Yeats and like Hopkins because they are, by ear, much closer to my given sensibility.

I do think poetry should sound like poetry. This is what disturbs me about a great deal of contemporary verse. I do not doubt the "sincerity of the poets," et cetera, but it just doesn't sound like poetry. It doesn't sound like anything. If you read it as prose it comes out as prose, and I hope that mine comes out as poetry.

IB: Your style in *Moving In Memory* is more relaxed than in your earlier books.

JR: I think I've gotten a lot looser and more relaxed, I want to say freer, not so many ballads and formal poems as earlier, yes, but still I do like music. And I like the poets who sound like poetry. This does not mean it must be sonnets. We're speaking of lyric poetry, I assume.

IB: What caused you to loosen up?

JR: I don't know. One doesn't want to be too old-fashioned. It's bad enough to rhyme—even slant rhyme. But it's even worse to write formal things. If I'd been born on a desert island, I'd probably be writing Elizabethan lyrics and ballads, but we can't do that anymore. We can't do it—it doesn't wash. Sometimes I do it, and I do it with my tongue in my cheek, and I'm quite surprised that a couple of reviews have not recognized that I'm doing it with my tongue in my cheek as a kind of nostalgic gesture—which is quite conscious. I know that this doesn't wash, but I still love it. I wish I was Isaac Watts who wrote a lot of hymns. The hymnal is a big influence in my poetry.

IB: Did you remember them from when you were a kid?

JR: In them days we went to church. I went to church until I came to college and then never since. But it's in your blood—it's fierce like the childhood poems—like "Hiawatha." It's just there and you remember it and it just keeps coming up. It's the background that I'm haunted by, by a straight Christian background and I can't get rid of it either. So there.

IB: What is your God like?

JR: I don't know. There is something there. But I'm not a church-goer. The church has gone the way of nature. It doesn't really exist in a meaningful way for me. I keep asking the religious questions because I can't avoid them. I think they're impor-tant. I just ask myself as I read about the black holes and often keep mourning for stricter, more doctrinaire support of the church, which I do not have.

IB: Now, let's have you name songs from the hymnal.

JR: I have thousands. I range from "Fairest Lord Jesus" to "Oh, God, Our Help in Ages Past" to "In Heavenly Love Abiding" to "On Jordan's Bank The Baptist Cried" to "Love Divine, All Loves Excelling," and I could go on and on. I mean, I know the whole 1940 Episcopal hymnal by heart.

IB: Do you have any strong Puritan qualities?

JR: Yes, I do. But that's a hard question to answer. I mean, I don't abide by them—I have some principles which I do not abide by. When I drink too much, I get very Puritanical with myself, for example, and I do believe in hard work, though I don't al-ways do it.

IB: Do you have a favorite poetic device?

JR: I use a lot of slant rhyme. It's the ear thing—I don't think you can just use iambic tetrameter, rhyming abab, except rarely. But I try to mute the music but still have it there. I like the poem to have some sort of ending, not just fade off into the far blue as so many do. I like to give the poem a shape that I think is a shape and I like it to be coherent and sound like a poem. But I never know what's going to come out when I start. The poem develops as you write it. Every time I've tried to write a poem to a specific theme with a specific end in mind, I fall flat on my face and can't do it. It just doesn't come out. It has to be more of this sort of dreamlike congeries of images that you discard a lot of. Then one fits in, and I just cannot write the end of the poem until I've written all the rest of the poem, and it all comes out organic. I believe in the organic nature of art, and I don't think you can have a scheme that you can fit something into. But I don't know what I believe. I don't formulate it all.

IB: Do you have any past lives you want to confess?

JR: (Laughs.) Not at all. I'm very entertained by a friend of mine who says it well. "You must have a fireplace so you can burn up all the papers you don't want people to see." And I said, "I don't have any papers I don't want people to see. They're perfectly welcome to go through everything in the house. There are no secrets." That's true.

IB: Well, what about those limericks?

JR: They're in a folder on my desk.

IB: I'll be right over. (Laughs.) If you had to be born in another age, what would it have been?

JR: I would have been born in nineteenth-century England in the country, naturally. Or I might have been born in Lewis and Clark's generation, the early-nineteenth century, frontier

America. Either one of those, but definitely in the country and probably male. If I'd been born in the twentieth century, which I was, I'd rather have been born in Boston than Baltimore.

IB: Why?

JR: Easier access to better scenery. A *real* intellectual tradition. I lived in Cambridge for two years, in Longfellow's house on Brattle Street.

IB: Do your family's roots go way back?

JR: Oh, yes, I think they were probably all indentured servants. My father's family came up from Virginia, but one of my grandmothers was a Bostonian. So we have New England roots and Southern roots. My mother's family was strictly Maryland, which was betwixt and between. But we always went in the summer when I was a child to New England, and I went to college in New England, so I really didn't go South until I went to Hollins to teach, and I'm very fond of both of them. But if I had to have my preference, it seems to be Northern.

IB: You seem to be a little Yankee.

JR: Yeah, a little Yankee. Though I have great sympathy with the Southern cause. I'm a great expert on Civil War songs. When I get drunk, I play Civil War songs.

IB: Give me a couple of lines.

JR: Who will care for Mother now? Soon with angels I'll be marching,
with bright laurels on my brow.
I have for my country fallen
But, who will care for Mother now?

They all go like that. They're awfully sentimental—marvelous songs.

IB: What do you like about the Civil War?

JR: I detest the Civil War; all I like about it is the music on both sides.

IB: Wallace Stevens has that quote about the mind being the violence from within protecting against the violence from without.

JR: I think that's quite accurate. You have to fight back with something. You have to put up something. You have to feel that you are something. I don't mean physically, but an internal or mental thing. And I think that's very important to a sense of stability—you have a lot to fight in the modern world, besides the traffic.

PHILIP LEVINE

Philip Levine was born in 1928 in Detroit. Levine earned a B.A. from Wayne State University and an M.F.A. from the University of Iowa. He has taught at a number of colleges and universities including the University of Iowa, California State University in Fresno, Princeton, California-Berkeley, Columbia, and Tufts.

Levine's earliest poetic influences included W. H. Auden, T. S. Eliot, Dylan Thomas, and particularly William Carlos Williams, whose own work measured the urban landscape. His first book, *On the Edge*, was published in 1963, followed by *Not This Pig*, which brought him to the attention of a wider audience. To date he has published seventeen books of poems, most recently *A Walk with Tom Jefferson.*

His awards include the Lenore Marshall Award, two Guggenheim Fellowships, and recognitions from the National Institute of Arts and Letters. He received an American Book Award and a National Book Critics Circle Award for his book *Ashes.* He has also received the Harriet Monroe Memorial Prize and the Ruth Lilly Poetry Prize of $25,000 in 1987.

Philip Levine is a tall, stark man, savvy, direct, quixotic, and imaginative. One sees the tough and tender balanced in his demeanor. He is a motorcycle racing fan and has traveled widely in Spain, where the cityscapes of Barcelona have found their way into his work. It is the urban life that he depicts so powerfully in his poetry.

INTERVIEW

IRV BROUGHTON: There are a lot of definite opinions and definite stands expressed in your poetry and yet as an intellectual it must be difficult sometimes to make decisions about what is right and what's wrong. Or do you find that a problem?

PHILIP LEVINE: Well, I think everybody finds it a problem. I'm just like everybody else. I try to believe that what I'm doing is right. Sometimes I see the right and don't do it and feel miserable. Sometimes I see something that might be the right thing to do and don't want to do it out of cowardice or because I feel I should defend myself. I'm a person who tends to defend myself. Sometimes I do the right thing and sometimes I don't. I don't think it has much to do with being an intellectual. I'm not sure I am an intellectual. My wife is not, and I don't see that her choices are really much different from mine or that the way she achieves them is different. After all, the most significant choices that the two of us make have to do with each other and our children and the little communities in which we live. No, I don't think it's any different for an intellectual.

IB: What sort of choices in regard to the community?

PL: My wife lives in a community of plants as well as one of people. She spends hours every day with growing vegetables, herbs, flowers, trees. She troubles over the well-being of birds. She also works a great deal for various causes; she gives a lot of time to the Women's International League for Peace and Freedom. I teach, so I'm involved with dozens of students. I write. In the larger community, I've spent a lot of time recently trying to get a man out of prison, a man I think is there unjustly. He was convicted of committing a crime in Fresno. It wasn't something I looked for; someone made an appeal to me. He felt I was in a position to help him, and he was powerless. I'm tired of it, it's a defeating experience to go and try to deal with judges, adult authorities, policemen, what have you. I'm not very good at it.

IB: Do you think of poetry as a kind of minority voice?

PL: No, I don't. A minority would tend to suggest a body of the populace. I think poetry is the voice of individuals. Poetry is the voice of man and woman, boy and girl. And sometimes one man or one woman might speak for all men and all women; sometimes he might speak very eloquently for a small portion of the population. I don't think you're thinking of portions of populations, minorities. I'm not. I don't know about my fellow poets. I don't know about the great poets. I don't think Emily Dickinson was thinking that the spiritual states that she was dealing with were minority states. Maybe she experienced certain emotions with an intensity that was unusual. I sort of go along with Wordsworth, the idea that the poet is very much like other people, but he has a verbal facility and, I suppose, a stubbornness to use it extraordinarily.

IB: Are you especially stubborn?

PL: Stubborn? I don't think of myself that way, but I've been told that so many times that it would be hard to honestly say no. I really don't feel that I'm stubborn. But people tell me I'm terrible, that I'm stubborn. Well, people who like me say it's good; people who don't say it's terrible. I really don't know. I guess in some ways I could draw evidence to the fact that I was stubborn, that without much encouragement, for example, except from a few individuals, I wrote and wrote and wrote and wrote, pretty anonymously. A young black woman, a high school student, not long ago in Providence, Rhode Island, when I was reading some poems and talking, this young woman said to me, "Where did you find the strength to write all those years when nobody read you and knew you existed?" Well, that's an extraordinary question to come from someone so young. I was immediately struck by how powerful her imagination was. I was so nonplussed that I didn't answer the question. And then she said to me, "Was there someone who pulled you along?" and I began to talk about the people who had, especially my mother. Then she spoke later on—she came up to me and spoke of her parents and how they had discouraged her and told her that a young black woman of her age—at that time she was only fifteen—had no time for frivolous things like poetry. They wanted her to barrel ahead toward medical school. She said, "And I stopped writing. And I've grown bitter." And I said, "But you're only eighteen. You can start again." I didn't start writing till I was in my twenties. She said, "No, I quit and I'm bitter."

IB: What started you writing in your twenties?

PL: Well, I think I began poetry when I was much younger but I didn't know it was poetry. Like most American teenagers, in our high school the poetry I was shown was so irrelevant, deadly, and it was presented in such a deadly manner, so much attention to scansion and not much else. It was almost utterly irrelevant poetry. "Snowbound" was no big problem for me. I mean, snow is no big fucking deal. But I had all kinds of problems with other things. The kind of emotions that as a teenager I was beginning to feel, like sexual feelings. The second World War was on, and I was very frightened of the idea of going in and getting my ass blown apart. Well, a lot of other people felt those fears. You can go back into the history of war poetry. And I remember at the age of eighteen, a woman gave me a copy of "Arms and the Boy" by Wilfred Owen. It was the first time that I saw these people had real feelings, this stuff wasn't written by the Count of Monte Cristo, it wasn't written by the King of England. It was written by a man with the same terror I had. I went to school with a group of guys who never really admitted their emotions to each other. It was amazing if we admitted them to ourselves. So, I'm sure that the fear that I felt was really general throughout that generation. It wasn't alluded to and in the movies the guys who felt it were scoundrels, they were motherfuckers, they were horrible, and we waited for them to get killed.

IB: There is a lot of sexuality in your poetry.

PL: I don't think so, I don't know. I never thought of myself as a very sexy writer in the sense that I really deal with it directly. There is a little fucking. Maybe I'm wrong. When I think of what Ginsberg can do in a poem, how open he is about what he does, I feel really like some Victorian aunt. I have a reticence to talk about these things. I don't feel bad about it because there are other poets who do it. It isn't that our poetry is lacking in it, it's being done.

IB: Do you think sex is a kind of energizing force?

PL: I don't know, not in my experience. I remember when I was very young, a poet whom I will leave unnamed said to me, "Levine, if you fuck more than once every ten days you won't ever amount to anything as a poet." Well, that just seemed like hocus-pocus to me and it still does seem like hocus-pocus. I think if a guy has a kind of neurotic obsession with fucking and has to fuck someone every seven or eight hours, it seems to me he would be spending, at my age, all of his energies. And there is a kind of neurotic fucking that one is aware of, that really doesn't seem to have too much to do with a need to make love or even rises out of what you might call being horny, which also sometimes doesn't have much to do with making love. You know, I think there are some very sexless people. I just don't see the connection myself. You know the one thing that poetry and sex have in common for me, I don't know about other people, is that making love is for me often a very healing experience. It's very hard to describe but—I don't want to talk that much about my love life—there have been times when my need to make love and really experience love and not just fucking was something essential not just physical. It went far, far deeper than that and had something to do with reassuring me that I was human and I was loved and could express my love. And I think writing poetry a lot of times has done that for me too, in that as I mentioned, I write often to heal myself. Finally, I hope my poetry might do something for other people and have written it so that it could. I try to make it clear and I write about other people, my poems are full of other people. It's people I think I like more than any other thing and am more awed by than almost anything. So in that sense there is a similarity. I don't think a hell of a lot about sex. In some of my poems I look back at my youth; I have a poem in *1933* called "First Love, 1945" where I have a couple making love for the first time. I'm very sympathetic to these people although they're just having a hell of a difficult time.

IB: What's your favorite Jewish proverb?

PL: "If you spit in his face, he'll say it's raining."

IB: Do you have another one?

PL: Oh, I have a lot of them but that goes beyond all the others. My mother has another one, "God hates a coward."

IB: You're quoted as saying something like you like animals, for they would say "Don't tread on me." This kind of philosophy seems to permeate your work, a kind of stubborn independence and dignity, and I think that goes along with your general philosophy of poetry.

PL: Yeah, I suppose the two things I just said in a way go too. I'm a man who has been broken down at times. I don't think defeat is a terrible thing. I've been defeated. I have in the beginning of one of my earlier poems, "Silent in America" from *Not This Pig*, the line from Whitman, "Vivas for those who have failed!" I grew up always threatened by failure. My life was crowded with failures, my own and other people's. And for me what always made the difference was the people who could get up. I don't care how much it hurts and how much they suffered and how long it took really, but the people who could get up from their failures and try again. And I guess if I live by one thing I hope I'm that kind of person. Sometimes it's taken me a long time to get up, and I've gotten awfully angry at me. And that's probably one of my problems, that I'm very impatient with myself. Sometimes I think I want me to be more, more stubborn, more resourceful. I hate myself when I'm sick, as though we aren't all sick. Well, that's when I'm being stupid, which is about half the time. Other times I'm a little more forgiving. Yeah, sure, those are the things that I've yowled about in my poetry. But obviously a guy who would talk that much about that in his poetry really doesn't feel that that's him. We hardly notice our own nature. I have had my nature described to me by some people who know me very well, and I've been surprised by what they have said. When I thought about it, it was obvious that they were right.

IB: What did they feel you were like?

PL: Well, I don't really want to talk about what they said. They had insights that I thought were profound and when first given to me were extremely surprising—that's me? That kind of person? Because it's where I'm together that I hardly notice it. It's where I'm kind of frayed and frazzled that . . .

IB: Is there any one character in your work that exemplifies this ability to get up and fight back, this tenacity?

PL: In my poems? In my poetry I suppose there are several. The prizefighter, Baby Villon. The guy who's lost an eye, and just has his leg shattered in "By Animals, By Men, and By Machines"; the poem takes place in a hospital, and he's singing even though he's just a wreck. There's my grandfather in my poem, "Zadie," in *1933*. There's a woman in the poem "To P. L." in *They Feed They Lion,* who finds the dead man and takes his boots, takes his knife, creates life out of death in a way.

IB: What about poetry and biography? Your poetry is personal, much more personal than some of your peers such as Merwin. How do you relate to those people and to the personal in poetry?

PL: You mean relate to those people like Merwin? Well, I love Bill Merwin's poetry, he's a marvelous poet. Obviously I really don't want to write his poetry. It's very different from my own. I think it's beautifully done. I really don't want to live in a world of poets who write my poetry. I want to live in a world of poets who write their poetry, and I'm glad to have his poetry and Ginsberg's poetry and Snyder's poetry because they have experienced worlds that I haven't, and they quicken my awareness where it's dead. When I began writing poetry, I had this heightened consciousness of how voiceless so many people were. It was that voicelessness that really got me—there were the newspapers, the radios, the books I read, and there in contrast to that were all the people who I lived with. And they never got one goddamn word of all those millions of words. What they were feeling with such power. Now I come from a people who speak. They weren't a bunch of meek jerks—I mean they really yelled and raged, and we knew what was down their throats and up their ass. And the people I lived with in the neighborhood were much the same. The black people, the Southerners, that I worked with, they got angry and they shouted and so one knew their feelings and shared them. Sometimes they didn't like you and they let you know. And I thought God almighty, here are all these fucking movies, all this radio garbage, and we never enter—we never enter. All the hundred and thirty million Americans there were when I was eighteen years old, and you could go to every goddamn movie in the United States, you could listen to the radio all day long and you'd hear the make-believe people and the hundred and thirty million never got their noses in it. And I was so conscious of this and infuriated by it. You know how idealistic young people are. I used to say, half jokingly but half seriously, I will be the spokesman for this. And then as I grew older, maybe twenty-five or twenty-six, my grandfather died and that whole dying came back to me. My father died when I was very young, and the power of death shocked me again and the power of change. The city of Detroit didn't change much during the war. There was very little building, we all drove old cars. But suddenly after the war there was the radical change in the world that had been my childhood world. It was disappearing, going under. Freeways were appearing, new factories, new places. And to me that old one was a magic world. Just as somebody living on a farm might look out at those woods and think of it as where he grew up. Jung talks about the spirits of the trees and all that. Those city things have spirits for me, too, curiously. And I said I'm going to capture this, I'm not going to let it die.

IB: Well, you're kind of rare in this time, as you seem to return to the city for roots, much the way most writers go to the land or to traditions perhaps more related to, I don't want to say family, but perhaps history. This is unusual.

PL: Yeah, I suppose one of the reasons that I felt it needed to be done was that it wasn't being done and the poets that really got me were the ones who were in a way doing it—Williams. And I loved a lot of the older poetry. My favorite poet when I was twenty, twenty-one, was Keats. I knew his life very well, I read every biography. There were some basic similarities in our lives that I didn't realize until I started to think about it. His father died when he was very young, he came from a family that was doing fairly well till the man died, then they were up against it, there were a lot of kids. His letters are full of the most incredible awareness of the world he lived in, its injustices, its passions, its pains. His poetry is not full of those awarenesses—his poetry is a poetry of a never-never land, beautifully, exquisitely written, but so much of those long narrative poems is placed in a mythological time or kind of a strange medieval world. At the same time he's written these incredible letters. There's a letter where he describes walking into Manchester and hearing the sound of the spinning wheels, and he says it's the most ugly sound he's ever heard. He talks about Scottish girls coming under the vindictive rule of the kirk. He talks about the plight of an Irish laboring man and the unspeakable conditions in which these people live, the crimes perpetrated against them. He says, "I would jump down Aetna for any public good," but he says, "I'm a poet, that's what I want to be." There is a kind of schizophrenia here. It never seems to strike him, he doesn't have to write propaganda but just a presentation of the reality of those lives. We don't know anything about the reality of most of those lives. Still they're hidden. You can find out if you go looking for it, but by and large you inherit a pack of lies about the past, very similar to the pack of lies you get about the present. And the kind of barbaric cruelty practiced against women, men, children in the so-called civilized countries of Europe and America, when there was no government to protect people. Government ought to protect people: now it's killing people. Unbelievable. And Keats must have known the world with fantastic intimacy. He was studying to be a surgeon at a London hospital. The hell he must have seen. But it's not there, nothing. Not in his poems.

IB: Keats said somewhere in one of his letters that the poet is the most unpoetical thing, that he's always assuming another body, another shape.

PL: Yeah, he says he could be a sparrow pecking about the gravel sooner than he could be a Coleridge, or Wordsworth, a know-it-all, philosopher—king-poet. And I think that kind of jibes with his notion of negative capabilities which I very much believe in. I think it describes the condition of the world. I don't know what the world is, I don't know how it got here, where it's going. I don't really know why I'm here. Yet I have to act, I have to choose, I have to live, and have that ability to accept it and say, "Well, I think it's x, but I don't know, but I'll live with my doubt." The ability to live with those kinds of doubts and not to demand final answers. And to love this world and all of its rigors and accept the hardness. I think it's a fantastic state of mind. That Keats was so young, what was he, twenty-four, and could articulate it so beautifully shows what a fantastic guy he was. I don't know anybody who articulates it any better. I know a lot of people who know everything, and I say to myself, "Jesus Christ, I'm forty-six, what a moron I am." They know everything, they know why there wasn't an earthquake, because some spiritual leader stopped it. I was told that the other day by a lovely, arrogant person. She was patient with my lack of faith, but I finally said to her, "Why don't you stop cheating? I got opinions and you got insurmountable Truth. Now let's meet as equals. You can marshall the garbage in your mind against the garbage in my mind." I've changed my mind too goddamn many times about too many things to announce anything with too much certainty. You know, about poetry, I don't like to tell people, "This is the poem, that is the poem." I don't write the way I did a long time ago, and I really hope I'm writing differently five years from now. I don't like the same poems I liked when I was younger. Why should I?

IB: Was your early poetry too tortured?

PL: No, it was too tight, too closed. If I'm tortured I'll write tortured poetry, but I don't think there's anything so hotsy-totsy about writing tortured poetry. Why imagine you're tortured when so many people are and are writing about it? But it was too closed, it wasn't letting enough of the world in. Even the language wasn't my language. Somebody after a reading said to me—well it was Ken Kesey and his buddy McClanahan and Wendell Berry—that at one point in the reading they didn't know whether I was talking or reading a poem. That I passed from speech into the poem imperceptibly.

IB: I felt that too.

PL :   I like that. What I like about it is it suggested that the language I speak is the language of my poetry, that the rhythm I speak in is the rhythm of my poetry. I was very pleased to hear that. There was a time that would have pissed me off. I mean speech is casual and passing, and poetry is forever. But I'm not convinced my poetry is going to last forever. I hope to God it outlasts me by a week or two. I would hate to be about seventy-five and get all these anthologies and find my poems are taken out and they got some younger fool in there who writes worse.

IB :   Is there a Jewish consciousness in American poetry? There is a lot of talk as regards the novel.

PL :   You know, someone was asking me about that and I didn't know how to answer the question. I still don't. I think the best Jewish-American writer was just about the first who was really good, and that is Henry Roth. There've been lots of good books, don't get me wrong, but I don't think anything even gets near *Call It Sleep*. The struggle of that kid is the struggle of every kid to deal with the magic and the harshness, the unknown and the alien. In this case New York City, the Catholic world, and the magic of the crucifix and the Son of God and the world of sex—all this enters his consciousness. I don't really know how Jewish my writing is. A man named Abe Chapman, a remarkable man, is doing a book on Jewish-American writers. The idea of a book like that doesn't thrill me, but because he's doing it, I have the feeling it will be very interesting. He came to a reading that I gave once, and he said a few things about what I took to be the Jewish spirit, which was that we are a people like other people and we've had the shit kicked out of us, and we've survived, and we have survived as what we were. The whole world has tried to make us something else. They've told us in a million ways that if you'll change we'll make it easier on you. And we didn't. And I'm immensely proud of my people from that point of view. And what he said to me was, in a sense, that that should be something to enlarge the spirit, so that one who has been hurt can feel for the other who is hurt. If there is any value in suffering it would be there. I'm not interested in being exclusively Jewish. I don't feel really any more comfortable with Jews than I do with non-Jews. I'm just not interested in that. I'm not interested in denying what I am and I'm not interested in loving it to the extent of failing to see that it's not very different from something else. If it's going to cut me off from other people whose griefs are mine then I don't need it. And I don't think that's what it was all about. But that's just one guy's look at it.

IB: I think Robert Mezey said something about only really feeling his Jewishness when he saw some Nazis. I don't know whether he meant that metaphorically or what.

PL: Yeah, I know what he means by that. Sometimes one runs into certain situations that are reminiscent of childhood, for example, during the Second World War when I grew up, there was a lot of anti-Semitism. I suppose it started with Adam. He was the first Jew, and I suppose the first one who came along who wasn't called "You, Yid," or something. But at any rate, I experienced a lot of it and very directly. I didn't get jobs, I was called names, I was beat up, and I was told not to be around here. In school, I was excluded from certain activities. I was unaware of a lot of this, when I was very young. But when I was older I became aware that there were little social activities, in eighth and ninth grade, that the black boys and the Jew boys didn't go to because it might have involved touching these pristine little WASPs. We didn't even know these things took place. It was only by accident that I found out that there was this whole social life that we were excluded from.

IB: How did you find out?

PL: Some dumb bunny told me. They must have killed him. It hurt to know that people who sat in the seat next to you and played basketball and baseball with you and seemed to be your friends were drawing an invisible line. And there was a point where it really did hurt, it was a shock to me. That getting beat up because you were a Jew, that hurt double.

IB: Did you fight back pretty strongly? Did you whip up on any of these people that first attacked you?

PL: Well, I would have to say, I didn't feel like losing, I didn't feel like being beat up, and you might say I got very conscious of this thing. I spent a lot of time learning how to fight and fighting. Still losing a lot but winning sometimes too. It was awful. In other words I became what you might call a tough guy. Once you looked like a tough guy, once you were willing to fight, you didn't fight much. And I think in a way it was something of a curse I carried probably into my thirties. A combativeness, a willingness to make it clear that I would fight physically. Well, I finally got so destroyed in a fight that that ended it.

IB: You obviously are a gentle person, yet a physical person. Is it hard to balance the two? What if somebody accosts you on the street? Do you think it would all come out?

PL: I don't know, I hope not. I don't know myself that well in those regards. Sometimes you go back to very old patterns to defend yourself. I got involved, in the early sixties, in a terrible, terrible fight. And nobody, I think, understood my response to it. A friend of mine was assaulted very brutally, and I was there. It was clear that if I was going to enter the fray and fight fair, that I was going to lose. I didn't fight fair; it was ridiculous. I hit one guy from behind with a beer can and laid him out. My friend was being kicked, really kicked by a guy who was in fact a college wrestler. And what finally happened was, there were two of them and two of us, but it was like two of them and about five-sixteenths of us on the same scale of quickness and power. We were men in our thirties and they were guys in their early twenties, big jocks.

IB: Where did this happen?

PL: Well, that doesn't matter, but what really matters was that nobody really understood my response to it which was that's the way it goes. If you hit a man with a beer can even though he's trying to kill your friend, and you don't win the fight, you're going to lose really hard. I wound up with a broken jaw and a concussion, a lot of minor injuries. I thought I had it coming because that was how deep that ethic was.

You know, an interesting thing happened yesterday. Wendell Berry, he's a very nice man, came up to me after the roundtable where I talked about my poetry and my feeling about the fact that I wasn't alienated from a body of readers, that in fact I wrote about these people, and I wanted them to read my poems. He said to me that I had said exactly the opposite in an interview in *The American Poetry Review*. And I said, "No, you didn't understand me," and gave him an explanation which seemed like a nice one. And I came home and began to dwell on it, and I realized that I was wrong, that Berry had gotten my meaning and that I had changed it to meet another side of my character. And I told him that when I saw him in the evening. He said, "Yes, I notice that you really do have almost two opposed ways of talking about your relationship to your readers, your poetry, your relationship to a lot of things," and I said, "You're right, I do." And what I had said in *The American Poetry Review* was something like "Well, nobody reads me in Detroit, I ain't got any readers, and I don't give a damn, that's great." But of course, I do give a damn and it's not great. But what happened as a result of saying that in print was that some people wrote me from Detroit, and they assured me they read me and that I was alive to them. A lot of people have read me and it's meant a lot to me to know that there are people who read my stuff. But I also have this other thing where one protects oneself. Sure, a poet who has no readers is a very vulnerable person, and I grew up in what might be called a kind of combative atmosphere. Yet I really wasn't a very combative person in a lot of ways. But I protected myself by pretending I was, and I still do it in a lot of situations. In fact, there was a certain flippancy in some of the things I said yesterday. I think that's why I don't like interviews because in many cases I don't say what I believe.

IB: Can you ever say it all?

PL: No, but I don't say what I believe, that's the difference. Of course, we know probably on a deeper level than we can enunciate, that we can actually express. But I really know something different and I won't say it. I could have said I don't choose to say the truth because lots of times you get fucked when you say the truth. I grew up in a world where a lot of people weren't to be trusted, and if you trusted people you were a sap. You were a schlemiel, a jerk. And I got had. I see it in my son now. My oldest son is very generous, he works hard, he makes some money and people take it away from him. They borrow and don't pay back, they cheat him. It's hard for me to say to him, "Mark, man, you just got to get harder. They borrow tools from you that cost you hundreds of dollars. Man, you got to work your butt off, and they rip you off." It hurts him; he has a generous nature, and he wants to share things. And he gets screwed all the time. And I see him and I get angry for him. On the other hand I don't want to say, "Be a real prick. If someone wants to borrow a button, say 'No, man, I don't lend buttons.'" You can go all the way down the line. As a person he's much more open, a much lovelier person, but people like that sometimes just get it, we have to protect ourselves sometimes, too.

IB: Well, you feel very greatly for other people, it's obvious from your poems. Doesn't that hurt, isn't that exhausting?

PL: I don't know. I get tired a lot of times, but I don't know that that's what's tiring me. I think that feeling powerfully for other people is energizing and sustaining. I remember a recent experience, failing very badly to help this guy in Folsom Prison, trying to do something, not meeting resistance but making discoveries that hurt because they made the whole case look bad.

And so, I had identified to such a degree with this guy in this long, long incarceration, and I just thought, "Well, there ain't nothin' we're gonna do that's gonna bring about a change." He's been there nine years already. And I'm much less patient than he is. Sometimes during the Vietnam War, there were times when I believed I really would never write again. It was just very hard for me to give myself the intimacy with myself, the luxury of all that silence and time alone to write poems. I felt so sickened by what *we* were doing, and I do feel very much an American. And I really felt my own voice, this American language, I felt it was nauseating. It did pass but to a degree I allowed myself to believe the war was ending as they tell us in the newspapers although I knew better. Sure, there are experiences that will stop you cold. You don't want to hear a human voice, not even your own.

IB: Do you think you're sometimes misunderstood in our time when you go down to the prison or to the ghetto? People say, "Oh, he's just a good liberal."

PL: Well, I don't know. It doesn't ever occur to me that I would be. I don't really go to the ghetto, in the first place. The ghetto was something of my past. In Fresno, I go to the other side of the town; on many occasions I cross the tracks, I know the whole town. I think anybody can go to the ghetto. But I don't live there. You're not wanted. It's made evident to you. You're not wanted, so what the hell, am I going to force myself on other people's lives just because I'm so beautiful? They have their right not to want me. The Folsom thing, no, I don't think you'd be misunderstood. There's no way to misunderstand, I mean, because it is so painful, so awful to have to go there, and so few people will do it. I've gotten many people to go with me and most of them don't go back. I have a couple of guys, a Chicano poet named Leonard Adame and a poet named Butch Benck in Fresno, who go with me, who feel something the way I feel. And I don't know what I feel frankly. I don't like to go there. And I don't exactly know why I go. I go I guess because nobody else will. If somebody else went I wouldn't. But I can't get anybody else to go, so I have to. I think somebody's got to. It's a kind of bearing witness. These guys are there, they're dying, their lives are unbelievable. And they are possessed of an incredible thing, they are incredible people. And there is a lot to be learned from them.

IB: What have you learned?

PL: Well, I've learned a lot about how men live. I learned a lot about what Detroit was when I grew up there. I met a man who was exactly my own age in Folsom. Our lives took us different ways. So I learned things about alternatives. I learned a lot about thieves, armed robbers, what kind of people they are, and how putting men in a condition like a cell means they'll act like shit. I see men in prison and I see how they act. I didn't know. The movies don't tell. I didn't go there to learn that, I didn't really want to learn it.

IB: Have you been to the South? You seem to feel a kind of affinity for the South in a sense that you've known the people who have come north after migrating.

PL: Yeah, I went south. My wife and I lived for a while in North Carolina in the mountains, Boone, North Carolina. My wife was teaching for a while at Florida State University in Tallahassee, and on my own when I was even younger I spent a lot of time traveling through the South.

IB: What do you think about the South? What's it do to you? Do you feel the tragedy of it, the kind of disintegration of it?

PL: I first went south as a boy. My brother had some kind of bronchial pneumonia, and so we went down there to live in a milder climate. Course, I was a little kid then, I can't remember much of it. Later on, yeah; what I saw in the South I had not seen in the North. It was really dramatized to me what was happening to the earth, to nature. Some of the landscape was still fantastically beautiful, but you could see what was going to happen in a few weeks. As far as the racial thing, the same went on in Detroit. It looked worse in Detroit. I don't know that it was worse, but it was so bad and there was so much police violence against black people and when I was a kid in Detroit there were these terrible riots over housing projects—that was during the war. Even before that, a guy ran for mayor of Detroit as a KKK write-in candidate, and if the Democrats and Republicans hadn't finagled the vote he would have won by ten thousand votes. And that was a vote of about four hundred thousand. Detroit was a KKK town, so bad it was just unbelievable. I saw a lot of the race riot of '42—there was no way you could not see it. And there was no question of what went on. Police in many cases stood idly by while gangs of thirty or forty white men would beat to death a black man, say in his sixties. Beat him to death. If you want to go into the archives you can find photographs.

IB: You wrote some short stories, and you ultimately used them elsewhere, didn't you?

PL: Yeah, I didn't write them with that intention. I wrote stories because I wanted to write stories. Bob Mezey when reading my new poetry said, "You're a terrific short story writer." And I looked at him, and he said, "I mean here in these poems. They're all stories." I was showing him some new poems which were all narrative. They were hidden there but they were structured around narrative. At one time I just felt kind of stopped up as far as poetry was concerned. There were a couple of things I wanted to write. I didn't know how to write them as poems. So I sat down and wrote three stories, two of which I think were quite successful as stories. One was just sort of a dry run, the first one. The second one was quite long, it must have been sixty typed pages. And it was basically a story about a marriage. But the background to it, especially the husband's background, was factory work. I don't think I got the story right, I don't think I got the marriage right, especially the wife, I didn't get her. I did better with the guy. I grew kind of disinterested in those two people. Their plight interested me, but I didn't make them people enough. The background was far and away the best thing. And it was the background I used, I got a couple of poems, probably two years later.

IB: What were the poems?

PL: "Blasting from Heaven" and "A New Life."

IB: Where do you pick up your narrative technique?

PL: Well, I began writing as a short story, fiction writer. I wanted to be a fiction writer. And I wrote a lot of fiction, I wrote a great many stories. I wrote a novel. I don't know what the stuff was like, I threw it all away, thank God. I love stories, I just love stories and I love character. So a lot of the elements that are in fiction I really like. But I don't have the temperament. I don't like the way they do that, those fiction writers. I burn, I mean, I really get hot and I stay that way for a couple of days; the whole thing of staying with a novel, I get so fussy and bored with it. And it just wasn't me. I hate things that I can't put together. I get this thing all scattered out, and it would be like—that novel that I couldn't put together—was like me walking around in a hundred pieces. I just feel so fragmented. But when I write a poem I have enough energy to just kind of sit on the son-of-a-bitch most of the time until I get it done. And even the long poems are a kind of torment.

IB: How long does the average poem take you to write?

PL: Well, it varies enormously. In the last year, last two years, there has been a change in the way I write, and I now can let a poem sit in the most fragmentary way for quite a while, say a month. Let it be completely fragmented and just put it over there and do other things. And I am getting much looser about these things.

IB: Why is that?

PL: I have no idea. I don't care, I'm glad. I'm happy that I can do another thing which I couldn't do.

IB: There seems to be a kind of body of substance, a heavy quality—not in a negative sense—to your poetic line, where Merwin has a less interconnected more detached line. What's your feeling about line?

PL: I don't think much about it. I really don't like to talk about that kind of thing. Well, I'm doing a lot of writing now and technique is a thing that might be fascinating if you weren't writing, but I'm writing so I really don't even want to look at those things from that point of view.

IB: Did your mother used to read you stories? Do you think you got your stories from this background?

PL: No, my grandfather was a great teller of fantastic tales and, there was a cat named, I think, the Baron Von Munchausen, a famous liar. My grandfather thought he was about the greatest. My grandfather loved to tell me wild impossible, improbable tales. There's a reference to one of his tales in the poem, "Saturday Sleeping." I talk about "the great talking dogs that saved the Jews." That is a character out of one of his tales, a huge dog who loved the Jews, who would live among the officers of the Czar, and would come bounding to the Jews to warn them and advise them. And it seemed like a happy tale in a way. But later in life I realized it was unbelievably bitter. What it said in effect was, from men we'll get nothing; if there'll be help it will come from dogs. But he was a man who endured a great deal, but never lost his humor. I loved those stories he told. I think he used to make them up. And later on in life I passed the tradition on and told stories to my own kids.

IB: Do you think you can inspire creativity in children?

PL: I think the problem isn't to inspire it, it's to stop defeating it. I think creativity is so natural in young people. The problem is we kill it. I've never really worked with children in that sense, but I've seen my own kids and other people's kids, and I was a child. And as I say, the urge to build, the urge to make, is so obviously there. I remember my little kid digging very complicated tunnels and things out in the back yard. We had been in Spain, and everything there was built by hand. When we got home he started with a shovel and a little bandana on his forehead the way the Spaniards put it. They were building houses; he too could begin a building. There he was, about eight, with a shovel and he would go out in the backyard and dig and dig and dig, dig all day. I mean, it was hard. If I told him to cut the lawn, he'd tell me to go fuck myself, or say, what are you going to pay me. But he would do this all day. And the kids, they take wood and smash together their own houses and paint them; they redesign their rooms all the time. We know how to do it, we know how to kill creativity. I suppose it's dangerous if these kids grow up naturally in a society as fucked as this one. How long would healthy people put up with this horse shit? We're so defeated by it, most of us, that by the time we're twenty we think we have no power.

IB: What does the little magazine mean to the poet?

PL: Everything. Without the little magazine, the small publisher, I never would have survived as a poet. I published my first book at thirty-five although I'd been writing very seriously for eleven uninterrupted years. It was with a small press. I'd been turned down, I'd been lied to, been promised, and all that shit by the big publishers. Finally, they didn't print it. But the small press took the chance. That's where poetry's been for a long time in America.

IB: What is your favorite obsession?

PL: When I was a little boy it was killing Hitler. I put myself to sleep a lot of nights dreaming sniper stuff in the middle of the Reich. It's a hell of a thing to grow up with. It hadn't occurred to me in a long time. Now I don't know what's my favorite. They're all crowding around for attention.

IB: Do you use dreams in your writing? Do you get up in the middle of the night to write?

PL: Very rarely. I have though. Oh, I don't know, I'm not in as much of a hurry as I used to be. I have actually written in dreams and then awakened and written down what I'd written in the dream. But that was a long time ago and hasn't happened lately. Yeah, I make discoveries about myself, about other people, my true feelings, and their feelings toward me. I think I see a lot of things in dreams that are very valid, that I am kind of blinded to in my ordinary life. Urgencies that pass me by suddenly speak to me in dreams—say the desperation of a friend who can't come out and say it, the needs of a child. Awake, I see the evidence, but I somehow don't gather it. It's all there, and I collect it in a dream and it speaks. A dream changed the way I write, changed my whole poetry. I dreamed once when I was in my middle thirties that a man named Eugene Watkins, a black man that I'd worked with in Detroit many years ago, called me on the phone and I was in Fresno and he was in Bakersfield. And we talked, small talk. It's a long ways from Detroit to Bakersfield, and he didn't know, he didn't say where he was going, but I assumed he was going to L.A., and I didn't invite him up to my house. And then I awakened and I said at first to myself, "My god, Levine, have you gone, are you such a middle-class asshole that you don't want that

268

guy here, that he wouldn't look right, a black factory worker from Detroit?" He had a bad marriage, his wife was a difficult woman, I thought. How was he going to fit into my life now? Does that kind of shit so concern you, that you'd turn your back on what you were? And he was a man, I remember, with missing fingers, and there was a way in which that suggested something kind of menacing. He was a very bright guy, too bright for those dumb jobs, and as such he lived in fantasy and would hurt himself. Often, you can do a factory job and just think about your dreams. It's great, but you just cut your fucking head off, too. I've seen it happen. Not heads, but fingers. At any rate, I was very angry with myself. "Jesus, Levine, you've come to this." And then about an hour or two later I realized that the dream was a warning. It wasn't what happened but what might happen, and I felt very elated, like getting another chance. I stopped everything I was doing, I quit teaching, and I just got in bed, and I wrote for about ten days, the first good poems I'd written about that part of my life.

IB: Do you ever dream of flight?

PL: The only thing I never dreamed of is an interview.

IB: You said during your reading you'd learned something when you went to the ghetto, walked back through the charred ghetto. Could you talk about that?

PL: I was frightened, it was very clear to me I was a little, middle-aged white guy. This was an angry place. They just had this goddamn insurrection, and there was a lot of damage done. I don't want to patronize people and I don't want to be patronized. They looked at me and they looked with anger. I represented the society that was killing them and their children. And that was a fact. That is a fact. I think we're all living off their pain.

IB: Did you say you learned who you were?

PL: Well, I didn't learn everything, but sure. I was reminded again of where and who I really was. And that in a way there is a kind of schizophrenia in me. I hate this white society, yet I'm a member of it. That's kind of what I learned.

IB: If humor eases the pain, why aren't poets more humorous? Or is poetry opposed to humor?

PL: Well, of course it's not opposed to humor. I guess it's hard to write funny poems, and a lot of what we want to write about today just ain't funny and there just ain't no way it's going to be funny. Kenneth Koch is a hell of a funny poet. Marge Piercy read a crab poem yesterday that was very funny. I've written a couple of funny poems. I love funny poems myself, I wish there were more. But as I say, so much of what we're concerned with just ain't funny and it's so goddamned hard to be funny about it.

IB: Can you write when you're tired?

PL: Yes, but I write badly.

IB: Where's the strangest place that you've come up with ideas? Have you ever written a poem on a doily?

PL: I worked out a poem in a class of bonehead English in my early teaching years. I had to go to class, and I told the kids to be cool. There I was writing some of it on the board and just having a great time with them, but I was actually writing a poem, seriously, 'cause it was coming to me right there. It's a damn good poem, it's in my first book.

IB: What's it called?

PL: "*L'homme et le bete*"—Man and beast. It's about the hanging of a pig. I couldn't stop writing. I was so much in the poem that nothing could stop me. And I went to the class and said, "Oh, be quiet, kids, come on." "What are we supposed to do?" "Oh just talk to each other." I loved those kids; it was one of my very favorite classes. They were wonderful kids. They were all told they were failing because they couldn't talk, they couldn't write. I said, man, we can learn this shit. And I had a great time with them. I think I convinced them they were human beings even though they'd gotten some Fs. It was a wonderful experience for me.

IB: What can the creative writing teacher give the student of poetry?

PL: Oh, he can give him a lot. He can give hope, he can encourage him, help him with all kinds of technical problems, he can expose him to writing that he wasn't aware of, he can get him through a lot of hard times, he can lend him money, he can give him affection, he can show him that older people aren't monsters. He can get a lot from him, he can receive the friendliness, the affection of the student. It's like, what can men and women give men and women? That's really all it is. Except that in this case, what can teachers give people who want to learn? What can a man or woman who knows something give to a person who wants to learn something? What can the carpenter give to the apprentice? Well, he can show him that's the way to hold the saw, fuck face. Or he can say, "you're not doing too well now, but I didn't at first either. Stick at it and you'll learn it." You can kill him if you want, but I'm not interested in killing them.

IB: How do you maintain a kind of discipline and yet not kill them?

PL: Well, I don't want to tell anyone how he ought to teach. I think if you got a talent for it and you're not too fucked-up personally so that you have to kill them, you're not jealous of what they might do, I think it's rather an easy thing to do. I think it's the most wonderful thing in the world. It's nice to teach and to feel their affection come back to you and to have them thankful that you've helped them. I got a little something that a student made, recently, that was really lovely that had something to do with that. I failed a lot of times in the sense that I haven't been as perceptive about talent as I should have been.

IB: Don't you think there's a lot of unfeeling academic poetry that's perfect in form but . . .

PL: There's very little poetry that's perfect in form. I think there is a lot of tepid poetry, yes, I do. I think there always will be a lot of tepid poetry. It's no problem. Those poems don't hurt anybody. They're all going to be forgotten. If you go back and say, well, all right, there was a poet living next to Whitman, and he wrote these so-so sonnets, I don't think they did Whitman any harm. Nobody reads them now. It's a fake issue. I'm always asked that question, as though it were a serious problem. It's not.

IB: So isn't it a moral kind of thing; I mean, can the poet always write sonnets and say, well I don't have to worry about my brother?

PL: I think poems that are written out of that kind of obligation and not out of need are going to be pretty dull. We write the poems we were given to write. There have been times in my life when I was utterly fascinated with a flower or form or box or grass and what have you, and sometimes I wrote about them and sometimes I didn't. I have poems in which I talk about natural phenomena and what they've meant to me. But Jesus Christ, you don't want to go around all day saying, "God, I got to lift the average income in this country or I'll just die." And I think it's a very presumptuous thing for anybody to tell anybody else what he ought to do. He ought to use that energy that he's blowing at the other guy's face with his bad breath to go home and write his own stuff.

IB: What do you like about pigs?

PL: I think I like the bacon part, then there's the chop.

IB: Does that run counter to your religion?

PL: No, a lot of Jews voted for Nixon. Talk about liking pigs . . .
No, not my personal religion.

IB: What do animals mean to you on another level? Do they each
specify different things?

PL: Oh, I haven't anything worked out, you mean a kind of . . .
no, like they're little symbols? No. Or big symbols, a rhinoceros
would be a pretty big symbol.

IB: You can fatten a pig up and he'd be a bigger symbol.

PL: No, I don't want to be a symbol. Look, let's say two pigs are
having an interview and one of them says, "I kind of like this
guy, Levine, what does he mean to you, what does he symbol-
ize to you? and the other pig says, "Well, I like Levine, he
doesn't eat pigs, he's Jewish." No, they're frivolous questions
to me because my mind doesn't go that way. Perhaps other
people have a whole symbolism worked out for fellows, the
beasts. I don't want to be a symbol.

GEORGE GARRETT

George Garrett was born June 11, 1929, in Orlando, Florida. He was educated at Sewanee Military Academy and The Hill School and attended Princeton University as both an undergraduate and graduate. He received his doctoral degree from Princeton in 1985. He served in the U.S. Army as Sergeant in Field Artillery, "Chief of Section" of 155 mm howitzer, in Austria, Italy, and Germany.

George has published over twenty books of his own (novels, short stories, poems, plays), including his remarkable *Death of the Fox*, which *Publisher's Weekly* called "one of the finest novels we have ever read . . . Mr. Garrett, a magnificent storyteller, opens out for us a vast world of the imagination." Another *magnum opus, The Succession,* evoked some of the same rich historical tracings. His short stories were recently collected in *An Evening Performance,* as were his poems in *The Collected Poems of George Garrett.* That wonderful, acerbic Garrett wit is to be found in a recent book, *Poison Pen,* published by Stuart Wright in 1986. He has also been editor or co-editor of more than a dozen books.

George has received awards from the Ford Foundation, American Academy in Rome, and National Endowment for the Arts and was granted a *Sewanee Review* Fellowship in Poetry. He has been a member of the faculties of Wesleyan, Rice, Princeton, Michigan, and Hollins College, where he began an ambitious program in writing and filmmaking. He is currently Hoynes Distinguished Professor of Creative Writing at the University of Virginia.

My interview with George Garrett took place in his office which was cluttered with a mélange of things—books at every angle and slant, posters on the wall, some of them even presentable. There was sitting room among the collages, doll houses, mobiles, and plastic banana tree—all the work of inventive students paying tribute to a person who truly honors creativity. George spoke rapidly, delivering his words in spurts like a comedian or boxer. (He was, in fact, a pugilist at one time, and he lost his only amateur fight, by decision, to the National Golden Gloves Champion.)

There is a staccato quality to nearly all his movements. And George is funny. "Anybody that wants to see the execution of Max Baer has got to pay more than fifty dollars for a ringside seat," he adds as he prepares for the interview.

INTERVIEW

IRV BROUGHTON: Frank Norris felt that the novel could express modern life better than painting, architecture, or poetry. Can you make much sense of that?

GEORGE GARRETT: Not really. I guess it would be a nice idea, except you can't live in a novel. And most of them, in spite of attractive jackets, can't make good wall decorations. As physical objects they're—depending on size—useful for doorstops and for windows that won't stay in place. I've frequently used novels to hold up the windows on a hot night in my house in Maine. Norris said that long before the film came along, too, didn't he? Perhaps he'd feel a little differently about this today. I'm not sure that that's what the novel is all about—containing modern life.

IB: What novel do you use to hold up the window?

GG: If you want it pretty high on a hot summer night, *Portrait of a Marriage* by Nicholson, Harold Nicholson. That's a very nice sized book. I think Peter Mattheson's *Far Tortuga* is an interesting shape. Modern library giants fit beautifully for just a kind of moderate level, keeping the window up. Over the years, I've used the plays of Eugene O'Neill a lot. That's true. Unfortunately, it rained a few times. It's in a very strange looking condition now. Poetry is not worth a damn for holding up windows or as a doorstop either. It's very decorative in rows, but you have to get so many of them, because they're thin.

IB: Did you ever use *Sunrise at Campobello?*

GG: No, I never have done that, but *Fear of Flying* held up my window for quite a while. Then the kids got a hold of it.

IB: Is there a poem of yours that hurts you to read?

GG: Emotionally?

IB: I've heard writers say that sometimes there's something of theirs that really hurts to read.

GG: There are a good many that hurt me to read. One keeps changing, and they hurt me to read because they're embarrassing. I wish I could fix them up. But, that's just technique. No, I don't think there are any. I mean that would be a strange duplicity, wouldn't it? Or a kind of hypocrisy if you are willing to write the poem, see it in print, and then announce that it's much too tender to be shared with the world. Quite aside from that kind of notion of coy hypocrisy, it's just the act of putting something down in the form and perhaps also the process of publication, the fact that it ceases to be a part of yourself in that sense. Perhaps this might not make any sense at all, but perhaps, when poems originate out of injuries or out of complex personal situations and things, which they often do, though not always—that's a mistake people make—the act of doing the poem is probably in some way therapeutic. I would think if the poem, after years, still hurt to read, the poem itself must be in some way unsuccessful, very unsuccessful. The cathartic quality of it did not begin even at the first level. What's really troubling the poet who feels that way is that he somehow didn't get it right.

IB: Tell me about growing up around Kissimmee. Was your imagination spurred by seeing all those cowboys and hitching posts there?

GG: When I was a child living in Kissimmee, Florida—although I was born in Orlando—the family had moved to Orlando, and we had a house in Kissimmee for a long time. Kissimmee was a real cow town. They had real live cowboys riding up and down the street. And hitching posts. And they had just begun to bring in, at that time, Brahma cattle from India, which are now, of course, the source of several breeds, and are all over

Florida. And actually, it was my father's law partner, a man named Pat Johnson, who first brought Brahma bulls and cattle into Florida. There had been cattle in Florida, but they were ill-adapted to the kinds of mosquitoes, bugs, pests, and parasites that Florida had. In those days a genuine experience was for an outlander to have the temerity to order a Florida steak. This caused great glee in restaurants and other places. The only thing I can tell you about a Florida steak from the early days in Kissimmee is that if you've ever had a chicken-fried steak in some place like Waxahatchee, Texas, that thing is like an aged sirloin from the Four Seasons compared to a Florida steak. I don't know why they carried it on the menu except that you could take a Florida steak and tie it around your foot with a piece of string, and you had a good pair of shoes. You could march all around Valley Forge with Florida steak on your feet. But we had cowboys and rattlesnakes, and it was a wild, kind of wonderful place. So was Orlando, which might be hard to believe in this day and age. Because, for a long, long time, Orlando, Florida, was a town of about twenty thousand. And then suddenly, with World War II, they put a huge air base there, and the population grew and grew and grew and then exploded into a massive sprawling megalopolis. It's so bad now with freeways that the last time I drove home, I couldn't find my own house. Partly this was because freeways cut me off from all the streets I knew. I drove and drove around Orlando, occasionally sighting a landmark and heading in that direction. Change and decay all around us. That's the great Southern theme, "change and decay."

IB: So you were spurred by seeing the cowboys?

GG: Maybe my imagination was "spurred by the cowboys," but I have never written any cowboy stories. I don't know why. (Laughs.) In retrospect, my imagination is still excited by recollections of what life was like then, and all of that experience of growing up in Florida at that time. I want to avoid, as a writer, becoming a victim of nostalgia, a direction Wright Morris says "leads to nothing." We want to head for the territory ahead, but it would be hard to grow up without being affected. Those were lively times and interesting times. The Depression was the last really democratic period we had in this country. I don't mean in the political party sense. I mean that when everybody was poor together it really wasn't so bad. We all maintained our status as we dwindled.

IB: You have a tremendous collection of Sir Walter Raleigh books. When did you start collecting them?

GG: Oh, about 1948–49, along in there.

IB: How many volumes?

GG: Well, they cover a few shelves. I haven't really looked at them in a while. There aren't many biographies, because they came along later. At the time I first got interested in Raleigh, there had not been a biography of Raleigh in many, many years. Other people must have noticed this, too, because they've been coming along ever since. There was one by Robert Lacey, who's very good. It's a field where a great many things have been done, and particularly in the 1970s. And I collect marvelous books about different aspects of Elizabethan England as I can. Like other books, they're very, very expensive. One of my prize possessions is a book—a very elegant book of "Tudor Royal Proclamations." They really are a lot of fun because they were read out by some herald, and you can flip through and find the point where, say, the Rebellion of 1569 was going on, and, you have never heard in modern life the vituperation of the kind that came as normal descriptive sequence of adjectives, dealing with the enemy in a case like that—"knaves," "rascals," "scroyles," "murderers"—and, it seems to have been kind of standard to savagely attack your enemies by means of a proclamation. And I enjoy that.

IB: Is that what you like most about the period?

GG: That's one of the pleasures of the period. It's a very loud pe-riod. One of the pleasures of the period is its difference, in so many ways, from anything that comes after, difference in thou-sands of little details of life. It engages the imagination quite a bit to try to conceive how it would be to live that way. It is not a simple case of working backwards to a simpler life. In some ways it's more complex than ours. An example: for a gentle-man, it took an hour to get dressed. You couldn't get dressed in some of those clothes by yourself, and even then, it would take about an hour, and you had to have people lacing up stuff for you. That makes for a very different thing. You can't run down to the Seven-Eleven if it takes you an hour to get laced up. That's a very small example. But the clothing, what they ate, how they lived their hours of the day, and everything else were so radically different. The more you get into it—it's almost like reading about moon people—you realize it's not a simpler form of life at all. It's the end of something, and something else be-gins after that. Something more familiar to us. That, and all the small aspects of it, is very terribly interesting to me.

The diet then was radically different. This might seem silly now, but what I'm trying to say is that we're just dealing with people who were people but very, very different in custom. It is hard for us to conceive of people who began the day, prior to the existence of coffee and tea which from the eighteenth cen-tury on people had, with a quart of ale for breakfast. It must have been quite different around—the things that they ate—a very good diet, but a heavy protein diet. We don't know a lot about certain things. They were crazy for distillation of things. Distilling excited them very much. And Elizabethans distilled all kinds of natural medicines and cordials. They were very se-cretive about this . . . and we don't even know what they were, except that their cure rate was just as good as what you get in the Massachusetts General Hospital. The biggest thing, the thing that interested me most about this period—historical fic-tion is not my only interest—is how we are the victims of a kind of myth, based pragmatically on looking at the world around us now and believing that there's some kind of linear progression from simpler ages to more complicated ages. Judging by the technological progressions that we see around us all the time, and by certain abstract notions, like evolutionary notions applied to human history, we have an idea that those people were versions of ourselves, but more or less like children in an earlier, more innocent form. And we also, secretly, if you think about it, in our imagination, assume that they were kind of dumb. They were dumb because they hadn't invented television. So that the act of imagining people who are just as complex and dimensional, and whose lives were in details radically different, and whose assumptions about reality were quite different is a very exciting thing. That's one reason, in the fiction that I've done and I'm doing now, that I go out of my way not to make analogies and comparisons to the present age. To begin at least, I think those analogies and comparisons are built on false premises. I cannot help, nor can the reader, making analogies, because we're living in the twentieth century. But what needs to be emphasized, then, is the strangeness and difference of the past. For the reader and writer today, the likenesses will be there anyway.

IB: What do you mean, the strangeness of the past, the difference of the past?

GG: Well, what we assume is—because this is the way the imagination works, and the lazy way—that they were people like ourselves in costume. Now think about that for a minute. When we try to imagine Romans, we even feel they must have felt a little silly in their costumes, as we would feel. This has one basis in reality. It is a part of our understanding that human beings haven't changed that much in imaginable history. But that basis of truth makes for a distortion. They didn't see themselves as running around in funny costumes. This is all very relatively simple-minded stuff, but it has to do with trying to engage the imagination in the strangeness of other human beings. I think the same thing applies, of course, in the contemporary world. You assume that John Dillinger has really got a consciousness like Irv Broughton, and this is the only way you can deal with the world. But of course, he doesn't. He is alike, but different, and that's the point I'm making. Stress, in my historical fiction, is on the difference. That's also a reaction to many, many historical books, in which the points are: a) why, they were almost like we are; and b) that they were fumbling their way towards getting where we are. And these things, while comforting to the contemporary mentality, are not very accurate.

IB: You deal a lot with the imagination. Do you want your writing to personify the imagination?

GG: What I would like from my writing is nothing grand, like the personification of the imagination, but the maximum use of the imagination and engaging the imagination of the reader. To do that, I would also like to have it as sensuous as possible. These are the proper realms of artistic experience, as distinguished from just discursive communication of one kind or another. I think imagination—its limits and its possibilities—is one of the great constant themes of all literature, regardless of form. Every poem and every novel and every play and every film is a test of the limits and the possibilities of the imagination because it engages the imagination. By this, I mean it's not a demonstration of the writer's wonderful imagination—it is a communication and a dialogue between the imagination of the writer and the engaged imagination of the reader. And that's what I would like to achieve now. Not to demonstrate the eccentricity of my fantasy life, or what have you.

IB: Would you say it's difficult to live in the world of the imagination?

GG: Do you remember what Julia Moore, the sweet singer of Michigan, said, addressing the bad criticism she had received? "Let them scoff as they may, the literary is very difficult to do." I think the literary is very difficult to do. (Laughs.)

IB: How do you control the imagination?

GG: I think imagination has to be controlled in many ways. For instance, it has to be controlled because you're speaking to someone else, and because reading is an interchange. The literary experience is an interchange, an intercourse, a dialogue. So, imagination is controlled, in that sense, from the outset, by the necessity of give and take with an imaginary reader, who is very real. Obviously, one could lie back on the couch and imagine and fantasize much more interesting stories than anyone will ever write, and could do this very easily—because you have no one, no audience other than yourself to concern yourself with. I'm not saying that people write, quote, "for an audience." But I'm saying that they write for an imaginary reader. And that very problem of engaging and involving a dimensional, imaginary reader is an enormous control on the looseness, and the enigmatic, elliptic quality of just uncontrolled imagination and dream-like fantasy. I really believe that it would be difficult beyond belief, and not particularly valuable, if we could in some weird way, tune in on each other's dreams. I don't think that would make any sense to anybody else, imagining some sort of technology whereby someone could point a laser at someone else's head and suddenly have their dreams. Those dreams, which are consciously uncontrolled imagination, would in large part be baffling and enigmatic and not of any special value. They might be entertaining to a reader, but they would not have much meaning.

IB: Bernard Berenson said that the really historical novel is impossible, because as we reconstruct the past scientifically, our artistic reconstructions suffer.

GG: Berenson has made some assumptions that I necessarily follow: that because the approach of many people to the past is scientific, or uses a kind of scientific methodology—that is, our approach to past events, people, history—the artist must also be in some way conditioned by this methodology. This is entirely possible, of course, and you can't escape metaphors, the great metaphors with which we do most of our thinking. Science is one of them. But fundamentally, a work of art, whether it deals with here and now, yesterday, ancient Rome, or prehistoric man—you name it—is an act of imagination, regardless of how it dresses itself. It's not on the level of what he means by scientific construction, what they meant by *scientia* in the Middle Ages: reasonable, logical. It takes jumps, leaps, blind hops, dances a little. Imagination is key to any work of art; it speaks from the imagination to the imagination, and although the quotation is an interesting and elegant one, it doesn't really interest me too much because you could argue, if you wanted to, precisely because what he says is true—if it is true—that the historical novel or historical fiction has more possibilities in that it requires a greater exercise of imagination under the circumstances of living in a world of, quote, "scientific construction." I don't know if that answers that question or not. It's just a methodology, a method which, like any other, can be gotten around, can be discarded, can even be used.

IB: What about adaptation? Gore Vidal thought that he'd failed miserably adapting Hemingway for television, which made him wonder about the original.

GG: Well, I envy his enormous confidence in making a remark like that. I think, though, what if he had difficulty translating the *Iliad?* I believe he's onto something there, but the forms are different. Anyway, I think it would be extremely difficult to adapt, as witness the fact that very, very few really good pictures have been made, adapted from his work. The prose qualities that make it great are not those that transfer very easily. I think probably the best piece of adaptation of Hemingway was Faulkner's complete rewrite of *To Have and Have Not* with Lauren Bacall and Humphrey Bogart. There's nothing of Hemingway in it except that it has boats. But in some way, it's more true to the spirit of Hemingway than any of the direct adaptations, where they've got the dialogue. You know, the dialogue doesn't carry very well. It reads wonderfully on a page. It has all sorts of resonance and all, and once you have people actually saying those things, it seems very stylized or unreal. Whereas, by some kind of ironic contrast, very stilted dialogue on the page, not stilted but old-fashioned (for example, Dickens, Conrad) plays beautifully in a movie. That's one of the problems of adaptation. Maybe adaptation of a good novel is impossible, as Frost says, defining poetry as what is lost in translation. I think something like *Tom Jones* was pretty good adaptation, not complete—they never are—but I don't think it reflects on the original that *Moby Dick* is very difficult to adapt to the screen.

IB: What is the greatest adaptation you've seen?

GG: Maybe, besides something like *Tom Jones, Tunes of Glory* was pretty good adaptation. That's one where Alec Guiness wears a kilt.

IB: There's something terribly McLuhanesque about adaptation, I mean the changing of media.

GG: That's really what it is. It's not a good idea to translate the novel into film, but this is what they do, and I hope they don't find out.

IB: George, you did the first black comedy motion picture, *Playground*.

GG: That's what Bosley Crowther said. It upset him quite a bit. He gave us about a B-minus. It was a funny thing, just when he was leaving the *Times* and it didn't make any difference.

IB: There's a certain black comedy to your—

GG: It's not black comedy, our use of blacks. We had one black actor who was really good, who played all the blacks all the way through the picture and very few people noticed this. It was a piece of social comment, like, "They all look alike." An assistant to a surgeon, an actor, a bell hop—every time the play called for a black, this guy was it. He didn't put on any makeup or anything. The final irony was showing it at a black university where they complained bitterly about his grammar in one scene, where he said, "I ain't got none." The thing was, it was the same guy all the way through the picture, but they hadn't noticed that. So we lost some of the social commentary on that, I guess.

IB: You dedicated your first book to Marianne Moore.

GG: It's kind of a complicated story. I'll try and make it as brief as possible. I first met Miss Moore when I was a college student and had gone up to Mount Holyoke College to read some poems for what was called a Glascock Memorial Reading. They gave a prize and, as it happened—I won probably the only prize I ever won—I won the Glascock Prize. We were staying in the girls' dorms—these little rooms assigned to us—and I came rolling back to the dorm, and there was an eleven o'clock curfew or something for the girls. There were a lot on the porch wildly saying "goodbye," necking with their boyfriends, and the night watchman was shooing the boys away. I just walked right past everybody and into the dorm, and loud outraged cries came from the porch—"Hey, what about him, how come he gets to go in there and blah, blah, blah." And the watchman said, straight-faced, without irony, "Oh, that's all right, he's a Glascock." So that caused great cheers and some jeers, and took a little of the pleasure of winning the prize away—being known far and wide as a Glascock, safe to spend the night in a girls' dorm. Anyway, at that time I didn't know any literary people at all, and I don't know any since, but though Miss Moore was relatively reclusive, she had come out for this thing, come up from Brooklyn. We ended up, entirely by accident (and it was, really), riding on the train together, back to New York. We talked about a lot of things, and not very much about literature. She was all interested in oranges, and I came from Florida and talked about oranges. I even arranged for her to get some special Valencia oranges from a small grove down there. She liked oranges very much, and we wrote some letters back and forth. Then, some years later, she was asked to introduce a young poet at the Museum of Modern Art. This was a series that they had where distinguished poets were introducing young nobodies, I guess. I was her young nobody on that program and gave my first sort of big poetry reading. Later, I was in the service and somewhat lost touch with Miss Moore, and I did what I gather is the unforgivable sin which was to write some prose, too, which put me in very bad repute. However, I've always been a great admirer of Miss Moore, and I'm very, very grateful to her for, in effect, my first public introduction. So when the first collection of poems came out, it seemed natural and appropriate to thank her for that by dedicating it to her. She had helped a great many other poets as well, and had not, it seemed anyway, received any particular response from them other than thank-you notes, and I thought really I ought to dedicate the book to her.

IB: Are you a Southern writer?

GG: Well, I have been so named a couple of times lately. And indeed, I did grow up in the South. I don't know. Obviously, I'm not an English writer, although I've written about Sir Walter Raleigh, or an urban Jewish writer, or a Western writer—but I don't know yet what all these regional things may mean or not mean.

IB: Frost was discovered in England. Where would you like to be discovered?

GG: What would I like to be doing when I'm discovered? I think I could get on just as well without. It's quite a different world, you know, than when Frost was around. Unless you're someone like Germaine Greer or Joe Namath, I don't know how you can ever be the same—put on a fright wig and an English accent. I don't know that there's any particular advantage to being discovered. They already have all this data on us in computer banks. What would be the advantage of more? It would be nice, yeah.

IB: At one time, in introducing Kay Boyle, you spoke of her influence on your writing.

GG: This again involves a story. When I was—I guess still in high school, very young, I spent a summer in Orlando doing not much of anything but reading wildly in the public library, and in the Albertson Public Library of Orlando, Florida—not famous for its great collections—somebody had collected a big long shelf of Kay Boyle books, which I stumbled upon just wandering in the stacks. That's sort of unusual for any public library. I don't know if it's still up to date, but they sure had everything up into the forties, and so I began reading them. I read everything they had. I read through these works, and they were tremendously exciting to me, the whole idea of what a short story could be, the poetry of the language, everything. In a sense, almost entirely by accident, Miss Boyle's work was my introduction, I suppose, to the modern writing. I came onto other things later in school, but it was a kind of heady, intoxicating summer of reading. I knew, of course, I'd known all along, that I wanted to write, in fact was writing things all along—very badly, but these books served as a tremendous jolt of energy and excitement and inspiration, and made a great difference, and made what would have been an otherwise boring summer, perhaps even a wasted summer, very purposeful, very exciting. The only disappointment was eventually—it takes awhile, because Miss Boyle's written a lot of books— eventually running out of Kay Boyle books to read.

IB: Did you hire researchers for the Raleigh novel?

GG: Yes and no. I think some very grand writers don't do any research at all. I spent years reading around, years on years, reading, backtracking, and still not covering all the ground. But at certain times I did, at very modest salaries I must tell you, get people to check certain things for me where I was unable to check myself. Here I particularly would like to thank a really brilliant lady, Mrs. Ruth Battestin, who happened to be in England twice during the period I was rewriting the book and is really good and really creative as a researcher. She was able to look up things and to check things that are referred to in books but had never really been checked out by other people, I think just passed on from book to book. She was a great help, and I think without her aid I shouldn't have been able to do it at all in the same way. On the basis of my questions and her really brilliant follow-through, a lot of this is submerged, hidden, some of it just results in a sentence or two, but it gives, I think, an unconscious authority to the writer. At least it makes the writer feel a little bit more at ease with his material. She was very helpful, as was her husband who joined us a little bit later and read through the manuscript, not primarily for literary things, but to see if I had committed any gross instant errors of fact. I was in Virginia, not able to get up to Princeton, and, though I knew pretty much what to look for, I had to have somebody to do it. But really, these people—the Battestins and a couple of Princeton boys—weren't making a living at it, barely cigarette money, so that it wasn't a grandiose sort of hiring of researchers or research staff or anything like that. Yes, I had some help. I took all the help I could get. I'm very grateful for it.

IB: Fellini dislikes the pretentious, but it's been said that he respects the ceremonial. Could this be said of you?

GG: I wish someone would say it. Yeah, that'd be really neat.

IB: I'll say it: George Garrett dislikes the pretentious, but . . .

GG: But he respects the preposterous. I see what you're talking
        about. No, I think that's great. The thing I like about Fellini,
        though, is that he's not afraid of the corny. He's my favorite
        motion picture director, but for me all those "ceremonial," and
        "pretentious" things don't worry me at all. I like it because he
        goes for the clown and the gags, and he builds his pictures
        on real, sort of gutsy Italian spaghetti notions of reality. He
        doesn't have this terrible dry quality that Antonioni, who
        wants to pretend he never had a plate of spaghetti in his life,
        does.

IB: What about *Frankenstein Meets the Spacemonster?*

GG: Yeah, it's our all-time success. It's considered by many motion-
        picture types to be one of the worst pictures ever made.

IB: Is it?

GG: I don't know. It's pretty interesting because the first time we
        saw it was in a drive-in theater, and they mixed up the reels,
        and it didn't make any difference at all. It could be like a very
        modern novel, just show it any way it comes. Those guys were
        wonderful to work with. They had an office—you had to buy a
        ticket to a forty-second street theater to get in their office. It
        was behind a door marked "Janitor," at the top of the stairs—
        something like the Portland Cement Company. We did all our
        correspondence by tape, and they sent me a serious tape, these
        two producers, on the subject of *Frankenstein Meets the Space
        Monster.*

IB: Well, you did it a little too seriously at first.

GG: No, at first we did it as a comedy, and they kept saying, "You
        can't have your horror and your comedy mixed. You gotta have

your horror in a horror picture, see." We went along. We had all the inside gags and named the characters after people we knew. Unfortunately, those two guys sold the picture to somebody else as a property, and the other people mixed up the two scripts, so that the farcical scenes from the earlier version mixed right in with the horror. In the scripts at typing time, we referred to Frankenstein all the time as Frank, and the fools did just like it in the script, "Oh my God, Frank is on the loose!"

IB: Henry Ford said, "History is bunk."

GG: Hum. Answer: "So they say." At least that's what Henry is supposed to have said. Then, I suppose if you're urgently involved in something as dramatically new and different as the mass-production automobile, it would be wiser not to think about the long lessons of history. Perhaps if Henry Ford had, he might have modified his invention to the extent that we wouldn't have to be backtracking now, making those monsters that run up and down the road half-safe and polluting the atmosphere. History might have given Mr. Ford a longer view, not necessarily causing him to wash his hands of technology and the grand prospects of mass production, but to consider some of the consequences right at the beginning, rather than the almost too late of now.

IB: Irving Stone distinguishes between the fictional novel and the biographical novel. Is there a difference?

GG: Well, I don't know. All of these categories, metaphors, games, seem to me useful insofar as they enable one to do something, to do work. They don't have to be rigid. I can't understand that distinction too well, except I presume what he's talking about is one of the things he does, which is write fiction about real people. I have some real people and some imaginary ones in this book. I'm not sure that the distinction leads very far, ex-

cept to help define the limits of what he intends to do. Mr.
Stone says he cannot write the fictional novel? Fine, fictional
novel, I presume, is anything made up. He feels he has to have
a basis in fact, more like a painter or sculptor who has to work
from a model? Right, many people work that way, whether
they call it, label it, name it, and justify it on the basis of distinctions or not. I hope that this particular book, *Death of the
Fox*, is kind of a mix of both. Since I presume, finally, the subject is the imagination in action anyway, I certainly envy Mr.
Irving Stone, indeed all the Irvings—even Irving Broughton—
their success and grandeur and the possibilities for furthering
their work, but I don't have to live with these arbitrary distinctions. Seriously, I never thought of this as an Irving Stone type
biographical novel. A fictional novel seems to me a redun-
dancy. A novel is a novel is a novel . . .

IB: How must the historical novelist *perform* to please the historian?

GG: This is a big problem, and I don't know yet, because at the
time I'm talking on this machine, the historians haven't given
me the once-over. Generally speaking, with a very few excep-
tions, they quite naturally take a different view of historical fiction. It's different. Its approach is different, and frequently
there's a certain disagreement about the facts. Now, if I were
doing this as a straight historical piece, I should be able to sort
out my case in areas, or doubtful areas, with many footnotes
and many persuasive arguments. Since I don't do this, I can
simply be a work of fiction, and I can be refuted; that is, the
expert historian can simply say, "Bullshit! That is not so! That
is not the case. He's wrong!" And there's no answer to that.
The historians do feel, I think, a little bit of possessiveness. It's
their turf. Why should these casual Johnny-come-latelies rush
in and interfere with the landscaped territory, turf, and history?

IB: Is it in fact possible to please the historian?

GG: Frankly, I don't think you can ever fully please the historians. Maybe a really good historian, an imaginary historian, doesn't feel threatened or possessive, and is at least interested, can sort of turn off the Inquisitor scholars long enough to let the imaginary aspects of a work of fiction work on him. In a sense, one has to be concerned about this, because historians can sort of do you in, and frequently do, as I've observed with perfectly fine historical works by writers. My solution, my way of handling this has been not to worry about that, since it's beyond worrying about, and to treat the historian, insofar as possible, as just another part of my imagined, imaginary reader, namely myself, reading the book. I think we could talk about this a long time, but it would be a bore. There are aspects of writing historical fiction that require a lot of choices anyway, and a kind of self-conscious rhetorical strategy, so you have to be conscious of this imagined and imaginary reader, but I don't say the historian is a separate reader.

IB: Do you think you'd like Sir Walter Raleigh?

GG: Well, I had very mixed feelings writing about him. Of course, I was writing from his point of view, so I had to be sympathetic. I doubt that we ever would have met. I might have been holding an arquebus or something in the background, but that's not really the same. About Garrett, there were some Garretts in Devon. One of them was a sea captain, and then there was another one that was referred to from time to time as "The Dreadful Pirate Garrett," but I never found out what he did . . . being a dreadful pirate was bad enough. It's like the abominable crime of buggery.

IB: There's some contrast between a black comedy motion picture and this lyric Raleigh novel.

GG: It has always seemed to me that we have, as writers or anything else, enough built-in inhibition and limitation without cultivating it. The obvious secret of success—if that's what interests you—is to establish a Brand X and to do that one thing.

IB: You haven't done that.

GG: Well, I don't want to, but I think that the actual inhibitions and natural inhibitions are strict enough to limit me, as to what subjects I've tried to extend, as far as I could, the extent of the range of what I can do. I hope I'll keep on doing this. The second novel I wrote (the English publisher really liked the first one), they got furious. They thought someone else had written it, and I was trying to help him out. Another thing, you probably do this yourself, I like to work on several things at one time, and in different stages. With the Raleigh novel, for example, it was difficult. You can't live four hundred years ago all the time. I was getting very involved in those things. It was a nice change of pace to do things like that Kim Novak book, or a black comedy.

IB: I heard they changed the street where you lived, and I was wondering, did this make you realize the transitoriness of existence?

GG: Well, not so much existence as fame. It really wasn't the street where I lived. It was the street where I worked . . . that doesn't rhyme. I have often passed the street where you worked. It was right near a place called the "Kissing Wall" in Rome, but this was at the American Academy, which was number five Via Angelo Massina, so named for one of the dead soldiers in Garibaldi's famous charge up the street to the Villa Pamphilli. I don't know if they made it, but there's a whole section of Rome absolutely full of gravestones and street names from that one fifteen-minute charge. It was like shooting fish in a barrel, really. Angelo Massina was one of the first ones, I guess. It's a big street, and they used to come down at night and cross out Angelo and put Giulietta.

IB: You're a laugher, and laughers, as one play has noted, are rare. Does this culture take the laugher seriously?

GG: No, but I assume they don't because they take the laughable position that we really ought to laugh starting at the top. I mean, if you take a real laugher like Agnew—now, we're taking him much too seriously. No, generally they don't take the laugher seriously, and there's great difficulty in communication, because the laugher has to laugh in order not to take things too seriously. People were really shocked, I remember, at Virginia, when Faulkner read those horrible scenes from *As I Lay Dying,* and kept breaking up laughing where they tried to set the guy's leg in concrete. I mean, people were very upset when he laughed at his own. There's a little passage where the policeman—Faulkner suddenly shifted point of view—smelled this family with a corpse coming before he could even see them on the road, see the buzzards and things. He laughed uproariously at that . . .

IB: You're known for your odd jobs. Are you bragging or complaining?

GG: I can't really do either one. It's just that we're not fit to do very much. I've been kicked out of the finest universities in the states of America. The list is amazing. I'm proud of that list. It's like a list of minor mountains, places I have been.

IB: Will reporting the extreme things as if they were average start one on the art of fiction, as Fitzgerald has said?

GG: I don't know why we couldn't treat the average things as if they were extreme things. Kafka, absolutely, absurdly, and very matter-of-factly said, "One morning Joseph K. woke up and discovered he'd been transformed into a gigantic Volkswagen." Well, I don't know. The world we're living in is so blatantly absurd, and the whole thing is one big Grand Canyon credibility gap. I don't think that there is an Indonesia. It's something made up for the six o'clock news. And it's really difficult for the fiction writer today. I suppose Fitzgerald was talking about understatement, and it has its place. You know, in California, they just had on the radio that they found a map of where this migrant foreman disposed of bodies. They found twenty so far, but the map indicates thirty-six. I don't think that's a good subject for fiction. I'll leave that for Truman Capote. Truman might be able to handle thirty-six. He hit it big with a couple of amateurs.

IB: What kind of man reads *Playboy?*

GG: Well, he's gotta be horny to start with and you know he's a real adherent, if you'll pardon the expression, of the *Playboy* philosophy. He's probably the guy that had acne real bad as a teenager, has aged along with Hefner. Gloria Steinem called their bluff and said they could be more mature and part of the revolution if they quit airbrushing, if they started to show the occasional beaver shot, and apparently it turns off college kids by the million. They don't want to see pubic hair. They want their pictures airbrushed.

IB: There, of all places . . .

GG: Right . . . I think it's a great mistake, probably, for publications to try to be "relevant." I read only this week *Vogue* magazine has hired Mirabella, whose purpose, she said, was to make it more relevant, and to have it not only fascinating but interesting, too.

IB: That's a great combination.

GG: I think most people's reactions will be the same as my wife's: "I'll never read *Vogue* magazine under the hairdryer again." If it gets rough, I mean, you gotta have someplace for an escape. Hefner puts real pubic hair in imaginary gardens, and you got trouble.

IB: That sounds a bit like Marianne Moore.

GG: I apologize to Miss Marianne Moore.

IB: Will reading *Playboy* make you foolish?

GG: It'll make you slap-happy for a very short while. But they have short memories, too. I've just been packing up my old books and my old copies of *Playboy*, and I came across all those wonderful things of Donna Michelle. There's a whole generation grown up that never heard of Donna Michelle.

IB: "She's round as a bell," you wrote in a poem.

GG: Yeah! And "Hey nonny ninny sing horney sing ho!" That's a very nice song. I'll never forget that one—classic of the literature.

IB: I understand you once made a medical footnote, George?

GG: True . . . but actually no. I confirmed the existence of a medical phenomenon. One day while I was teaching at Virginia I came out with a hideous, incredible, loathsome rash of some kind or another; first I thought probably it was something typically plebeian, proletarian, of the kind that I might get any time in Florida. You've been there. You have impetigo, ringworm, fungus, all these lovely things. But this was in Charlottesville, and it had been a long time since I had any little goody like that. My friendly doctor, who was honest anyway, said, "Beats me." And then I began to think it might even be all in my head. Everybody was psyching out in those days, working for Big Fred Bowers, and I thought maybe the thing was just another psycho thing, or perhaps the outward and visible sign of my inward and spiritual no-goodness. So anyway, they sent me across the street to the University Medical School to see a dermatologist, a youngish doctor who usually sighed and was soft-spoken. He jumped up and down when he saw me because

I proved something that he had read about in a footnote but had never seen an example of in dermatology, and he wanted to use me to fool his dermatology class. This odd sort of thing I had was a strep throat which did not manifest itself in fever or even a sore throat or any signs or tokens thereof, just in this weird rash. I came and sat proudly nude and bespeckled with rash in a little room, and they poked and looked and asked questions. I could answer yes or no but was not to volunteer any information.

Well, this was fine. I did that, and not one of his brilliant students asked to see the throat where, apparently, one look at least would have made it possible. And then they all went off to discuss this case in class, and one med student came bopping in, very late, wearing a dirty white jacket, obviously hung-over, red-eyed, and unshaven, and said, "Oh, God—have I got a hangover. I'm late for class. What are we supposed to do?" And I said, "Look at the throat," and he did and went off to class. And I'd like to think that he became a star and is a hung-over dermatologist somewhere bringing the light of science and wisdom to his patients. I have always thought that on an imaginative kind of basis, if a doctor is dedicated to health, if his ideal is good health, then it must be inevitable that the doctor develops a contempt for the unhealthy, that is, lack of health. That's his enemy. His patients all have something disgusting and contemptible about them, just by being sick. To conclude the story then, about imagination, truth, et cetera.

This hypothesis of mine was at any rate confirmed by my final conversation with the great dermatologist. He thanked me for participating in his little experiment, not knowing, by the way, that I had come to the comfort of the drunken bum of the class, and gave me some medicine and then attempted to give me some advice. The advice was a little difficult to follow, because he suggested various things that might be therapeutic, but then again might be bad for me—he didn't know. In point of fact, what he said was, "The summer's coming on, sun-bathing may be wonderful for this condition and it'll all go away; and on the other hand it may aggravate it and make it worse than ever. Bathing in the sea may be just the ticket to solve your little problem here, on the other hand it may make it horrible beyond belief. It's going to have to be—ho ho—a system of trial and error, you see. You'll have to try things and see what happens." Well, I'll have to admit that the prospect of trying and losing, et cetera, dismayed me a bit. I wasn't caught up in the scientific constructions that Berenson talks about. I really thought maybe the doctor could give me better advice than that. So, when he concluded his description of things with I might as well flip a coin, I said something like (as nicely as possible), "You don't know a hell of a lot about this, do you, Doctor?" There was a pause, and he smiled very sweetly—a kind of sweet smile and a smirk combined—and looked right at me and said, "No, that's true, but I don't *have* it, do I?" End of conversation. And I somehow feel that's what all our doctors must feel, even if they don't articulate it, about us when we come drag-assing in with our ailments. We should keep ourselves far removed from the idea of perfect health and eternal life everlasting.

IB: Do you think the jocks will inherit the earth?

GG: The jocks?!! It will be sort of noisy if they do. I don't know what's happening to jocks these days; you've got these guys writing the real inside story of the locker room in baseball, football . . . pretty soon we'll know what happened on that Ping-Pong tour, behind the scenes. I don't think we should worry too much about the jocks. My old jock friend, Bill Robinson, down in Florida was telling me about going to a track meet. All the guys have long hair now, and at a distance they looked like really crazy, freaked-out kids, but he walked up and down the track and the first thing that struck him was how much more uptight the contemporary long-haired jock is than the jock of his age, who would go around laughing and scratching between races. That's too bad. We're probably getting a different class of jock. Now you've got upper-class people running the four-minute mile. Where all this leads I don't know.

It's a problem. They're writing books while they're running the mile relay.

IB: George Plimpton has put a lot of would-be jock writers out of business.

GG: Yes, he has. He's tried to cover all the bases, as they say. He's kind of my favorite Walter Mitty character of our times. Better he should be putting jocks out of business than writers, now, don't you think?

IB: Do you think we'll ever have another Renaissance man?

GG: (Laughs.) This question derives naturally from discussion of Plimpton? He's as rich as a Renaissance man. Maybe Joe Namath! No, I don't really think that, white shoes or not. I think we worry too much about the Renaissance men. Actually they had their problems, too.

IB: What were their problems?

GG: Oh . . . some of the usual ones, health, money, sex, food, and in those days, when you lost, you lost your head, too, literally, which made it a little more serious game. I mean, all you lose now is everything you own, and you end up on welfare. That's not so bad. I've been there.

IB: Are writers good spellers? Are you a good speller?

GG: I used to be. There are certain words that I lapse. Perhaps it's the onset of senility. But the farther I get away from the spelling bees that we used to have in the Delaney Street Grammar School, the worse it gets. Also, my children have taken all my portable size dictionaries away, and if I want to check something out, I have only the Random House Dictionary, which is like lifting a set of bar bells. When there is a word that I've forgotten, I just go along with whatever the current form is.

Some writers are very good spellers though. I'm impressed. Of course, you can't really tell, because what we see—let's just study the handwritten manuscript—is, after all, the printed virgin . . . ver . . . (Laughs.) I'll take that back . . . version . . .

IB: It was just a case of misspelling.

GG: That's a good title. I'd like to pause . . . I'd like to copyright that title, *The Printed Virgin.* But what we see is the printed version. And, I do think from that we conclude, with some authority, that if most of the words are spelled correctly in a book, the publishing house has a good speller on the staff somewhere. But a good many of them evidently don't. Of course, another thing to do is only use words you know how to spell.

IB: Simenon says he uses, I think, less than a thousand different words in his writing. What do you think about that? You use a large vocabulary in your historical novels.

GG: Well, I thought that they ought to be sprinkled through, like a little parsley, you know. There was a thing about Elizabethans, they loved big words, and some of them had very big mouths, and loved to express themselves that way. I'm interested that you say that about Simenon because he's wonderful in the economy with which he sketches scenes and moves things in and out. You can learn a lot from him. I would presume that the range of vocabulary of a story should, in some way, approximate the range of the subject and should work with the subject and the scope of consciousness of the characters, and that sort of thing. I carefully avoid characters with vocabularies superior to my own, so that I won't have to spend hours going through the dictionary.

IB: Talk about maintaining the momentum of a long book.

GG: In the old days—back in the 1960s—there was always the possibility of getting some speed and that would help, but finally in the late sixties, I was getting pretty addicted to that shit, and so I had to quit. And now, the momentum has to be artifically aroused by being threatened by law suits by the publisher. That got me to finish *The Succession.* I was working away, minding my own business, and all of a sudden I got a letter from Doubleday saying, "We're going to sue your ass off if you don't get this in right away." I had to get a lawyer and discuss it and everything.

IB: Do you use dreams in your work?

GG: Sometimes. I'm not heavily into it. The most obvious example is where I just say, "This is a dream that I had," and it really happened. That's in the story "A Wreath for Garibaldi." I tend to dream conventional anxiety dreams. I used to dream in school that I had done my term paper. I would sleep on merrily in the morning, and it would be horror when I realized I only dreamed that I had done it. In "A Wreath for Garibaldi" I literally dreamed that I got up and put a wreath on Garibaldi's grave. The irony of that dream was that I couldn't find the tombstone. I dreamed myself walking around the park there and looking to lay my wreath down, and I couldn't find the tomb, and I realized that someone had mounds of flowers all over it—you couldn't see it.

IB: Any recurring theme to your dreams?

GG: Besides Christie Brinkley? No, I can't get her in my dreams. "Tonight, Christie, it's you and me—on a desert island in the Pacific." Then I go to sleep and dream I'm back in the army, shining my shoes. The only persistent theme is that they're not symbolic. I don't know how to explain this. I just haven't been to the right psychiatrist. My dreams are exactly what they're about. If it's about anxiety, in the dream I'm very anxious. If it's about sex, in the dream I have sex or don't get it, et cetera. I think my dreams have more to do with digestion than anything else. If I could just find the right food . . .

IB: What was the hardest thing about writing *The Succession?*

GG: Figuring out a structure for it. I knew it was going to be in parts. There would be all these different characters. At some point I realized it would be all these different characters, in different years, and they wouldn't know each other. But, since they're all in the past, they would be simultaneous for the reader now. Right? Then I had a problem. I had the messenger that opens the book up, and the way it is now, I keep coming back to him, and he keeps riding, riding, riding. It takes him the entire book to get to London. But, originally, I had him all in one block like everybody else, and nothing seemed to relate too well. All of a sudden, I got the idea that the messenger could be broken up and be in between each of these chapters, and he would still be trying to get to London with this news from way back in 1560. Also, I thought I'd put one other Nabokovian thing in there which is that much later in the story, in 1603, there's a guy who rides north to Scotland with news of the death of Elizabeth, and there's some indication that these two guys pass each other—it's very slight, but it's there.

IB: What are the pitfalls about writing a long book?

GG: Well, you're not making any money while you're doing it. You're spending all your time doing it, and all your buddies are writing skinny books and getting rich and famous. The other thing is if you're writing a long book you know nobody's ever going to read the whole thing. The minimalists are very elegant, even when they write about proletarian things. Basically, the secret of Anne Beattie, Raymond Carver, and Richard Ford is that their minimalism, even when they're writing about blue collar people, is very elegant and elitist; and they consider you like a guy sitting there with a huge serving of meat and potatoes

and pizza if you're writing a big book. You're disgusting to
them. So, all the time you're writing it, you're thinking, "Well,
so I'm disgusting to all the minimalists. So fucking what?"
After I finished my book I was exhausted, and I picked up
Wilfred Sheed's essays, and in one of them he said something
that goes like this: "It makes no sense to spend ten years writing a book that will last no more than one." Well, in point of
fact, that's true. The season for any book except Stephen King's
is less than a year. But that's not really the life of a book, it's the
commercial life of a book. Books live on in libraries. Someday
in some dusty place—this is an exciting idea for my books—
somebody will reach up and find it. It's there until the acid-
rich paper used by crummy American publishers turns it to
ashes, which may happen, too. I'm not talking about posterity.
I don't know about that.

IB: David Slavitt calls you a Christian novelist. Does that mean
      your books will be saved?

GG: I think he means I'm not Jewish. He wants his friends to know
      that I don't know what he means by that. Everybody's got to be
      something, right?
          I've been in two anthologies as a black writer. There was a
      story I wrote once about a knife fight in high school, and the
      story was something that took place in my presence in Or-
      lando, Florida, when I was in junior high school. Now, I didn't
      mention race at all in that story. For one thing, it happened
      during the period when schools were segregated. It didn't
      make sense for me to mention that those kids were white be-
      cause they were. Or, as is often the case with something that
      really happened, I may have been sketchy with some of the de-
      tails. I may have assumed that readers knew more than what I
      was saying. The only way you could conclude that the people
      in that story were black was that they went to public schools,
      which everyone did for a long time; that they fought with
      knives; and that they talked to each other crudely in Southern
      dialect, right? That's it. But two black guys editing an an-

thology in the sixties of contemporary black writing wrote to me. They were from Chicago and didn't know much about the South. And I didn't realize until I saw the anthology that everyone in it was black. They just said, "We've seen your story. We think it's really good. We'd like to use it in our anthology." So I said, "Terrific. It's yours." Then another black anthology that originated in Canada—*What's Happenin' Baby?*—just picked it up directly from the other anthology.

IB: Where does *Poison Pen* fit in, if you'll pardon the expression?

GG: Irv, a lot of people have asked that question, starting with my family and my New York publishers. Fortunately, I don't have to be a critic of my own work. But since there isn't any other critic of my work around, that I know of (except Richard Dillard, who has just written a book for University of Southern Carolina Press titled *Understanding George Garrett,* which he calls "Ugg" as in U.G.G.). I have thought of this: It's relationship to the heavier, more serious novels is like a satyr play in Greek drama where between a couple of those tragedies they used to have a satyr play in which people came out and did slapstick and cleansed the palate, right? Similarly, Japanese Noh drama—monkey plays, where people would come racing back in monkey suits—did exactly the same thing. This was again a cleansing of being too serious and too self-indulgent. That's part of it. I was doing these things parallel. *Poison Pen* is like *The Succession* and even like *Death of the Fox* a little bit in its documentary quality—there are all kinds of documents in there—and its epistolary quality. It also might represent a somewhat belated response to the twentieth century by somebody whose time and pressures have forced him to live a lot of time in the sixteenth century. In other words, every once in a while I had to surface and look around, and I would see a really fucked up world which is reflected in *Poison Pen.* Plus, I think there's some element of truth in it. That is, a lot of people that I respect—I've noticed this more since I was doing this—are disturbed about the qualities of American life that are totally bogus, or in the old-fashioned view are bogus, because they only exist as publicity. The theme of the book is given to Susan toward the end. She says, "Public life is an illusion . . . only private life is real." I guess that's what it's about. This guy's a little bit like Terry Southern's *Magic Christian,* in that respect, going around thinking up tricks and insulting people.

IB: Did you ever get so geared to one of the longer projects that you felt the flavor of it sneak into your other writing?

GG: Once in a while. You have to watch that. You don't really want to be writing in a style that's supposed to be reminiscent of the sixteenth century, and all of a sudden have something creep into your story about two GIs and Linz, Austria. That would fuck everything up. That's another reason for a safety valve to break out of the mind set. You have to kind of hypnotise yourself to do this historical stuff.

IB: Meaning?

GG: For the time you're doing it, you have to believe you're really there and that it matters, it counts, and that you don't know how it's going to turn out and all this other stuff. And that way leads to madness if you carry it over to your life. So as mad as *Poison Pen* is, I did leave out a few things, including "Jane Amour, Space Nurse."

IB: What did Christie Brinkley say when she saw *Poison Pen?*

GG: I don't know what she said. I know that she got a copy of it, because a woman novelist from Greensboro, North Carolina, was sharing a duplex—she had one-half of it, and Christie Brinkley and Billy Joel had the other. But I think this woman chickened out and got the doorman to slip it to her. So, Christie Brinkley must think because of this that I'm totally bananas. I would like to persuade her otherwise, but I don't want to talk to Billy Joel about any of it. He doesn't look like a very friendly guy—probably yells at the help, don't you think? But surely she will tire of him eventually, by which time I'll be 82.

IB: Did you lose any friends or gain any friends due to *Poison Pen?*

GG: I don't think either one. I got only one letter from someone who felt he had been maligned, and I was able to reassure him by telling him exactly what it said. Then I got a lot of letters from poets who were left out of the insult list. Many of them said, "I thought you were my friend, and I'm not in there." And I thought they would rather not be in there, but that's not true. I came to the conclusion that if you're a poet in America today, you want to be on any list, no matter what it is.

IB: Anything else we've overlooked?

GG: I don't know. One thing, maybe. John Ciardi's concept of the unimportant poem was an influence on *Poison Pen.* I was really hung up with the idea of how you maintain high and pretentious grandeur at all times, when I heard Ciardi say, years ago, "I'm trying to write unimportant poems." I figured out what he was trying to say, which is that you don't have to be important all the time.

URSULA K. LE GUIN

Ursula Le Guin was born in 1929 in Berkeley, California, the daughter of Theodora Kroeber, a writer, and Alfred L. Kroeber, an anthropologist. She graduated from Radcliffe College and received her M.A. from Columbia University.

Author of a wide range of material, her work includes novels, short stories, poems, and books for young readers. Her fifteen novels include *Always Coming Home,* a classic work in which she manages to imagine a whole culture in a most ambitious way—down to creating music for the culture. An earlier novel, *The Left Hand of Darkness,* was widely received in the sixties. She has written over sixty short stories, which are collected in three volumes; the latest is *The Compass Rose.* She has published four volumes of poetry, including *Wild Oats and Fireweed,* three books of criticism, and ten books for young readers including *Catwings* and *Catwings Return.* Ms. Le Guin has also been recorded reading her work.

The Le Guin honors are many including: a Newberry Medal; a Boston Globe-Hornbook Award; the Prix Lectures-Jeunesse (Paris); a Gandalf Award; and Hugos for *Buffalo Gals, The Dispossessed,* "The Word for World is Forest," "The Ones Who Walk Far Away from Omelas," and *The Left Hand of Darkness;* as well as three Nebulas for "The Day before the Revolution," *The Dispossessed,* and *The Left Hand of Darkness.* In 1972 she received the National Book Award for *The Farthest Shore* and in 1986 a Janet Heidinger Kafka Award for *Always Coming Home.*

As the sun dapped through the window like a continuous bolt from a ray gun, Ursula Le Guin manipulated a carved pipe, shaking and gesturing with it. We pulled the drapes over the insistent sun and began the interview.

1974

IRV BROUGHTON: When did you first feel confident about your writing?

URSULA LE GUIN: I tried to publish from age nineteen on, rather lackadaisically and timidly. I was urged by my father into publishing some of my early poetry; he acted as my agent. He was then about eighty and leading a full life as an anthropologist. He said, "It's time you got something published; you're just writing for yourself, really." But it did become a necessity to me to publish. I began to realize that I must publish, I must communicate if I call myself an artist. When I was about twenty-six or twenty-seven, then I really made an effort to get published. But up to then my stuff wasn't terribly good, and I really wasn't eager to publish it.

IB: Writing is, for many, a process.

UL: Writing is simply a major part of the way I live . . . like having kids or being a member of a family or cooking meals. It's one of the things I do, one of the important things I do. But of course one tries to do it well, and since it's an act of communication, a public act, one is obliged to try to do it well because other people are involved in it. After all, the readers—you owe them an obligation.

IB: What about personal growth?

UL: Well, I started out writing poetry, then I wrote short stories, then I wrote novels—that's all part of growth. Novelists, you know, don't usually start until rather late. Some of them didn't start writing until they're forty or over. And I have also learned something, thank God! The only excuse for getting older is that you do keep learning.

IB: What do you think about the hacks in the field?

UL: Kill . . . kill . . . I don't like hacks. I don't like hack musicians, I don't like hack painters, and I don't like hack writers. I do take art seriously and I don't like people using it cynically. It really makes me very mad. Very mad indeed.

IB: Cynically?

UL: Yes, to make money out of it, to make fame out of it—using it as a device for their profit. Now very great writers do this, of course—Dickens used his art in that sense for fame and fortune. But to use it and *not try to make it good*, that's hacking and that's what I hate.

IB: What about writing as self-expression, pleasure? People are entitled to that, are they not?

UL: People are entitled to do absolutely anything, so long as it doesn't do harm to others. To write, paint, or play the fiddle— for one's own pleasure is a lovely thing, a truly human act. The difference between the amateur and the artist is one of degree, not of kind. It is, however, a very great difference. The difference between the amateur and the "professional" is one of kind, not of degree: it is an economic difference—the professional gets paid. That does not, however, make him an artist. It may make him a hack.

IB: Stanley Hyman did a tribute to his late wife Shirley Jackson and noted how surprised people were that the author of disturbing and grim fiction should be a wife and mother and an apparently happy one.

UL: Being a wife and mother is supposed to be a consuming occupation, therefore you couldn't do anything else. And then the fact that Shirley Jackson wrote the kind of books she did. I suppose people think: I wonder if she strangled her children.

IB: How can the science fiction writer be believed today?

UL: It may be easier to believe science fiction writers than it is to believe normal fiction writers, because science fiction can reflect this incredible, exorbitant world we live in much more faithfully than a novel which tries to pretend that the old social norms still exist, or that what happens in *Peyton Place* really matters. For example, one of the American science fiction writers I admire most is Philip K. Dick, and Philip K. Dick's world involves immense tracts of pure insanity. It's a world which is always in danger of falling to pieces. It is an accurate picture of what is going on in a lot of people's heads and how the world actually does affect us—this weird, disjointed, unexpected world we're living in now. Well now, Phil Dick reflects that by using a sane, matter-of-fact prose to describe the completely insane things that happen in his novels. It is a way of mirroring reality. *Peyton Place* is a fine trivial example of non-realism. What reality is that reflecting? Nothing. A literary pseudo-reality where everybody goes to bed all the time with each other. It doesn't exist, you know; it has no relevance. It is escapism. Whereas serious science fiction is a modern literary device for handling this insane world we live in.

IB: A literary device?

UL: Yes, a tool fitted to the job. Like the right size of screwdriver.

IB: You consider yourself a feminist?

UL: Yes, I have all my life. A more or less unconscious one until 1974.

IB: How do you mean that?

UL: Well, in sixty-seven or sixty-eight there was no feminist movement. It died as a movement after the First World War. My feminism before the women's movement started consisted simply of the fact that I wasn't going to let any men put me down because I wasn't a man.

IB: Your book *The Left Hand of Darkness* was used a lot by the women's movement.

UL: It still is. Women's studies groups often read it as a textbook in a course or as a discussion subject for a group. Because one of the things I was trying to do in the book was to get away from stereotyped roles of manhood and womanhood. I did so by the "simple" trick of making the characters both men and women.

IB: I understand your initials got you in trouble.

UL: My agent sent *Playboy* a story before I was a well-known writer—as "U. K. Le Guin." They accepted the story, contracted for it, paid me for it, and then she told them that my name was Ursula K. Le Guin. So they wrote me a letter asking to use my first two initials only—I believe this is a direct quote—"Because many of our readers are frightened of stories by women." And I felt somewhat bound by the fact that my agent and I had in a sense deceived them; they had a right to continue our deception. I came to them as U. K.; they could present me to their readers as U. K. So I said, "Sure." Since then I have felt that, had the women's movement been going then, I don't think I could have done that in conscience. I would have realized that I was copping out. But at the time I thought it was funny. And I wrote them—you know in *Playboy* they have a little blurb about the writers in it—and they sent me this form to fill out. They wanted to know my hobbies, my interests, and so on. Well, anything I said would give away the fact that I was the wrong sex. So I wrote for them across this whole space—"The stories of U. K. Le Guin are not written by U. K. Le Guin but by another person of the same name," and they printed that. I gave them an out.

IB: The women's movement has been helpful to you?

UL: It could help me help other people. I've never felt that I much needed help, because I had an extremely good start in life from my parents who simply weren't sexist. They weren't prejudiced for boys and against girls or the other way around either. They just set us all off on equal footing—sons and daughter. And so I have been able to hack it without worrying about it very much. But a lot of other people aren't. A lot of women, particularly, are hassled. They need all the help they can get, because they've been set off on the wrong foot and have to pretend to be something they aren't. And here's where you get the solidarity, as in any movement—any even slightly revolutionary movement. And then to allow myself to come out as "U. K. Le Guin" was letting them down, letting the others down; therefore, I feel bad about it now. And doubt I would have done it had my consciousness been raised a little bit.

IB: For a long time it was said that science fiction was going to do in the psychological novel.

UL: There are very few writers capable of writing psychological novels in any field of fiction. I don't know quite what you mean by psychological novels. You mean one where the characters have real emotions? Yes. Oh, it's being done in science fiction—occasionally.

IB: You've criticized science fiction for not being imaginative in terms of the social movements.

UL: In terms of society. The man-woman thing's a perfect example of it. In most science fiction until quite recently, women either didn't exist, or if they existed, they were these little stereotyped figures that squeaked. Or conceivably, the very ultimate possibility, there was an elderly woman scientist that never married and wore glasses. And that was fifty-three percent of humanity, represented either by absence or by these few stock figures. Well, this is not looking at the world as it is and society as it is. Then when we get into social imagination, we've thought up a lot of fancy hardware in science fiction but have not been imaginative about society. The society usually presented in stock classic science fiction is an extrapolation of free enterprise capitalism, or an extrapolation of the British Empire of the 1880s, and nothing further. There's no Marxism; often there's not even any democracy. This is American science fiction I'm talking about, by the way, not science fiction from the rest of the world. American imagination thinking about getting to another world. When they get there, they find a feudal society, they find an intergalactic empire exactly like the British Empire, or they find the Rotary Club. There's a current reaction going on against the squeaking female carried off by the monster, saying "Oh captain, save me." Some of us are using rather extraordinarily courageous, independent women characters.

IB: In the science fiction story isn't it difficult to have to set up a whole world and then people it? There's an inherent difficulty, it seems, in setting that great construct up and then making human people.

UL: Well, you may not be setting up a whole world. You may very well be using this one a few years in the future, but, yes, it's very difficult to write a real novel which is also science fiction. It's what I try to do, and I am aware of the difficulties. In science fiction writing, if your interest is technological, then your hardware's going to occupy so much space, you're going to be spending so much time on that, and perhaps on the social and political system, that it's hard to develop your people as well. Whatever your science fiction element is, it's always going to be rubbing elbows with the novelistic parts of it, and perhaps crowding it to the side so that there's a sort of combat going on within. It's hard to do, but I do think it's worth doing. I think some of the most interesting novels of the 1960s have been science fiction novels. And most of the least interesting novels of the 1960s have been non-science fiction novels.

IB: Why would you say that?

UL: What, the latter part of my statement? People talk about "the novel is dead"; well, it seems to me they're talking about what we in science fiction call the "mainstream novel," which does seem to be in a poverty-stricken condition at the moment.

IB: Have you ever written diaries or anything like that?

UL: I keep a journal—I think most writers do—where you write down sometimes thoughts, sometimes ideas, sometimes what's going through your mind. And when you'd like to write a letter to the newspaper—but it's too much trouble, you write it down, get rid of it.

IB: I heard a professor say female writers were, as a rule, more concerned with description than men.

UL: I don't think that's true. It's interesting that in a writing workshop or contest where authorship is concealed nobody can usually tell whether a woman or man wrote the story.

IB: C. S. Lewis talks about how science fiction separates from the ranks of the novel and sometimes becomes a new form which he refers to as a pseudo-history. He feels that there's the same quality of texture and so on—broad general movements and tones.

UL: That's very nice. That isn't true of all science fiction, but there's Cordwainer Smith with his future history, which was clearly worked out on paper and in his mind. He only gives you a glance of it in each story, but you get this exciting sense of reading a history of a people you never knew about, and it gives you this sort of resonance which a good history book does. The sense of space and time being large which is very exciting and beautiful.

IB: Is that what you like about science fiction?

UL: That's one of the things I like, yes. The expansion, the opening doors, instead of being shut in a small closed room. You're in a room with all the doors open and you can see the sky.

IB: Which do you think science fiction is more important in defining: the infiniteness or the finiteness of the universe?

UL: I don't know. I think I could argue both. I think one of the most interesting things science fiction has done and is doing, in Stanislaw Lem for instance, is showing the infiniteness of the universe and the fact that we are not going to be able to understand everything—that we cannot assume that our mind is of the same potential size as the universe. Lem thinks it's not. He thinks that we will not be able to understand everything no matter how long we go on with thinking and using signs. And he gives to me a most exhilarating picture of a fairly incomprehensible universe but a very beautiful one, which of course is what we all are faced with right here and now. Terrifying, but also beautiful.

IB: How much do you have to know about science to write science fiction?

UL: It is good to know something about at least one field, so that you know how scientists think and how science is done, if you're going to have any science or even any pseudo-science in your stories. But there is a requirement: that a science fiction writer be *interested* in science. He may hate it; I think Ray Bradbury hates it. I know he hates technology, and I rather think he hates science. But he's interested in it. It's got down into his subconscious and it comes up in the form of horrors and monsters. But he takes it seriously. My main criticism of much modern fiction is that it doesn't involve science and technology, socially and in personal terms; in other words, it excludes most of the actual, physical world we live in, and the relationships of human beings to their world. By concentrating exclusively on people it becomes irrelevant to people. Whereas good science fiction includes us in the universe.

IB: Do science fiction fans get a kick out of finding flaws in science fiction writers' logic?

UL: Yes, the logic and the details, oh yes. If you make a mistake, you're going to get letters about it.

IB: Has this happened to you?

UL: It would have happened to me—now let me put in a good word for *Playboy* here. In the story that *Playboy* published, I had made a bad mistake in my genetics. *Playboy* apparently sent it to a genetics expert, because it had to do with cloning, and he or she caught this thing. And there wasn't time for me to rewrite the sentence, so they rewrote it and airmailed it to me and said, "Is this all right?" I said, "Yes, yes, of course, thank you!" That was neat. I appreciated that, because I would have got some angry geneticists on the telephone or something. "You got your X and Y's mixed up, kid!"

IB: What do you think of the confessional kind of writing?

UL: I haven't read much of it because it is not my meat. The ego that fills the universe is very boring, really. The novels of the great writers are not confessional. They are deeply *personal*—profoundly individual.

IB: Do science fiction writers worry about being "scooped" by the morning papers?

319

UL: Yes, we worry, and unless one is very knowledgeable in some field, one is scooped. I wrote a book, *The Lathe of Heaven*, which involved sleep and dream research. Well, I was up on my sleep and dream research, fine. I loved to read about that stuff and I was well educated in it when I wrote the book. But I had a machine in the book called the "Augmentor" which had a kind of feedback effect to the brain, which augmented certain things the brain was doing in sleep. Then I found out the Russians and the Israelis had been using it for seven years already when I wrote the book, so I had to improve my Augmentor a little bit.

IB: Isn't it a dangerous occupation, that places everything on words?

UL: Yeah, it's a mug's game.

IB: It seems like there's at times a self-indulgence in some science fiction writing that's a little difficult to appreciate.

UL: You mean the wish-fulfillment type thing where you get the hero defending us from the alien fleet single-handed? Sure. And that's part of this hangover from the pulp days. It's also because an awful lot of teenage boys read science fiction. I think what a lot of the writers don't realize is that a lot of teenage girls do too. Those wish-fulfillment sort of things tend to be very male-oriented, and it turns the girls off a lot. I ceased to read science fiction partly for that reason—because I was tired of bureaucratic heroes.

IB: C. S. Lewis, referring to science fiction, once said, "If you have a religion, it must be cosmic; therefore, it seems odd to me that this genre was so late in arriving"—at the theological area.

UL: I am an atheist and I always have been; I have a great deal of trouble with C. S. Lewis, with the way his mind works. I don't really know what he's talking about. I admire the first book of his trilogy, as a novel. He was one of the first writers to invent alien creatures who were truly alien and truly sympathetic. I think those Martians of his are magnificent. And the second two books of his trilogy I consider an abomination, because he started preaching. I do not like to preach, or be preached at.

IB: What qualities of science do you find in yourself? Any?

UL: If I have any relation to the scientific temperament, it's probably some genetic inheritance from my father. I like solid facts and solid artifacts. I like to know about things, where they came from and what they are.

IB: He was in anthropology? What did he do?

UL: He was a professor at the University of California, a cultural anthropologist. He worked in Peru and in California and wrote some standard texts.

IB: Did you travel with him?

UL: No, he was in his fifties when I was born, and his traveling was mostly earlier. But we had Indian friends who would come and stay and many anthropologists circulating around, so I was fairly well plunged into anthropological life in that sense.

IB: How does this come out in your writing?

UL: Well, I think in the sense I just said. I'm interested in other cultures. I have this great advantage of not being brought up ethnocentric, of not being culture-bound. Of course, we're all culture-bound in that we grow up in one culture. But I grew up amongst people who spent their life thinking about other cultures and about the way others thought—different races, different people. I thought this was the way everybody was. The world came as kind of a shock when I realized everybody wasn't an anthropologist or an Indian and wasn't interested in facts and artifacts and the structure of society. All this shows up very clearly in my books. My father did the real thing; I make it up.

IB: Would you agree with Isak Dinesen's idea, "All sorrows can be borne if you put them in a story"?

UL: That's nice, and I like Isak Dinesen. Yes, but it is kind of a tautology, because if you can put them in a story, it means you're already bearing them. You are bearing them as a woman bears her child.

1988

IB: You spoke years ago of being in awe of poetry? Are you still in awe of poetry?

UL: Sure. I started out writing poetry. I've always written poetry. My awe of it is related to the awe I feel for music. Poetry partakes more directly of the irrational than most prose. It's uncanny. It's taken me a long time to find my voice as a poet. I feel I'm still and always will be trying to find it more clearly.

IB: What does your poetry owe your science fiction writing or vice versa?

UL: I don't know. I suppose one of the most useful things about writing serious science fiction or fantasy—repeat, if you're taking it seriously—is a kind of discipline. Things have got to be coherent if you're inventing a world, whether in science fiction terms or in fantasy terms. It's got to hang together. You're not relying upon the coherence of the everyday world to hold your invented world together, you have to do it yourself, and so this gives one a certain discipline in making sure everything does hang together in whatever it is you're writing.

IB: There seems to be a strong feminine thread in your poetry. It comes out in your novels, but also in your poetry. Do you think a poem is an extra good vehicle for that?

UL: I'm leery of saying that one chooses to express something in such and such a form because then you get into this thing of writing as self-expression which is a very low form of writing. I find myself tongue-tied, (as you can see) if you talk about "expressing"—as if one were an orange and the juice was being squeezed out. As I have increasingly found my voice as a woman, thanks to feminism and feminist theory and criticism and feminine solidarity during the last ten to fifteen years, as I've been able to speak less as a kind of genderless object in the male mode and more directly as a woman and a woman writer, a lot of it has come out as poetry. It is one of the things that made me feel my poetry really grew up: I could write from the body out.

IB: Has feminism affected your self-concept?

UL: Yes, it's given me more confidence to be a woman. It has helped women be women and not just reflections of men, particularly, as Virginia Woolfe said, "magnifying reflections" of men. And it's not easy on either women or men to have this new kind of consciousness, because men feel something is being taken from them, and that's true. When women refuse or cease to serve as "magnifying mirrors," men have to find their own self-image. So a lot of people have felt kind of frightened and lonely in the process of this—what you might call—gentle revolution.

IB: Your mother influenced you, didn't she?

UL: What the literary influence was, God knows. She started writing long after I did, but she was successful well before I was, so it was interesting catching up to each other. Women are often interested that a woman who had four children and was a classic housewife could start writing in her fifties and become a genuinely good artist and successful writer.

IB: Did you compare notes?

UL: She saw my work mostly when it was pretty near finished, because I don't show first drafts. She was the other kind of writer—she would show things that weren't finished yet and say "What shall I do? What shall I do?" and we would sit around and talk. Actually, what you do with that type of writer is let them talk about it until they see where they want to go next. And my mother sometimes did that. She had some very hard books to write. *Ishi* was terribly hard.

IB: Anything you learned from her?

UL: No. She was fifty—she was thirty when I was born—so I was finding my own way by then.

IB: How did it feel when she came to you to show you something?

UL: Oh, it was lovely. I mean, here we were doing the same thing, fighting the same difficult word battle and able to talk shop with each other. It was absolutely lovely.

IB: Do you ever second-guess an ending of a book?

UL: If you mean you think you know where a book's going and it isn't going there, it has happened. I think generally one learns fairly early as a novelist, particularly as a novelist because a novel is a commitment of a month or years to a job, that you've got to know the general direction of your work. If you start off without knowing where it's going, or with a total mistake, you're likely to waste several weeks or months and find yourself at a dead end, because it really had no direction in the first place. But one can make a mistake. My book *The Eye of the Heron* is a fairly simple science fiction story, a little planet upon which there are two colonies—one a bunch of pacifists and the other a very patriarchal and macho culture—a thought experiment. OK, we've got these aggressive people and these Ghandian pacifists, and both of them think that their way is right. Both of them think that they know what they're doing. All that seems very straightforward. What I didn't know when I planned out the book was that the hero was going to have to be killed by the middle of the book, and that he wasn't the hero, that the hero was actually a girl from the aggressive culture, only she isn't really a hero either. So the writing would go along for a while and then stop and I would be stuck. "What on earth? What's wrong? It isn't going right." And then I would have to painfully figure out what had to happen. And it really was painful that I had to kill Lev off, that he was insisting upon getting himself killed. It's a hard thing to do to a nice young hero, to a person who is, after all, a part of yourself. That is the one case I can think of where the book knew where it was going, and I was unable to accept it.

IB: Ever run into a hero or character you genuinely don't like?

UL: There's a voice character, a viewpoint character, in *The Word for World is Forest* whose name is Davidson. He was a pretty terrifying voice for me to write because he's a highly aggressive, sadistic man. But then, he is part of me, obviously. I wrote him and accept him as part of myself.

IB: How do you find yourself dealing with that?

UL: I just let him talk. You're kind of inside his head and essentially you're listening to his thought so it was kind of like, "OK. That's how Davidson thinks."

IB: You're a political being.

UL: Aren't we all? I deny that I'm more political than anyone else. I happen to practice an art which lends itself to being clearly political—writing, an art which cannot hide its political grounds the way a nonverbal art can. I have to *defend* my politics more than a dancer might, for instance, or a composer.

IB: We live in a world of massive forces. Do you draw on these?

UL: Well, of course. To pretend that writing could be nonpolitical, could be nonmotivated by the forces that move our society and our world—to pretend that is mere self-deception. To pretend that there is some kind of pure art that rises above politics in the larger sense, I think is a fraud. All art is political. And I think consciousness of this is a rather good thing. Unconsciousness, pretense that one can be nonpolitical, somehow escapes commitment, and I think that damages art in the long run. An example of this is the place of women in art. Take painting—the endless painting of naked women. This is not supposed to mean anything. They're just painted because they're beautiful. But, of course, it does mean something politically: It means we have a clothed man painting a naked woman. It means that women are seen as objects by men who are perceiving subjects. This is a good example of artists saying, "But I'm not political," and saying it in all good faith, believing it, but not admitting the fact that we are working within a politics of the relationships between men and women.

IB: Where did you learn to read a novel?

UL: I don't know. I've written all my life. I devour books. As soon as I literally learned to read I was reading narratives, and I do it continuously. To me, it's a central part of my being a writer—to read the same kind of thing that I write, poetry, narrative fiction, and nonfiction.

IB: Some writers speak of having trouble reading certain types of books when they're writing.

UL: Oh, absolutely. Most novelists don't read novels when they're engaged upon a novel because if you read a powerful style, it's going to derail you, either consciously or unconsciously. "Oh shit, I wish I could write like that." Then if you start doing it, it'll derail what you're doing, you'll lose your own voice. It has to be a pretty good book to do that to anybody as old as I am.

IB: Did that used to happen to you?

UL: Oh, when I was a kid, of course. I would read D. H. Lawrence and then I would turn out an absolute dreadful ten pages of D. H. Lawrence, or Tolstoy, or what have you, but only when I was a kid. The process of becoming a writer is the process of learning your own voice, and how to speak in your language, not somebody else's. It was along in my mid-to-late twenties that I began to get the skill to talk my own language.

IB: The concept of thought experiments is interesting. I guess it's a physicist's concept, isn't it?

UL: Yeah, right. I came upon that reading physics for peasants. I think Schrodinger is who I learned it from, in talking about his own famous quantum thought experiment with the cat in the box. I wrote a story called *Schrodinger's Cat*. I won't go into the whole experiment, but it was obviously an excellent metaphor for a certain kind of science fiction.

IB: Ever gotten so involved in mixing fact and fiction that at some point, maybe for just a moment, you lose track of which is which?

UL: Well, one has a longing to stay in the book. This isn't only true of the book I may be writing. It can be true of the book I may be reading. But I would say that a genuine confusion there would be very dangerous and would be verging upon lack of control as an artist. It's something that an artist would have to be careful of.

IB: I guess I'm talking about the magic one likes to be led by.

UL: Confusing the fictional world with the real world is really bad stuff. I've had people who believed my novels and that's one reason I have an unlisted phone number. They are confusing fiction with their lives, and their lives tend to be somehow slurred by drugs and stuff. These people are frightened and sometimes frightening. But there's another aspect to this. In a mystical sense, there is a superior reality to a great work of art, to a real solid work of art, a very good novel or poem, and that heightens one's ordinary reality. It makes life more real. We're talking two very different things here. A mere confusion of fiction with life is to me flying saucer country—I don't go there.

IB: You refer to yourself as "the most arboreal science fiction writer." Tell me about this.

UL: Trees are interesting to write about because, particularly in the Pacific Northwest, we are so surrounded by them. They are these presences that many people don't even see. They don't realize trees have different leaves, even. And here are these lives standing silently all around us, amongst which we exist.

IB: We see icescape in your work. Ever go up to the mountains for stimulus when writing something like that?

UL: I'm a Californian. My ice and snow is basically of the mind. I didn't see snow fall until I was seventeen years old and went east. So it's always been magical. If I'd grown up with it, I'd possibly despise it. To me snow is always a miracle, but I don't need to go where it is.

IB: Talk about *Always Coming Home*. You invented a complete culture in that. What was the day-to-day nuts and bolts of that? That was pretty exhaustive.

UL: Yes, it took a long time. I had to think myself into these people's minds—people who perceive the world very different from the way we do. It was a sort of mental archeology, mental anthropology. I couldn't just decide, "Oh, they think this and they think that." It was a process of growing it all together, because their attitude on one thing was going to influence their attitude on everything else. And that had to be *my* attitude because I was writing their literature. So it was a very long process of thinking myself into their skin. In this case, by the way, going to the place where it actually happens was not only helpful but probably essential. The Napa Valley's a place I've known all my life, but being there during the central four months of writing the book was necessary. I had to be there to be writing on that ground because it was centrally important to me that the book be grounded in real earth, real dirt—adobe dirt.

IB: So what was the hardest thing about it?

UL: Trying to put it all together. Trying not to leave things out. You know, a novelist's job is largely leaving things out. Getting the story flowing clear of all the junk around it—the river banks. Well, in this book, I wanted to include the river banks. Not only the river, but the banks of the river and the bed of the river and the trees over the river. So in some ways I had to unlearn everything I'd learned about writing a book.

IB: Wasn't *Always Coming Home* a kind of quest for self-knowledge? Did you feel it that way?

UL: No, I don't feel it that way. I just wanted to write that place. I wanted to write it right; therefore, it had to be inhabited by the

IB: right inhabitants. There are a lot of neat people in Napa Valley, but the present day agriculture is kind of criminal—it's all one crop. It's all high-money vineyard, isn't it? That's no way to use that valley. It's one way but not the right way.

IB: How long did the book take to write?

UL: Well, the actual writing was probably a year and a half, but the getting ready to be able to write it was three or four years, roughly. I was kind of getting my head in place.

IB: How did you do that?

UL: I don't know. It's underground material. It's what Gary Snyder calls "composting." You know, stuff has to go down inside of you, get into the dark and turn into something else, before you can use it in art. If you use raw experience, straight experience, you're doing journalism which is another discipline.

IB: Talk about the origins of the music tape that accompanied the novel.

UL: Well, I was, oh, halfway—better than that—through the book. I was longing to hear the music of the songs that I was able to write by then, because a lot of the poetry was obviously sung. I was doing a radio play for KSOR in Oregon, an original radio play, and they got some original music for it. And the guy that did it was Todd Barton, the music director of the Ashland Shakespeare Festival. Todd and I got on well and I liked his music, so I got up my courage and said, "Would you be interested in writing music for a nonexistent people?" And he didn't think very long; he said, "Yeah." And I could not have found a man better qualified, because he's not only a good composer, but because of doing music to all those plays, Todd is savvy about any number of musical styles. So he didn't fall into the trap of writing music like anybody else—like the Jav-

anese or the Koreans or whatever. He is sophisticated enough
that he could develop a genuinely different musical style and a
very pleasing one, I think.

IB: Did the music feed your writing?

UL: Yes, when we started working together, and of course, when
Peggy, the artist, got in on it too. I was in control, I was the big
honcho, because somebody had to be able to say, "Yeah, this is
right. This is the way they would do it." Or, "No, I don't think
this is quite right, you know." Somebody had to coordinate all
our work—the music, the visual, the textual. And that was
me. But it became very much a collaboration. Peggy's pictures
would feed my sense of what things looked like there, and
Todd's music would make me feel as the people felt. And I had
to invent the language for Todd's singers to sing in. We
couldn't have them singing in English. So very late on, essentially when the book was written, I had to go back and invent
the language. I had until then been translating from a nonexistent language. Then I had to make a partially existent language, so we could have our songs. That was fairly hard work,
but fun.

IB: I guess! So that would be the hardest book to write.

UL: I guess it was the biggest undertaking.

IB: Did you ever want to actually *live* in one of the worlds you've
created?

UL: No, no. I live here.

IB: Do you use dreams in your writing?

UL: I have done it. While I'm actually writing a book, I tend not to
have very vivid dreams. It's as if the material were going into

the writing. But I have started several poems and a story or two from dream material.

IB: For example?

UL: There are dream poems in a couple of my books of poetry. They are titled "Dream Poem."

IB: And the story?

UL: I don't know a good example. It would be simply something in a story that a dream helped me solve or see my way clear. Actually, rather than dreams, the most useful time, the really sacred time to me is between sleeping and waking in the morning. It's not dream state. It's waking state when one is still in touch with the unconscious, but the conscious mind is able to direct the seeking a bit. And that, that is my most useful time as an artist.

IB: Isaac Asimov says he isn't a good sleeper because he wakes up and starts thinking—writing in his head.

UL: Right. But I wouldn't put it that way. I'm a good sleeper, and I need sleep. But if I can wake really, *really* early in the morning and be undisturbed for half an hour or so, as I was saying, that is a very, very good thing. That's a time when a lot of work can be done.

IB: How many hours do you work a day?

UL: It varies enormously, but essentially all morning. From seven to noon is pretty much my real writing time. Letters and crap take up the afternoon.

IB: Do you ever get on a roll and go all day or all night?

UL: Well, since my children are grown, I can do that. It used to be impossible. You know, I'm nearly sixty, and I don't have that kind of energy anymore. Very seldom. I've been surprised lately that I *could* actually write all day sometimes, because normally three or four hours of real writing is enough for the day. But I have spent eight and nine hour days writing this year.

IB: I would think just creating the names that you create would be a full-time job for some writers.

UL: Well, that's just a gift, I guess.

IB: Did you used to make up a lot of names when you were a child?

UL: Oh yeah. I made stories with my brothers. We played narrative games with stuffed animals, with toy soldiers, or acting out parts ourselves. The way kids do, you know. And most of those would involve names.

IB: So how do you make up names?

UL: It's a process of listening. You have to just sit around and listen to it until it's right. Some of them come easily. If I can't get a character's name, then I know there's something wrong with the character, or with the conception of the story. And this is just as true in mundane fiction or non-sci-fi, or whatever you want to call it. In my stories that *The New Yorker* has been publishing, these are about absolutely ordinary people in an ordinary world, but their names are just as important. If I don't know that she's called "Jane," I can't write about her. It's the same thing exactly as making up an exotic or invented name.

IB: Do you ever change a character's name halfway through if you feel the character isn't going right?

UL: No. That's got to *be* right.

IB: Do you track your characters like a bloodhound, as Faulkner was said to have done?

UL: My characters are more within me than that. I don't know where I would track them to. This thing of tracking, as though something were going away from you and you had to follow it—that simply makes no sense. That has no resonance to me. The character is something that happens as I write.

IB: Do you take notes and keep notes and things?

UL: I write so many kinds of books; in some of them notes would be appropriate. For instance, in *Always Coming Home* I didn't know how many kinds of oak grew in California. I had to make a considerable study and indeed I took notes. It's a small example of the kind of research or reading that I did for that book. Educating myself to the flora and fauna and climate and geology of California, because I wanted to get it right. In a book like *The Beginning Place*, what would I take notes about? I know supermarkets and I know the imagination, and it takes place in the ground between a supermarket and Elfland, so there was nothing to research. Nothing to take notes about.

IB: In 1942 you wrote an origin-of-life-on-earth story that was rejected. How did you feel?

UL: At age twelve?

IB: You were twelve then?

UL: I was twelve in 1942. I was delighted to have a genuine rejection slip. (Laughs.) It meant I was a real writer, with a real rejection slip. At twelve years old, I think that was fairly natural.

IB: Did you put it on your wall?

UL: I had it for years. I have no idea what has become of it.

IB: The scientist in your stories is frequently a lonely type. Is that kind of a metaphor, mixing of metaphors with science, or is that kind of the plight of the artist to the lonely trade?

UL: I think my scientists often could be seen as artists, to some extent, when I was writing with male protagonists.

IB: John D. McDonald one time asked me a kind of rhetorical question which I think is interesting. He said, "Could the writer write something if they didn't think it was unique?" What are your views on that?

UL: Well, earlier you asked me something about "hacks." My response then was that a hack writer is a person who is writing something that they know isn't original or they haven't put their mind and heart into. And that's what makes a second-rate writer, or a "hack." To me, writing is my central way of being. It's the best way I know how to *be*. How to live my life. My life is my writing, so I'm going to try to do *my* writing, not somebody else's.

IB: Do you have a favorite story?

UL: No. Well, it's always the one I'm working on.

IB: One of your characters, Shevek in *The Dispossessed*, delights in the "verbal splendor." What is your view on "verbal splendor" as a writer? I mean, you obviously write with a beautiful flair . . .

UL: Well, I enjoy it. You know, that's a huge question, and you're opening a can of worms about a yard around. Are we talking prose here or are we talking poetry?

IB: We're talking prose.

UL: OK. I essentially grew up in the, I would say, Tolstoyian school of trying to make the writing transparent. The most important thing is that the writing be almost transparent, that the person reading the novel or short story not be aware of the writing as "beautiful," in the sense that that beauty brings you out of the narrative. The narrative is the dominant thing in the story. And clarity of style is probably the first virtue of style. I still believe this, more or less. But I've always had kind of an oral approach to my writing. I do hear it. I hear the sound of it. Many people go straight from eye to brain. I don't. That's why I'm now so interested in oral literature and poetry for tape and stuff like that. But it's always influenced my prose style in that if the sentence doesn't have a kind of cadence, if it doesn't read aloud well, it's not a right sentence to me. And the same with a paragraph. I can tell you the kind of writing I *don't* like, that might be more useful. Vladimir Nabokov—to me, his is not a good prose style. It is self-conscious, self-reflective, rather posturing, goes in for a lot of fancy vocabulary; it is always bringing me up short. I want to say, "Oh, stop showing off, Vladimir, get on with it." It's a rather intolerant position to be sure. But then a writer like Kipling comes to mind, whose style is very idiosyncratic, rather strange, and, particularly in his finest things, in some of the children's books, is deliberately rather splendid and very rhythmical and totally oral. I love it. Well, maybe because being a native English speaker, he did it better than Nabokov. Anyway, it depends on the writer how I respond to verbal splendor in prose.

IB: You first tackled a mainstream novel with *Malafrena?*

UL: First published one.

IB: Did that feel different to you?

UL: *Malafrena* was begun earlier than any of the other published books. The early versions or sketches for it go back into, oh, really just post-college days, I guess. I'm a little dim about it now. And I think one can see it's a very old-fashioned novel. It's written like a nineteenth-century novel because that is largely what I was reading, particularly the English and Russians.

IB: What do you owe Jane Austen?

UL: Endless pleasure. Years and years of delight.

IB: What did you learn from Jane Austen?

UL: A great deal about life.

IB: For example?

UL: I can't give you an example. You don't get fortune cookie maxims from a great novelist. You learn what life is like and what people are like.

IB: Gertrude Stein said, "I'm writing for myself and strangers."

UL: (Laughs.) That is nice. That is funny!

IB: You say you are anti-progress. Can you talk about that?

UL: (Laughs.) Did I say that?

IB: Yeah.

UL: I was probably driven to it. Anyway, thank you for the chance to clarify it, because "anti-progress" sounds silly. Sounds like destroy the machinery and return to the land with a wooden hoe. This is not quite my style. But the myth of progress, the idea that we *must* progress and that progress is continual economic growth and continual technological complication, oh, I think that is a very destructive myth that has long outlived its time. We need new understandings of how we live in the world.

IB: Frank Herbert said something about time being literal in our particular culture.

UL: I don't know what he meant. But in *Always Coming Home*, I was trying to get a different sense of time than our clock-bound one. I wonder if he was talking about the fact that we think time is a thing because we have the clocks to measure it by. We think that our measurement of the process and existence of time, we—what's the word—we reify it. I bet that's what Frank was talking about. And I was trying to get clear away from that in *Always Coming Home*. To perceive time in a more cyclical, bodily sense, than we generally do.

IB: He said there was this conception we held of the future. We refer to it as "the future" as if there was *one* future.

UL: That's sweet. He had a lovely mind, Frank did.

MILLER WILLIAMS

Miller Williams was selling refrigerators in a Sears store in Macon, Georgia, when he met John Ciardi—an incident he details in the interview—and his life changed abruptly.

This meeting lead to a fellowship to Bread Loaf Writers Conference where he met Robert Frost. "It was a wild, bumpy, and wonderful two weeks," he says. He made his living for a while after Bread Loaf working as an editor in New York, where he stayed with novelist Dick Yates in a basement apartment on Seventh Street. Then the illness of his first wife took them and their three small children to Baton Rouge, where he ended up selling tires for Montgomery Ward and household insulation door-to-door in the evenings.

After about a year, Louisiana State University hired him to teach freshman English on the basis of his poetry publications in *Poetry*, *Saturday Review*, and other journals. Soon after this Williams won the Amy Lowell Traveling Scholarship in Poetry from Harvard, with which he and his family lived a year in Chile, where he learned Spanish and took an interest in translation.

After two more years at L.S.U., he joined the English Department at Loyola University in New Orleans, where he founded *The New Orleans Review*, but left over a censorship dispute; he spent 1970 at the University of Mexico as a Fulbright Professor and went from there to the University of Arkansas, where he holds the title of University Professor.

Over the years additional awards and recognitions have included the Henry Bellaman Poetry Prize, the Prix de Rome for literature, and a Doctor of Humanities degree from Lander College. Miller Williams has published more than twenty-five books, including a history of American railroads, critical works on John Ciardi and John Crowe Ransom, translations from the Romanesco of Guiseppe Belli and the Spanish of Nicanor Parra, college texts on poetry, including *Patterns in Poetry: An Encyclopedia of Forms*, and several volumes of poetry, including *Imperfect Love* and *Living on the Surface*, his new and selected poems.

INTERVIEW

IRV BROUGHTON: Did Robert Frost influence you at all?

MILLER WILLIAMS: I'm a disciple of Robert Frost in that I believe in craft. His marvelous sense of craft, his control of the line, his use of sound, his obvious attention to the way consonants and syllables bump against each other when a line is read out loud . . . these things were clear to me as I began to read Frost and I wanted to be that good a craftsman. I had the same sense of admiration for John Crowe Ransom, and I wanted to be that good a craftsman. I don't think that in either case I wanted to be that *kind* of craftsman. No, in that way I wasn't influenced. I admired how well they could make words work; in that sense only I would say that I was influenced by Frost and Ransom in a way that I wasn't influenced, say, by some of the looser handlers of words, some of the people that seemed to me a little more casual in their sense of line, who paid a little less attention to what a line is and how it sounds, how particles of words move against one another.

IB: You seem to place considerable emphasis on the line. What does line mean to you, how does it function in a poem of yours or in a good poem that you read?

MW: As I read, and as I write, I see the line as having the same relationship to the poem that a scene in fiction has and a paragraph has in exposition. The line is the unit the poem is built of. I don't think we can build anything very effectively in art or architecture, in civil engineering, or education, if we simply have a cosmic vision of the whole. We have to think in terms of the units that make up this whole, in the same way that a film editor has to be concerned with each frame and not simply with the movie. I know there are people who believe that too much attention to the line, the unit, the smaller part, hobbles a poet, keeps the poet from being able to swing free, and this would be

341

true if the metaphor for poet were "bird." I don't think it is; I think the metaphor for poet is more likely "train," or "car," or even "human being on a ladder." So that to be free we have to have the limitation of the track or the road or the ladder with the rungs on it. If we're going to get anywhere. I could live a little while with the concept of a poem's lines as rungs on a ladder. We have to go up a particular way and one rung at a time. There is that sense of progression, of going somewhere. A line ought to be a unit of information, a unit of syntax, and a unit of rhythm. I guess I would say that each line ought to be a poem-in-little, so that it has its own statement and its own rhythmical resolution, its own sense of beginning and ending and shape, and that the sum total of these builds the poem.

IB: Who most influenced your feeling about the line? Any single poet?

MW: I don't know how much of it came just from reading in the tradition. I think the line is important to me partly because I've found it useful and satisfying to order everything I do, to know what parts make up a day, what parts make up a trip. I have to order my world. But I smiled when you asked me where I got a sense of line, what poet I got it from, because I don't think I got it from a poet one would find in an anthology. I'm not trying to be evasive or funny when I say that my sense of line as line came from growing up listening to blues and country music. The blues singer and composer, the country music singer and composer, have to understand the line. I got my sense of line in great part from Robert Johnson and Hank Williams.

IB: Did you ever know Robert Johnson or Hank Williams?

MW: Yeah, well, I met Hank Williams. I was with him for a very short while, about an hour and a half. This was just shortly before he died. He had given a concert at a school where I was teaching. I was a young instructor and I admired him a great deal. When the concert was over, I went up on stage and said, "Mr. Williams, my name is Williams and I'd like to buy you a drink." To me it was just a way of saying "Hello," and "I like what you're doing," but things turned out that I did get to talk with him for a little while. I was, as I said, a brand new college teacher. I liked to hear myself called "prof." I was barely an instructor on a one year appointment, but I was smoking a briar pipe and wearing a tweed coat and drinking scotch, because I knew that college professors did these things. The briar pipe bit my tongue, and the tweed coat on a hot Louisiana night was about to itch me to death, and the scotch was making me sick. I was trying to be as comfortable and convincingly bright-young-college-professor as I could be. What I was, actually, was a dull young jackass and I don't know why he saw anything in me to keep him there even for a few minutes. But he was friendly and open and I was in awe of him and embarrassed to show it. I'm not proud of the kind of thing he must have seen, but when he had to go we stood up and—well—he had seen through me as if I were cellophane. He put his hand on my shoulder and after we'd said goodbye he stopped and said, "You know, you oughta drink beer, Williams, 'cause you gotta beer drinkin' soul."

That had an immediate and lasting effect on me. I still have sham moments, but when I begin to slip into them I remember that skinny old codger putting his hand on my shoulder and saying that line. What he was saying, of course, was, "You're really a nice guy at heart. Why do you put on such a . . . why do you put on all this phony baloney?" He was dead shortly after that. I was driving back from a bi-racial, we used to call it, a bi-racial youth congress in Columbia, South Carolina, where a group of mainly young people had met to plan demonstrations of various sorts to further the cause of school integration in the South. It was about 1:30 in the morning, New Year's Day, 1953. I was somewhere in South Carolina or Georgia, listening to the radio, when a voice interrupted the country music to say that Hank Williams had just been found dead in his Cadillac. The last words he had said to me came heavy at the moment, and I wanted to pull off the side of the road and cry. Then I thought if I did, he would say there was something a little phony about it; take off the tweed coat and drive home. And that's what I did.

IB: Do you have any one obsession, or one thing—it might not affect your life directly, it might just be an image, a type of person, or a . . . ?

MW: I want to go to the stars. That's an obsession with me, I suppose. I want to live long enough to die on a space flight. I don't mean some petty stuff like going to Mars. I mean, I want to go out there, really all the way out. A trip where you would expect that no one would be back for maybe three generations. I want to do that.

IB: Would you like to have your children come along and represent you in the return years later?

MW: They couldn't live long enough. One would expect to conceive children on the trip and then let them have theirs, and then theirs or their children, would come back. A trip like this is going to have to start off with a few people, maybe with twenty people, with room for six hundred. They'll build their colony as they go.

IB: That's Biblical, isn't it? Noah's Ark?

MW: I wouldn't object to that at all. The Bible is a myth system; almost everything that we can imagine doing is biblical.

IB: Are you religious?

MW: There's a colony of people in Fayetteville who say among themselves that they're sentimental about Jesus. My older daughter is Lucinda Williams, the songwriter and singer, what a country music person would call a picker. When she sings "Amazing Grace," I'm terribly moved. But it wouldn't be fair to say that I believe. It's important, though, for me to say also that I don't disbelieve, either. I did an article once called, "On Doubting the Non-Existence of God." That gets close to where I am. Dylan Thomas said that he wanted to write religious poems by a man who didn't believe in God, or something like that. I think it's impossible not to be religious when you're raised in the culture I came out of.

IB: In the South, you mean?

MW: No, no, I mean in the United States. It's as impossible for me to be unreligious as it is for an American Catholic not to be a Calvinist. In the United States, even Jews are Calvinists. We're taught that sin and pleasure are the same thing and that you pay for it tomorrow. This isn't true in most other countries. We believe that to have pleasure outside the sight of God, where we must believe we exist, is blasphemy and, therefore, inevitably to be punished. Thereby comes the pain that follows pleasure. This is supposed to be simply Bible-belt Protestant theology, but almost everybody in the United States braces when things are going well. In this sense, we're all religious. We can't escape our myth system. I believe in God as genuinely as I believe in Thor, and I'm not sure that I don't believe in Thor.

IB: What would your god be like?

MW: I can't relate to that question directly, because I can't conceive of a god who would know my name. I can't conceive of a personal god at all. I guess I would have to respond purely as a deist. My father, not an ordinary Methodist preacher, didn't believe in hell. When this was revealed to a Baptist preacher in our small Arkansas town, he said, "I'll tell you this for sure: he won't be there twenty minutes till he'll change his mind."

IB: There seems to be guilt in your writings. There are a lot of religious references and whatnot; in fact, it seems to permeate your writing, this religious influence, one way or another.

MW: I'd have to start on a broader scale. I think all of literature is about four things only, four topics: sex, death, religion, and the will to power. Or let's say love, mortality, awe, and ambition. These are our four concerns. Not very much poetry today deals with religious problems, because we're living in a particularly secular age. My poems and stories seem to deal inordinately with religion only because they deal as much with religion as they do with sex and death and ambition. The body of American poetry is curiously awry in that it virtually ignores the god-hunger of people.

IB: What are you trying to say in your poems? What would you like to say over and over again?

MW: That we are bound together as human beings by two elements, two things that we have in common: we're all lonely and we're all frightened. This, I guess, is what my poetry says, poem by poem. And this is what makes us human. Out of this grows compassion, patience, companionship, all the qualities that allow people to live together without killing each other.

IB: Were you lonely as a child?

MW: Oh, yeah. I hate to say that when I was eleven I felt an existential loneliness. If I start talking like that, I'm going to feel Hank Williams' hand on my shoulder again. I think that I was hungry to get closer to some human being than I had ever been able to get.

IB: How did your friendship with Kenneth Patchen start?

MW: Not very long before he died, when I was working on the anthology I did for Random House, the *Contemporary Poetry in*

346

America, I contacted him in the normal order of things and asked permission to use certain poems. He wrote to say that the poems I had asked for had been used in anthology after anthology, that he had done other work he thought was worth including, and if it wasn't, certainly, they ought to stop including him after a while, because nobody could ride forever on three or four poems. He was especially interested in my using some of his picture poems. He said that if I weren't willing to do this, he would rather be left out. I wrote him a long letter telling him how I felt about his poetry and, for some reason, about a lot of other things. He called me. I picked up the phone and he said, "Miller," and I said, "Yes," and he said, "This is Kenneth." I don't think we ever used each other's last names. He was dead in a couple of years.

IB: Your degrees are in biology, right?

MW: Right. I taught physiology and related biology courses in college for years before I switched over and became part of an English department. I simply decided I wasn't a biologist; I was an interpreter of a biology textbook. I wasn't helping to shape the field I was working in. I did one interesting piece of independent research during all those years, on the function of the parathyroids in the dog. That wasn't enough. I was no more a biologist than a teacher of poetry is a poet. I was writing poetry and short stories and criticism, and one day a biology student asked me a question I knew I would have known the answer to if I had been reading the literature closely enough. I had read all the literary journals. So I went to the department head and said I wanted out.

IB: You had read all the literary journals, and not the . . .

MW: Not the *Journal of Physiology.* Not that quarter. So I said I wanted out and I went to Sears and got a job selling refrigerators. I had decided a long time before that there wasn't anything special about being a college teacher. The academic world is no more or less sleazy, petty, politically corrupt, capitalistic, ego-driven, or dirty, than the world of commerce, law, or the ministry. A person selling insurance can be doing a much more noble work than a lot of people teaching English. And a person selling shoes at Montgomery Ward may be living in a more tightly protected ivory tower than a person teaching history at a university.

IB: Did you ever have any doubts that you were doing the right thing?

MW: No, I never had any doubts, because I thought in my case it was more honest to sell refrigerators.

IB: When you started out in poetry, did you have trouble looking at things with enough subjectivity?

MW: I don't see the worlds of science and art as divided between classical and romantic or objective and subjective. In fact, I hardly find them separate at all. The scientist and the artist have something much more importantly in common, in any case, than any difference between them. Both the good poet and the good scientist, living in a world of apparent formlessness and chaos, try to discover the form that's inherent in that chaos. To use a scientific metaphor, it's much as if we have a super-saturated solution, and by lowering the temperature of the solution or introducing a crystal of the solute into the solution, we cause the solid to crystalize out and get a marvelous, breathtakingly beautiful structure, sometimes, of crystals formed in this test tube. The structure we're seeing was already inherently there. It became manifest from within. What the scientist, the artist, the statesman, and the civil engineer have to do is draw out of the apparent chaos of our world the order that's naturally, if invisibly, within it. When people try to impose an order which is not inherent, bridges fall and we become tired of poems and theories that don't hold up, and political systems collapse. I'm not trying to find a unified field theory for all of human endeavor, but I do think it's important that we understand that poetry, painting, the dance, sculpture, bio-physics, civil engineering, all have to be aimed at discovering and drawing out, for our delight and insight, that order which is hidden in the apparent chaos we live in. This comes to my mind often because, as a person trained in the sciences, I'm frequently asked, "How do you reconcile the conflicts between the worlds of science and the arts?" and I don't see any.

IB: Can you talk with scientists? Do you have trouble talking with them, communicating with them, on an interpersonal level? Can you still do that?

MW: Sure, except that the sense of the truth of their own vision often precludes doubt. This is not found among the great scientists. It was never true of Steinmetz, or Einstein, or Newton, or Mendel. But the scientist one generally finds on the college campus is too rarely blessed with what John Ciardi called, "the grace of uncertainty." This sometimes makes it a little difficult to talk to them.

IB: You mention John Ciardi. Ciardi's been a great influence on you?

MW: When I was selling refrigerators at Sears—this was in Macon, Georgia—he came down there to give a talk. Back in 1960. My wife and I crashed the party given for him after the reading. I was married then to a good woman named Lucy, and we sat around and listened to him talk. And as we started to leave, we shook hands and he said, "I'm glad to meet you," and she said we hadn't met at all or he would have known there was another poet in the room. I was mortified. He said, "Who's this?" and she said, "My husband, right here," and he said, "I'd like to read some of his poems," and she said, "Sure you would," and he said, "Really, have him send some of his poems," and she said, "Sure you would," and he said, "Really, have him send me some." There I was, saying nothing. I was thirty. I had done nothing except write poems and put them in a box, thinking there might come a time when in Macon, Georgia, there would be someone I could show them to. We left. I didn't believe he'd meant it, or that he'd remember the incident. But he got our address from someone there, and in about two weeks I got a letter from him. It said, "I thought you were going to send me some poems. P.S. Tell your wife I like her way of going." So I sent him some, and he wrote back and he said he wanted to publish them in the *Saturday Review*, if that was all right, and would I accept a fellowship to the Bread Loaf Writers Conference. That seems a long, long time ago. I don't think there's been a year at Bread Loaf like that before or since. On the staff were Robert Frost, John Ciardi, Howard Nemerov, Dudley Fitts, and John Nims. That was just the poetry staff. Among the fellows and scholars were Robert Huff, Lew Turco, Milton Kessler, Richard Frost, and A. R. Ammons.

IB: You do both poetry translations and your own poetry. How do you value writing the one as opposed to the other?

MW: My poetry, certainly, is more important to me than my translations. It has its genesis within me. But I wouldn't want to give up either. I give at least as much time to the translation of a poem as I do to the writing of one of my own. There's a special strain, a special pressure, involved in translation, where one has to be true to three or four things at once: the original poet's sense of language, that poem's style and statement, and one's own sense of language, and the cultures of both nations. This puts some challenging and exciting pressure on the translator. There's another pressure that's particularly strong, at least on me, when I translate. When I'm writing my own poem, if I screw up, then I have only myself to answer for. So I have only myself to answer *to*. If I screw up when I'm translating a poem by Rilke, or a short story by Enrique Lihn, then I have to answer not only to myself but to them, and I have to answer to them in very direct and moral terms. Whether the person is dead or alive, is here or not, speaks English or not, that person is always looking over my shoulder as a moral presence.

IB: Do you think that translation has helped your own poetry any?

MW: I think so. In part, because a translator has got to learn to justify every preposition, every article. A translator sometimes is forced to add a word or leave out a word, to substitute one word for another. In order to justify this, one has to understand precisely why a word, maybe just a preposition or an article, is there in the first place. It's awfully easy in one's own poetry to get into the habit of thinking in terms of phrases. When you're translating, you can't do that; you have to wonder, "Why did he use that part of speech?" Any translation is a tough exercise in attention to detail.

IB: What image of the South is most indelible in your memory? Is there any one particular scene, or happening, or gathering, or anything that really seems to epitomize the South to you?

MW: I don't know how to answer that. In the introduction to *Southern Writing in the Sixties*, Bill Corrington and I tried to lay out what we believed the South was. I'm not sure that I would stand by all of that now. I'm not sure how much I would have bought it all whole-cloth then. Since we wrote it together, there had to be some compromise. But it's interesting that not only Southerners, but those who are not from the South, think of the South as a different place. Bulletins announcing writers' conferences often say Southern poet. They don't mention the region that anyone else at the conference has come from. There's something different that not only the Southerner senses; I'm not sure that this is always a good thing, but it's there.

IB: I believe you met Flannery O'Connor?

MW: We were friends from, oh, I have to think how many years it was now—from 1957 until she died. Which is not very long; she died in 1964. I was with Harcourt Brace as a textbook salesman, a college traveler. She was published by Harcourt Brace at that time, and lived in my territory, in Milledgeville, just twenty-nine miles from Macon. I went over and knocked on her door and said, "You're a marvelous writer, and I'd like to know you." She said, "Have a seat here on the porch and we'll talk," and we did and kept talking, for what? seven years. She was a good woman. Tough. She let my children chase her peacocks. She kept insisting she knew nothing of poetry. She wrote religiously for two hours every morning. She sat down at her typewriter at ten o'clock and she wrote till noon and she stopped. I could see her in her room, through the front porch window. I could see her as I drove up. She wouldn't come out if I'd misjudged the time and arrived before twelve o'clock. I didn't mean for her to, of course. Not until she'd finished. Then she would come out and sit on the front porch, and we'd talk and her mother would fix a tray with little cubes of watermelon with a toothpick in each one and Coca-Cola for each of us, and we'd talk—about her stories mostly. She would read my poetry, but she would always say, "I don't know what to say about poetry. I really don't, I wouldn't know how to make a comment about it." She would sometimes get poems in the mail, books from people who admired her and wanted to send her their poetry. She would ask me to look at them. "I don't know what it's supposed to do," she would say, "how it's supposed to work." Which seemed to me a little strange for someone who understood the English language as well as Flannery did. I guess I never quite believed her.

IB: What marks her most in your memory?

MW: Her ability to show a real, a true interest in other people. And to make her own obvious, and agonizing, affliction almost invisible, so that you forgot about it. She was on two aluminum crutches, of course, and could barely move. But she was concerned that I had a comfortable chair. And that the Coca-Cola was cold, and that the children not be bored while we talked. This wasn't something she decided to put on; it was an honest concern. I asked her one time, "What's your favorite among your own stories?" She said the one that she was most pleased to have written was "The Artificial Nigger," that this held more of what she meant for her stories to say than any other she'd done. This is curious in light of the fact that almost all of the anthologies, certainly freshman and sophomore college texts that use Flannery O'Conner stories, use "A Good Man is Hard to Find," which she said was way down the line. Close behind "The Artificial Nigger"—for her—was "The River," the story of the little boy who watched baptisms and then got caught in a pig pen and found out that pigs were not like Porky Pig. It was a significant matter to Flannery that she didn't publish her stories in the major, mass-circulation, slick magazines. Almost all had their first publication in university quarterlies. She believed very much in the quarterlies. She thought this was where, and I think she was right—where the best writing was being printed. It was then. I think it still is.

IB: You had a good magazine there in *The New Orleans Review.* Could you talk a little about that?

MW: Loyola University wanted a journal that might serve, in part, as a public relations venture. I think this is legitimate on the part of a university, a way of saying to prospective students and faculty, "We care enough to do this." And I had thought for a long time that I would like to publish a magazine of discovery, a magazine in which we would print primarily work by people who were virtually unknown. We had a budget of twenty-five thousand dollars a year, a full-time secretary, a business manager, and an art director-layout man. Bill Corrington was editor-at-large, and I had money to send him to such places as Atlanta and New York for interviews. I learned a lot. One thing I learned was how hard it is to edit a magazine, even with money. I don't see how anyone edits one without it. It also made me impatient with people who take forever to let me know whether they want to publish my poems or not. No editor needs months to accept or reject a poem.

IB: How should a poem work?

MW: I like for a poem's meaning not to be immediately and fully accessible to me as a reader. I want it to be just on my edge of comprehension, but just on this side of incomprehensibility, not just on the other side. Let me start back and say it this way: I don't think a poem exists on the page. A poem exists when the imagination of the poet and the imagination of the reader confront one another inside the act of language we call a poem. And I think that the reader should be prepared to put as much energy into that confrontation as the poet does. The imagination of the reader ought to work on as high a level as the poet's. I want to reach for what the poet is saying, but I want it to be reachable. "Gerontion," for instance, does not leap out at me. As a matter of fact, I'm still not sure, reading by reading, exactly what the yellow smoke is in Prufrock, but my imagination gets itself around these elements in confrontation with the poet's imagination. In the midst of that act of language. In a very real way we work together to make the poem. A reader works with a poet to make the poem a dramatic reality.

IB: Tell me, if you have a heart transplant, do you think you could exist having someone else's heart?

MW: Oh, sure. That wouldn't bother me. I think I would have a lot more trouble with a hand transplant.

IB: Why?

MW: Well, the heart's simply an impersonal pump that sends the blood around. We surely don't take seriously the old sense of the heart as the seat of anything psychic. But the hand is a very personal, intimate thing. Your first sexual relations with yourself and then your first sexual relations with others are with the

354

hand. Getting a piece of meat out from between your teeth or picking your nose or scratching your head, the hand does all these things. I think it would be awfully hard to live with someone else's hand. While I was teaching in Mexico—no, this was when I was teaching in Chile—I kept making a gesture. It was as if you were very lightly tossing an apple. Up and down in your hands, just with a motion of the wrist. Maybe feeling the weight of a cabbage. This is an extremely obscene gesture in Latin America. Roughly equal to the popping of the thumb from the upper teeth in Italy, "giving someone a fig," or giving someone the finger in this country. I did it continually as I lectured; I would emphasize points by bouncing an imaginary softball in my hand. Some of the students finally came to me and asked me please not to do that any more. I said, "Why?" The young woman who was speaking for them raised her middle finger, a lovely finger, wrapped all her other fingers tightly into her fist, and stuck it up between my eyes, right against my forehead, and said, "Would you like me to do this to you?" I tried from then on to lecture with my hands in my pockets or clasped firmly behind me.

IB: If you weren't a poet, what are the forms you'd pursue?

MW: I'll tell you what I'd like to pursue. I'd like to be able to play the piano and sing like Ray Charles. That's really what I would like to do. I'd trade with him now, if I could. But Ray Charles is much more likely to write poetry than I am to sing. Beyond that, I would like to paint.

IB: Why?

MW: I like the sense of physical involvement in the art, the sense of actually moving your hands to make them go where the lines are. It's one thing for Wallace Stevens to talk about the blackbirds, and make us feel them, see them, that is. It's one thing for Archibald MacLeish to say a poem should be dumb, like an old medallion to the thumb. We may feel our thumb running over the old medallion, and this is fine. For the *reader*. But in painting, the *artist* has the sensory experience, feels the paint under his fingers. I'd like to do that. My five senses get hungry very, very quickly. I remember when my mother finally let me do something I had asked to do for a long time, which was to run both hands down into a box of Crisco. Back in the thirties, Crisco came in a kind of oil-paper carton. I don't know if you've ever seen those. They were much like butter cartons, the same relative dimensions, but big. Enough to hold a couple of pounds of Crisco. And when you opened it up, it was as irresistible as new snow on a hillside. Perfectly smooth, untouched, soft and deep.

IB: What about your parents, what were they like?

MW: My father was a socialist, an integrationist, a pacifist. He spoke for Sacco and Vanzetti. He may have held the first sit-in in the South, in 1946. He was a minister in North Little Rock during the 1957 integration crisis, and preached against Faubus then. He believed that the role of the church had to be a social role, and that the faith that mattered was horizontal, between people, not primarily vertical. That God would take care of that, and that what we had to take care of was ourselves and our fellow creatures. He and my mother raised six children to adulthood. There were eleven originally. There were evenings of reading aloud. We had *McGuffey's Readers,* and *Foxe's Book of Martyrs,* Latin, Shakespeare, and the Greek plays, and an old wind-up Victrola we still had in the late thirties played Chopin and Bach and blues and country music. My parents taught by homily and by axiom, as well as by example. I remember being told, for instance, when I complained about a meal my sister had cooked when my parents were away, "It's them that draws the water leaves the bucket in the well." And I remember being told, "You haven't fixed your bike until you've put your tools away." These sorts of things sound easy, but together with example and discipline and a love you don't question from parents that you know are gutsy and often unpopular for good cause, they helped make a home I'm pleased to have come from. My parents were instrumental in the formation of the old Southern Tenant Farmers' Union in the South, organizing the sharecroppers. They voted for Norman Thomas every time he ran for president. They never were Christian in the sense of historical Christianity, although my father, as I've said, was a minister. He wanted to call himself a Christian, but he never believed in what he called the black magic of the Christian faith. Jesus was a man to him, and if most people worshipped him instead of following him, it was because it was easier. Who could be expected to be like God? But if you see Jesus doing as Jesus did, and he was a man, then you have to look at yourself in a very hard light. Essentially his faith was that Jesus was the Son of God, not because God named him son, but because Jesus recognized the Fatherhood. And that anyone could do that, that the divinity of Jesus was available to anybody. This is not traditional Methodism.

IB: You said there were eleven children originally.

MW: Well, my mother and father lost five children. This was not unusual on a farm or in a small town in the South, or maybe most anywhere, during the first decades of this century. Diphtheria, whooping cough, the 1917–18 flu epidemic.

IB: Did you ever know any of the brothers or sisters that you lost?

MW: No, not really.

IB: But did it mark you? Did it hurt? Do you feel their presence or anything?

MW: Yeah, we all felt the presences, because my parents continued to speak of them as if they were a part of the family. Not in any dark way. I think even Jordan feels that my brother Bowen, who died in the 1918 epidemic, is her brother-in-law. He simply has stayed around the house. In a very comfortable way. My parents were not afraid of death. Shortly before my father died, he talked about it. He told Jordan that he just hated to die with Nixon still in the White House. He didn't believe he was going to anything that we would recognize as heaven. He thought that he would have immortality as long as those people who knew him remembered him, and this was all he wanted. I don't think he would have chosen anything else, if he'd had a choice. But whatever shaped me, as far as my home life is concerned, was the encouragement from my parents that their children think for themselves and go their own way, without feeling that they were being untrue to anything they came from. That they not tell themselves easy lies. That they read hard books, and listen to good music, and not hurt anyone.

IB: You like gadgets, mechanical things, don't you?

MW: Yeah.

IB: Is fixing something like writing a poem?

MW: In the sense that it brings order out of chaos, it may be. I like the feeling I get when I write a poem, or when I fix an automatic garbage disposal or an electric typewriter, an adding machine, or a child's battery-driven toy. I feel almost as if I had invented the thing. It's not un-akin to the feeling I have when I finish a poem and think, "that works."

IB: How would you like to be saved, if you were saved?

MW: If I were to return to the church, I would become either an old-world Catholic, or a hell-fire-and-brimstone, foot-stompin', hymn-shoutin' Southern Protestant. I would either have me a meaningful ritual or a meaningful participation. But it would have to involve either my mind, or my guts, very deeply. It would not be a respectable liberal Methodism, or a nice Episcopalian kind of Catholicism. I would either give myself completely to old world, medieval ritual, or I would hump the pew and shout.

IB: Is ritual important to you?

MW: When I speak of bringing order out of chaos, it's ritual I'm talking about. The way in which we do something, the restraints we put on ourselves, the moves, the stylized moves we make that tie us not only to each other, but to the past, are the visible signs or those very thin threads that hold everything together. This is why repetition is an important poetic device. Repetition is in the nature of ritual. Remember I've said that what people have in common is that we're all lonely and we're all afraid. The less ritual there is, the more independent is every act from every other act, and the more removed from every life is every other life. It's through ritual that we come together. Whether it's saying "Amen" on every tenth phrase of a sermon, or marching up the steps to the Temple. All art embodies ritual. That may be why art flourishes as faith weakens, because we replace one ritual with another. Ritual can be defined maybe as a visible sign of the sense of continuity. Between people back through time, and between people around the world at the same time. Ritual is an antidote to that fear and a bridge over loneliness. When we lose ritual, our sense of ritual, we lose too much of what holds us together. Poetry is certainly part of this. All art is a part of it. Hell, Mae West knew this. "It's not what I do, it's how I do it . . . it's not what I say, it's how I say it." That's what we mean by ritual. God, she understood ritual.

IB: The term "poet" has lots of connotations, doesn't it?

MW: In 1962, I guess, I was invited to speak and read and hold conferences at a writers' conference somewhere in Louisiana. After I was invited, the directors of the conference wrote to John Ciardi and asked him if I was "all right." He wrote back to them, and said, "Miller Williams is a pervert, communist, dope addict, but this is more than compensated for by the fact that he is such a militant Afro-American." For some reason, maybe because they thought they really had an interesting kind of freak on their hands, the way they thought poets were supposed to be, they went ahead and invited me. But they asked me if I would be good enough to bring my own bed linen. I did talk to their young ones. Always, though, in the presence of an elder. "Poet" has all kinds of connotations.